MW00491001

Esoteric Secrets of Meditation and Magic

Volume 2: The Early Writings

by
Paul Foster Case

First published as 'Section C' and 'Section D'
by Paul Foster Case circa 1924 - 1925

ISBN 978-0-9818977-3-8
© Copyright 2008 Fraternity of the Hidden Light

All rights reserved. No reproduction, copy, or transmission of this publication may be made without written permission from the Fraternity of the Hidden Light. No paragraph of this publication may be reproduced, copied, or transmitted save with written permission or in accordance with the provision of the Copyright Act of 1956 (as amended).

The Fraternity of the Hidden Light is a world-wide organization working according to the Pattern of the True and Invisible Rosicrucian Order with Lodges, Pronaoi, and Study Groups in major cities around the globe.

Please visit our web site at www.lvx.org for a location near you.

Table of Contents

Foreward   v

Introduction   vii

Section C: Esoteric Secrets of Meditation   1

Practice of Concentration   3

Qabalistic Meditation   13

The Power of Mind   23

Watchful Introspection   35

Contemplations of the Adepti   45

Evolution of Homo Spiritualis   55

Mastership   65

The True Creative Self   75

The Perfect Stone   85

Section D : Esoteric Secrets of Magic   93

The Secret Force   95

The Magical Circle   105

The Magical Altar   117

Platonic Solids   125

The Four Maxims   137

The Great Arcanum   149

An Introduction to the Fraternity of the Hidden Light   175

Publications available from the Fraternity of the Hidden Light

Occult Fundamentals and Spiritual Unfoldment - Volume 1 : The Early Writings
    By Paul Foster Case

Esoteric Secrets of Meditation and Magic - Volume 2 : The Early Writings
    By Paul Foster Case

The Broken Seal – NEW Expanded Edition
    By Paul A. Clark

Sepher Sapphires : A Treatise on Gematria - The Magical Language : Volume 1
    By Wade Coleman

Sepher Sapphires : A Treatise on Gematria - The Magical Language : Volume 2
    By Wade Coleman

Please visit us at www.lvx.org/books for the latest
Fraternity of the Hidden Light publications

Foreward

In 1924, Paul Foster Case expanded his First Year Course by developing two advanced lecture series which he entitled Section C: 'Concentration' and Section D: 'Magic'. The lectures built upon the material in the 'First Year Course' (which had become known at this time as Section A: 'The Life Power' and Section B: 'The Seven Steps to Spiritual Unfoldment'). The Fraternity of the Hidden Light has recently published both of these lecture series as "Occult Fundamentals and Spiritual Unfoldment - Volume 1: The Early Writings." This current volume provides the two additional lecture series that complete the original fundamental course structure of Paul Case.

Section C, 'Concentration', expounds the esoteric secrets of Meditation. This section is a very advanced series of lessons that not only develops the essential skill of concentration but commences the student upon the 'Path of Return' with a series of powerful "Qabalistic Meditations." These Meditations have a tendency to facilitate deep spiritual experience in those who are prepared and chose to participate. This lesson series indeed represents some of the most advanced material written by Paul Case.

Section D, 'Magic', provides the esoteric secrets of Magic in a very rare exposition of the fundamental tenets of magical practice by one of the greatest occultists of the 20th century. Here again is material published by Paul Case that cannot be found in any of his later developed lesson series and provides insight into the "tools of the trade" practiced by Golden Dawn enthusiasts today.

Paul Case's students completed the 'First Year Course' or 'Section A' and 'Section B' before beginning the two advanced lesson series found in this volume. Likewise, I recommend all aspiring students to first proceed with each lesson of the first volume of the 'Early Writings' series, "Occult Fundamentals and Spiritual Unfoldment" two weeks at a time. Armed with this essential background, the serious student should have no problem tackling the very advanced lesson material found in this current volume.

As with the first volume of the 'Early Writing Series', Francois Cartier has lovingly typeset the text, added Hebrew and Greek font, and meticulously restored the diagrams from old mimeographs. Truly without Francois' assistance, this book would not exist today.

Enjoy!

Tony DeLuce
Laguna Niguel, CA
October 12, 2008

Introduction

Have you ever noticed that in all the Hollywood movies, when it comes down to dealing with the forces of Evil, who gets the call for the battle? The Priest or Minister! Half of the time, they lose. The Evil invades their consecrated church and they usually end up having to sacrifice their life in order to fend off the powers of darkness.

Sound familiar? It should. I can think of half a dozen plots where this happened. Not a very satisfying outcome, is it? You would think with God on their side they'd be better at this.

Perhaps they picked the wrong professional to champion their cause. As an ordained minister, I can testify that battling spiritual evil was not one of the emphasized courses at seminary! Unless we can talk them to submission! We had to take Homiletics or the art of delivering sermons every semester.

So, who better fits the job description of providing guidance along the uncharted by-ways of consciousness and steering the lost seeker around the pitfalls they may encounter. Just who is better suited to act as the guardian who stands between the naïve explorer and the forces of the shadow? Who?

The person of the Magus, the master of occult knowledge and the adept of the mystical sciences of the inner side of consciousness and the powers of nature is the person that fulfills these requirements. The illuminated soul, who has struggled up the mountain of spiritual evolution and is dedicated to serving humanity in need, is a candidate at which we might look. We glimpse this individual in the fictional accounts such as "The Lost Horizon," "John Silence," The Secrets of Dr. Taverner," and my own, "The Broken Seal."

What is not realized by most of the readers of these works is that this fictional archetype is actually based upon the lives of real men and women. Those that have through self discipline and sacrifice have proceeded a little further down the road of spiritual development than the rest of us and have paused to turn and extend a helping hand to those in need. The senior adepti of the esoteric traditions have dedicated their lives to serve humanity and seem truly mythical in our modern, materialistic age. But they are not. They exist, in the real world, right now and are doing their quiet but vital work.

A survey of history reveals that some of the most important events are linked to these individuals. Francis Bacon conceived the founding of the Royal Society of England and its subsequent role in modern Freemasonry. Dr. John Dee foretold the sinking of the Spanish Armada. The French Revolution and the crown heads (no pun intended) were connected to the Comte de St. Germain. Even the American Revolution had its mysterious "Professor." And these are just the more public examples.

Dr. Paul Foster Case is an excellent example of the Magus. His life story that I outlined in Volume I of this series is replete with faithful encounters and initiations. His prodigious volumes of teachings, still largely unknown outside of The Builders of the Adytum, the organization he founded and its successor The Fraternity of the Hidden Light, provide insight and guidance not found of a quality elsewhere. All who come into contact with them will testify that they bear the signature of one who truly knows and has experienced as contrasted to one who only writes about.

In the present volume of the early writings, he speaks more clearly and openly as an initiate about the inner secrets of meditation and magic than ever before or since.

The practice of meditation is the foundation of any serious system of consciousness development. In his lessons on this subject he exhibits his extensive knowledge of both the Eastern and Western traditions. These lessons provide sure, step-by-step guidance in mastering these critical skills.

In his discussion of Magic, we are privileged to be able to gain true insight into a subject about which so much nonsense and misinformation has been published. With the guidance of this great initiate, we penetrate to the adytum of the true teaching of this essential subject of the Mysteries.

Paul Case's goal in his writings was to help the aspiring student develop their latent powers that would lead to realizations within them selves. This transformation would allow them to contact their true inner teacher and the Inner Hierarchy of the Inner School that they might unite with them to help others. This dedication to the betterment of humanity is one of the hallmarks of the true Magus. They are content to remain in the background letting others take the credit when necessary, all the while working for the upliftment of genuine seekers.

These early writings present a process that followed conscientiously will lead the earnest student to that ever illusive goal of Self-knowledge.

I close this introduction to "Esoteric Secrets of Meditation and Magic," with the words from an ancient document that Paul Case would have been intimately familiar:

Sub Umbra Alarum Tuarum, Jehovah.

May you rest beneath the shadow of His wings whose name is peace, Jehovah.

Paul A. Clark,
Covina, California
November 2008

Section C
Esoteric Secrets of Meditation

Practice of Concentration

"Be well grounded in theory before you attempt to practice" is an alchemical maxim, and since our work in this Section is really a phase of alchemy, we shall do well to heed the admonition. Since the revival of interest in the Ageless Wisdom hundreds of books about concentration have been published, but it is surprising how vague many of them seem to be concerning a matter which is surely of great importance -- just what concentration is, and what force it seeks to control.

Our first care shall be to get this clear. We shall begin with some specific examples, rather than with definitions, because we believe this method will make it easier for you to see the principle at work in the various instances.

Up in the Catskills a little stream flows down the mountain side. A child could wade from bank to bank without any difficulty. Here in New York the water from that same stream and others like it rushes from the nozzle of a firehouse with enough force to knock a man down.

A chemist puts a solution in a retort and boils it. Thus he makes the solution stronger, and calls it a concentrated extract. In much the same way metals are said to be <u>concentrated</u> from ore. The ore is put into crucibles, heat is applied, and the pure metal is separated from the dross.

A general brings up battalion after battalion from various parts of his army and masses their strength against a single sector of the enemy's line. The newspapers tell us that he has concentrated his forces at that point.

In each of the foregoing instances something has been made stronger or purer by massing its component parts in a smaller area than they occupied before. The soldiers are brought closer together. The metal scattered through the ore is fused into a single ingot. The chemist's work of distillation crowds the molecules of his solution in close formation. The water pouring from the firehouse combines the forces of several little streams.

Concentration, then, may be defined as the packing together of units of force. This definition includes all the examples we have given, because the units, whether they be metals, molecules, drops of water or soldiers, are all built up from the One Power which you studied in the first lesson of Section A. Every kind of concentration on the physical plane is a condensation of the force of electrons, a packing together of units of electro-magnetic force.

When this fact is taken into consideration, it becomes evident that some so-called definitions of concentration must be incorrect. It is impossible to "concentrate attention," because <u>attention</u> is only a name for one of the mind's ways of acting -- the way, in fact, whereby we affect the particular kind of energy mass-formation which we are now beginning to study. The act of attention is the means which enables us to concentrate, but that act is not what we should regard as the subject of the operation, any more than a chemist's crucible or retort is the thing worked upon in the examples mentioned above.

That we misuse language when we speak of concentrating our minds may not be so apparent, for it is true that our practice enables us to intensify the strength of what William James used to call "mind-stuff." Yet we prefer not to run counter to accepted use of terms unless that use can be shown to be wholly wrong, and this cannot be said of the modern psychological use of the word "mind." Modern psychologists do not think of that word as denoting a substance, nor do they regard mind as a special kind of energy. For them "mind" means the sum-total of the conscious states of an individual, and this is not what we shall be occupied with in our practice.

Yet there is no particular difficulty in finding out just what it is that we shall learn to concentrate. We have seen that all physical substances are modes of One Thing. So, too, are all other substances, or if you prefer, forces. The One Thing is the Astral Light of Eliphas Levi, the Prana of the Hindus, the Ruach of the Qabalists.

Swami Vivekananda, you remember, says that Prana is the energy manifested in all modes of force, from thought-force down to the lowest physical activities. When Qabalists say that the Rauch in man includes the powers of all the Sephiroth from Chesed to Yesod, they also identify Ruach with the force which takes form as thought. Some Qabalists attribute to the six Sephiroth just mentioned the following states of mind:

CHESED	:	Memory
GEBURAH	:	The Personal "Will"
TIPHARETH	:	Imagination
NETZACH	:	Desire
HOD	:	Reason
YESOD	:	The Subconscious

Thus Ruach is the Qabalistic designation for that in us which takes form as thought, for the specific activities of the One Thing which are classified as mental states. Ruach is thus the Hebrew equivalent of the Sanskrit term Chitta, which is variously translated as "the thinking principle," "mind-stuff," or "the psychic nature."

The reason for comparing Ruach with Chitta thus early in our study is that one of the best text-books on the practice of concentration is a Hindu work, the Yoga Sutras of Patanjali. Here are three translations of the second sentence in that book:

a.   Concentration is the hindering of the modifications of the thinking principle.

b.   Yoga is restraining the mind-stuff (Chitta) from taking various forms (Vrittis).

c.   Union, spiritual consciousness, is gained through control of the versatile psychic nature.

The first version is from an old edition of the Sutras, now out of print, published in Bombay by the Theosophical Society. The second is that of the Swami Vivekananda. The third is that of Charles Johnston, whose translation of Patanjali we prefer to either of the others. In this particular instance, however, "control" seems to be a weaker verb than "hindering" or "restraint," because it does not make quite so evident the fact that the thinking principle is governed by right use of the principle of limitation, by checking and circumscribing its activity.

Precisely this limitation or checking is what always accomplishes any sort of concentration. Whenever you decrease the area wherein some force operates you increase the intensity and purity of that force. Sunlight passing through a window gives a pleasant sensation of warmth. Pack the same light-rays together by passing them through a convex lens, and they will burn your hand. In like manner, we intensify the force of the Ruach by limiting the range of its activity.

You have learned something about the Qabalistic meaning of the noun רוח, Ruach in The First Year Course. Now that we know this term designates what we are going to concentrate, we need to make ourselves thoroughly acquainted with its esoteric interpretation.

The first letter, ר, was once a crude picture of the human face which symbolized the synthesis of the five senses, because the head and face contain organs of every sense. The letter also refers to the brain-centers in the front part of the head, these being the organs of mental activity relating particularly to the functions of the conscious, or objective, mind. Thus the first letter of Ruach indicates that this term designates a force which is directly connected with sensation and with waking consciousness.

Among the heavenly bodies the letter ר corresponds to the sun. It is the symbol of solar light and heat, the sign of the fundamental mode in which the cosmic life-force becomes available for human use.

The value of knowing this is that it will make all our exercises in concentration more definite. We shall always feel that we are learning how to direct a real force, and we shall think of that force as being one with whose effects we have been familiar all of our lives. What we are setting out to control is not a nebulous abstraction, neither is it some new, strange, uncanny power hidden away somewhere within us. It is sunshine, the radiant energy of the nucleus of this world system. On this account the basic test of alchemy, <u>The Emerald Table</u>, calls the Great Work the "Operation of the Sun."

We are sadly mistaken if we think that this force is either good or evil. Furthermore, skill in concentration will not make us good, neither will it make us bad. Many writers on the subject, Patanjali among them, complicate the matter by injecting ethical considerations into their books. The truth is that one may gain great skill in the art of controlling the mental modifications of the Astral Light and still be a very selfish, even a criminal, person. There is no mysterious law which keeps a bad man from learning how to concentrate; any more than there is a law which prevents him from learning how to wire a house for electric light. The solar force is not benefic nor malefic in itself. The same sunlight which makes plants grow in a garden kills a man lost in the desert.

Hence Qabalists assign a pair of opposites to the letter ר – ZRO (=277), fruitfulness, seed, sperm, and ShMMH (=385), devastation, desolation, sterility. Reduce the values of these words, and you will see that the first reduction is 16 and the final reduction 7. This means that fruitfulness and desolation are identical except in outward aspect. They are opposite but complementary aspects of a single cause-in-action.

Finally, the path of the letter ר is that of the Collective Intelligence. This is the path of the synthesis of the planetary light-rays in solar force. The adjective "collective" is KLLI (90), and you will do well to give considerable thought to the meanings suggested by the letter-sequence of this word.

5

Note that its numeration, 90, identifies it with the letter Tzaddi, to which the faculty of meditation is assigned. Lack of space forbids any attempt to explain these details, even if the rule in teaching occultism did not require that the pupil must be left to find out as much as possible for himself. Here are the sign-posts. Your part is to find out where they lead.

Summing up all this (and it is just the beginning of what might be written concerning the letter ר), we find that the first letter of the Hebrew name for the thinking principle indicates that this force is:

1. The particular modification of the cosmic life-force which brain-cells transform into sensations and their interpretation by the waking consciousness;

2. A physical force with which we are all familiar, none other than sunlight;

3. A force which is neither good nor evil, promoting fruitfulness and growth, or causing devastation and sterility according to the way in which it is used;

4. A force which is the synthesis of all forces, even as Prana is said by Swami Vivekananda to be "the sum-total of all cosmic energies."

Coming now to the second letter of Ruach, which is ו, we learn from its name, Nail, that Ruach must be supposed to include the connective or conjunctive quality suggested by the nail symbol. We must also remember that the old pictograph represented a hook on which something is hung. Thus in addition to the ideas about Ruach derived from the letter ר, we learn from ו that the thinking principle whose modifications we are going to limit is a power which joins something together, as nails join boards, and a power which holds something suspended, as a hook holds an overcoat.

This is perfectly correct, because Ruach is the connecting medium between all expressions of the Life-Power. The mistake we are continually making is the supposition that the thinking principle is something inside of us, in our skulls, when in reality it is a force flowing through us which at the same time connects us with every other mode of existence, with stars and stones as truly as with men and animals.

Ruach is also like the hook which holds up your overcoat because it is the support of personality. Your whole personal life is a combination of mental states preceding from the activity of this thinking principle.

The function assigned by Qabalists to the letter ו is hearing, שמעה (415). By metathesis the same letters spell מעשה, work, action, employment, the function assigned to Lamed. If you will refer to the Tarot card corresponding to ו, you will see that the Hierophant is instructing two kneeling figures. He represents the voice of the Higher Self, which instructs both the conscious and subconscious modes of human mentality when they keep silence and listen.

In order to enter that silence, in order to become aware of the bond existing between ourselves and the rest of the cosmos, in order to be instructed in the principles of the Great Work, we must learn to listen; and as one cannot listen attentively at the same time that he is talking, so is it impossible to hear the Inner Voice until the unvoiced speech of personal thinking is silenced.

This is the control of the psychic nature which we seek when we practice concentration. The limitation we impose on the thinking principle is the limitation of silence. To this fact the last of the four ancient occult maxims (BE SILENT) refers, as well as to control of the spoken word.

Observe that there is a subtle Qabalistic correspondence between the first two letters of RVCh, Ruach. ר is the sign of the sun. ו has a particular correspondence to the sixth Sephirah, TIPHARETH, the sphere of the sun. Furthermore, as the letter of יהוה which is attributed to Microprosopus (the Lesser Countenance, or SON, including the Sephiroth from Chesed to Yesod), ו is itself a symbol of the psychic nature, Ruach, inasmuch as Ruach comprises these same six Sephiroth, as was said on page 2.

We are well aware that these intricacies of the Qabalah are rather terrifying at first, but we cannot too earnestly counsel you to study them until you have really made them your own. This one example of the way in which many details of the Secret Wisdom may be summed up by a single letter is itself an exercise in concentration. When the sight or thought of ו makes you think of all that we have written in the last two pages, you will have made a step in the direction of that unification of consciousness which is the real object of this work. As all things are from One on the Path of Descent, so all things are absorbed into that One as we progress along the Path of Return. Hence, you see, these details of correspondence and cross-correspondence are by no means so far removed from the main subject of these lessons as may appear at a first reading. When you set yourself to incorporating them into your brain-cells, instead of being content to remember that they are written down somewhere in these lessons, you are actually practicing concentration.

On, the final letter of Ruach, means, as you know, a field or a fence. The primitive pictograph represented a hedge enclosing a field set apart for cultivation. This is a direct reference to the underlying principle of limitation which is applied in every concentration exercise.

The function assigned to ח is speech, and speech is the externalization of mental states through the medium of sound. Thus mastery of words plays a prominent part in exercises for developing skill in concentration. This mastery begins in very simple ways. He who would become adept in concentration must think of language as a field to be cultivated with utmost care. He must learn to say what he means, and must be careful to mean what he says.

Here in America this advice is sadly needed. Nowhere in the world is language more abused. One need not be a pedant or a precisionist in order to use speech aright; but whoever wishes to succeed in practical occultism must address himself to the study of the dictionary. The spectacle of an aspirant sitting down to concentrate on the tip of his nose when his daily misuse of language makes two-thirds of his thought almost unintelligible is one which brings a weary smile to the lips of Those who Know. It may not seem to be "very occult" to look up words in a dictionary, but when one realizes that every misused word weakens the force of one's thinking, when one knows that slipshod speech wastes mental force, the desirability of the dictionary habit becomes almost painfully evident.

Accuracy and variety in the use of ordinary words is but a preliminary to the mastery of speech aimed at by occultism. Besides the sound combinations defined in our lexicons there are special words which are truly magical. One such is the Tetragrammaton, יהוה. Another is the ancient mystery name, IAO. Yet another is the noun L.V.X. The Hindus have many of these words of power, and they have a great number of books describing methods for using such words in concentration. This science is called mantrayoga. Variations of it are practiced throughout the Orient by devotees of different faiths. The Sufis, Mohammedan mystics, often use the sentence Hua allahu alazi lailaha Hua, "He is God, and there is no other God than He," for this purpose, and the spread of the Theosophical movement has made Western occult students familiar with Aum Mani Padmi Hum, "O the Jewel in the Lotus."

The books of the practical Qabalah contain a great deal of information along the same lines. It was to Moses' proficiency in mantrayoga that St. Stephen referred when he said the great lawgiver was "mighty in words and deeds." The Greek verb λεγει, "he speaks", is a technical mystery-term identical with the Sanskrit mantra.

Moses, of course, received his knowledge of this subject in the course of his initiation into the Egyptian mysteries. St. Stephen, indeed, implied as much in the passage just quoted, for he said this, "Moses was learned in all the wisdom of the Egyptians." Egyptian magic abounds in references to the occult use of sound. Most Egyptologists try to explain the Egyptian use of "words of power" as being a superstition rooted in the false belief that there is a mysterious connection between a man's name and his personality, so that there must be a connection between the secret name of a god and his powers. Without entering into any discussion as to whether or not the said belief is altogether without foundation in fact, let us say that when rightly pronounced, the Egyptian chekau, "words of power," are just as effective as ever they were.

Not a few Hebrew divine names are simply rearrangements of Egyptian originals. Among them is this very word Ruach which we are studying now. The ו in רוח is pronounced almost like O, and thus רוח is simply a metathesis of the Egyptian god-name of the god Horus, and there is a close correspondence between esoteric Egyptian conceptions of this god and the Qabalistic teaching concerning Ruach.

Among the Hebrew words of power are the divine and angelic names attributed to the Sephiroth. The full effect of these words is not secured unless they be intoned according to the musical cadences represented by the sequence of the letters. The name Ehieh, for example, gives the tonal sequence:

(Letters)	א	ה	י	ה
	A	H	I	H
(Notes)	E	C	F	C

Keys to the intonation of these names will be given in the lessons to come. The fundamentals will be found in the lesson on color and sound in The First Year Course. Let us warn you, however, against rash experimentation with these names. When you begin the practical exercises of this section you will have ample opportunity to find out for yourself that these are really "words of power." Attempts at unguided pioneering in this field of experimentation will be likely to teach you by bitter experience that the proverb about a little knowledge is only too true. It is unwise to be in too much of a hurry to utilize the high-tension currents of the Astral Light.

The letter Ch is also attributed to the path named Intelligence of the House of Influence בית השפע (=867). "Thence are drawn the arcana and the concealed meanings which repose in the shadow

8

thereof," says the Qabalistic commentary. Whenever a technical term employed by the Sages of Israel includes the letter ח we may know that the word has some reference to drawing forth knowledge hidden in the subconscious, to the elucidation of mysteries, to the bringing to concealed meanings to the surface.

"Intelligence of the House of Influence" means "Consciousness of that wherein influence dwells." The word "influence suggests flowing force, or a current of energy which fills a receptacle. Recall in this connection the words of Eliphas Levi concerning the Astral Light. "We are, in fact, saturated with this light and continually project it to make room for more: by this projection the personal atmosphere is created." The state of consciousness represented by this path is also that in which we realize that every mode of existence is but a temporary abode of flowing forces.

To get at the deeper meaning of the letter ח, it will be well to study the seventh major trump of the Tarot. You may derive some benefit, also, from laying out the Tarot Keys corresponding to the letters of בית השפע. Simply place the cards in this order on a table, and see if they evoke any impressions from your inner consciousness. Do not try to <u>make</u> them tell you something. Let no sense of strain enter into this experiment. Simply look at the cards and wait. After a while, when you have quieted your thoughts a little, hints as to the hidden meaning of the path of ח will begin to come to you. Note them down. Even when you do not seem to succeed very well in your efforts to make these bits of personal revelation articulate, you will find that they help you more than anything you can get from books or teachers.

We may now sum up all that we have learned about the Hebrew name for the thinking principle as follows:

1. Sunlight transformed by the brain into sensations, emotions and thoughts is the cause of the operation of this principle (ר).

2. This principle is the connecting medium which joins every human being to all the other things and creatures in the universe (ו).

3. It is a power which can be modified by means of mental imagery, and especially by mental imagery expressed in sound-vibrations (ח).

When we take these facts into consideration it becomes evident that whatever success we have in learning how to concentrate must have far-reaching consequences. The force we shall be working with does not belong to us. It is not locked up in our skulls, or coiled up like a snake at the base of our spines (even though a certain expression of this force is correctly, if somewhat fantastically, described in Hindu books as a fiery serpent coiled in the lowest center of the sympathetic nervous system.) In concentration we are utilizing the power which sends worlds whirling through space, the power which lights our homes, the power which drives trains through the subways, the power which endows human speech, as Eliphas Levi says, with a universal reverberation and success. We are using electricity, and the only reason we prefer to call in Ruach is that "electricity" means literally "the force generated by rubbing amber," while רוח, besides being an older term, is one skillfully devised by its initiated inventors for the purpose of giving clues to the higher phases of the operation of this subtle force.

In working with such a force as this we need to use care. When we were busy putting on the finishing touches at our New York office, the janitor, with the best intentions in the world, tried to play electrician. We had a desk light which needed a longer cord in order to connect it with a wall-socket in another room. George knew the theory of wiring well enough, but he chose the wrong kind of a plug. When he tried to make the connection the result was a short-circuit which blew out the main fuse in the basement, darkened the building from top to bottom, kept George from getting his supper that evening, evoked an explosion of sulphurous comment from the overworked electrician sent out by the lighting company, and cost me two dollars to calm that person's ruffled scientific sensibilities. The moral of this tale is: Don't short-circuit the current we have established by forming this group of students.

Some readers of these pages may have advanced to a point far beyond the elementary instruction which will be given in this section. It they have, they will understand the force of this warning and will be the first to heed it. For they will realize that as students of this course, we are making, link by link, what Levi calls the Magic Chain. We are not particularly fond of this image, because it suggests bondage. What we are doing is rather more like connecting up the units of a living electric circuit. Whatever injures one of us puts more or less strain upon the rest.

No man lives unto himself. He who enters a group of students like this needs particularly to remember this old truth. Of this you may be sure, if you are impatient to get on, your feeling is an infallible indication that you have need to go slowly. Remember that a magician should work as if he had all eternity in which to finish his operation. He should work that way because the emotional mood involved is in harmony with a fact of which we need continually to remind ourselves. Each of us is really immortal, and time does not bind immortals. We have all the time there is, and all eternity besides. We can well afford to make good each step as we go along. We cannot afford to do anything else. Thus we shall grow easily and almost imperceptibly, but surely, out of the seeming limitations of our present state of consciousness into the freedom of the consciousness beyond thought which is the goal of our work.

In the next lesson we shall explain the first steps in the special concentration exercises which have been prepared for the students in this section. Before that lesson, you will do well to make sure that the foundation you received in The First Year Course has been properly laid.

Your first care should be to find out whether you really know the Tree of Life. Can you draw it from memory? Can you place all the paths correctly, with their numbers, names and letters? Do you know the attributions to each letter? If not, you need to get busy right away. For the exercises you will have to do will not permit you to depend upon the lessons, or upon notes of any kind. If we say, "Picture the 27th Path," you don't want to be obliged to go through the whole Tree of Life until you come to it. You must know instantly that this is the path of Mars, that its name is Active or Exciting Intelligence, that the corresponding Hebrew letters of Peh, that its color is red, its note C, and its Tarot Key THE TOWER. The picture of THE TOWER should flash before your mental gaze like a picture thrown on a screen, unless you happen to be one of those people whose auditory images are stronger than their visual ones. If so, you will probably hear an inner voice describing the card in detail.

The point is that you should have the impression of the Tarot Key and of all that goes with it, all at once, and as a whole, just as when you see a red rose you do not get impressions piecemeal, but recognize the flower at a glance.

Provide yourself with a notebook in which to record the details of your experiments. We shall tell you in the next lesson just how to keep this record, and it should be understood now that not a little depends upon whether you attend to this important matter exactly as directed.

You will also need a string of wooden beads, and for certain symbolic reasons, the number of the beads should be 108. Get the beads and the string, which should be a strong one, and thread them yourself. On no account let anybody else do this for you, and say nothing to anybody about what you are doing, unless that person is one when you know to be a member of this class. Do not even show your beads to anybody, or leave them lying around where they will excite comment. String the beads rather loosely, in twelve groups of nine, with a good-sized knot between each group. Be sure to get wooden beads, and let them be plain ones, preferably black or dark indigo. (The color refers to the limiting power of Saturn, which is employed in all concentration exercises.)

All this will be more or less trouble. It is meant to be. In these days we have to devise new tests to take the place of those imposed in the older forms of initiation, and if you do not know by this time that the work of the Builders is a form of initiation you ought to stick a pin in yourself to find out whether you are really awake. If we do not explain the reasons for this particular set of directions, it is because we think most of the students in this section will be able to divine them. Those who aren't need practice in divination.

This string of beads is not for the purpose of helping you to count vain repetitions. It is intended to enable you to keep an accurate record of the "breaks" in you concentration practice. A "break" is what happens when attention wanders from the object selected for concentration. In the early stages of your practice you will find that the breaks will take you several times around the string. The day that you go just once around will be, as we used to say in a certain "very occult" society, "a marked one in your career." It will not be necessary for you to review the whole Tree of Life before the next lesson. Our work this year begins in Malkuth, and takes us upward through the Tree. In the next lesson you will find specific exercises relating to the 32nd, 30th and 31st paths, and it may be well for you to confine your review work to those paths, their attributions, and the corresponding Tarot Keys.

We must not omit to say that it is not the object of this course of ten lessons to make you an adept in concentration at the end of ten weeks. In that time we hope to be able to explain something of the technique, and we expect that your preliminary experiments in this work will make some noticeable changes in your states of consciousness before the ten weeks are up. But it would be very unfair for us not to make it perfectly clear that this course is intended simply to tell you how to do something which will require months of practice before you gain any unusual degree of skill, and years of hard work before you attain to the higher grades of adeptship in concentration and meditation.

These instructions are given now, so that you may be able to enter into our practical wor as intelligently as possible. In some senses, every phase of that work is an exercise in concentration and meditation. And though our curriculum is designed to be completed in four years, it must not be supposed that at the end of that time you will have become a perfect Yogi. What we do hope to bring about in the minds of our affiliates is an intelligent understanding of the principles and methods of the Ageless Wisdom, a synthesis of the esoteric doctrines and practices of the Orient and the Occident.

How soon any affiliate will develop the higher aspects of consciousness, how soon he will begin to exercise the powers of one who knows by the fruits of experimentation that he is truly "the depository of the power of God," -- these are questions which nobody can answer.

The most that we can do is to lay before you the specifications of the work. Whether you build quickly or slowly, well or ill, depends wholly upon yourself. It depends a good deal, too, upon the accuracy with which you follow these instructions, and upon the degree of patience that you exercise.

Not to frighten you, but to make you realize that you are beginning something which is difficult, and often discouraging, let me remind you that one of the Upanishads says that he who would succeed in controlling the mental phases of the Life-Power must have as much patience as would be required to dip up the ocean, drop by drop, with a blade of grass.

Qabalistic Meditation

Now that you understand what concentration works with, what force it limits and intensifies, you are ready to begin to study the practical side of the work. In order to follow the first part of this lesson you will have to use the Tarot. Take out the major trumps entitled the MAGICIAN, STRENGTH and THE DEVIL, and place them on a table before you. Put THE MAGICIAN at the top, STRENGTH in the middle and THE DEVIL below.

The first thing to be observed about this arrangement is that STRENGTH, the middle card, bears a number which is the mean arithmetical term between the numbers of the MAGICIAN and THE DEVIL.

The mean term between two numbers is half their sum, and in the Tarot a card whose number is the mean between the numbers of two other cards represents the equilibrium between a pair of opposites symbolized by those two cards. Thus 10 is the mean between 1 and 19, 2 and 18, 3 and 17, 4 and 16, and so on. In this instance the pair of opposites is THE MAGICIAN and THE DEVIL. STRENGTH is the equilibrating activity which reconciles them.

In the preceding lesson we reached the conclusion that the force which we are to learn to concentrate is the L.V.X., or the Astral Light concerning which Eliphas Levi wrote at such length. This is the force which he tells us "was adored in the secret rites of the Sabbath or the Temple under the symbolic figure of Baphomet, or of the androgyne goat of Mendes." (Remember that the Sabbath was the so-called "Sabbath of the Sorcerers," a survival of the old pagan mystery cults, and that the Temple was not that of the Jews, but of the original Knights Templar.) Levi informs us also that the Astral Light is "the devil of esoteric dogmatism, and is really the blind force which souls must conquer, in order to detach themselves from the chains of earth."

THE DEVIL, therefore, represents this force, and we may now add somewhat to the interpretation of this picture given in the First Year Course. Very penetrating students of the earlier lessons may already have arrived at an understanding of what we are about to say; but because the science revealed and concealed by means of these pictorial symbols is one that leads to command of potent forces, (and that without any regard to the mentality or morals of the person who employs them, beyond such mentality as is required to grasp and apply the laws whereby those forces are called into activity), the First Year work on the Tarot purposely leaves many things unsaid. Nowhere is there any deliberate attempt to throw dust in the eyes of the reader by resorting to misstatements, but there are many intentional omissions, because we know that by no means every one who begins the Builder's Work will persevere in it until the end.

The first thing to consider about the DEVIL is the number 15. This conceals several details of the Ageless Wisdom in a subtle way. Has it ever occurred to you that XV includes two of the letters of L.V.X.? You see that it does, of course, as soon as I speak of it, and perhaps you may be inclined to ask, "What of it?"

Just this, the adepts who combined their knowledge in the production of the Tarot overlooked nothing that their ingenuity could devise in the way of providing clues to the meaning of the pictures, and one reason why the DEVIL is numbered XV is that X and V represent L.V.X. minus the L.

L is Lamed, which as a verb means "to instruct," and as a noun signifies "an ox-goad." Thus L.V.X. minus L suggests the absence of the equilibrating and directive quality represented by the 11th major trump, JUSTICE. In other words, the DEVIL is the Astral Light as it works in the realms of nature below man, where it is truly a fatal force, working by the mathematical law of averages. This is what Levi means by saying that it is the blind force which souls must conquer.

From the same source to which we owe the Book of Tokens, we received in 1919 the following statement about the DEVIL:

"The Devil is a figure of the Creative Fire encased in Matter, and he is also the 'god of them that walk in darkness' (i.e., the darkness of ignorance, or want of instruction, XV, or L.V.X. minus L. – P.F.C.). For they see the Source of All as a creative power ungoverned by Law; but God follows the Law of His own being, which is Love. Love misunderstood, materialized, and perverted, is the veritable Devil. Therefore are the human figures in chains, and the Pentagram inverted." (The Pentagram, through its correspondence to 5, is a symbol of the Mars-force and of man. Its inversion is the sign of a human misunderstanding and misuse of the Mars-force which inverts human consciousness, and turns man upside down. This inversion and misunderstanding are nowhere more thoroughly exemplified than in the teachings and practices of certain deluded souls who imagine that they are practicing regeneration.)

In other words, the DEVIL is a picture symbolizing the false conception of the Life-Power held by those who are wanting in knowledge of its real nature. The DEVIL is what theologians call God, as that Power is imagined by people who have not yet arrived by practical experimentation at an understanding of Its true nature. We say "by practical experimentation," because Qabalists identify instruction or knowledge with work, as you may see by referring to the attributions of the letter Lamed.

On the other hand, although the DEVIL symbolizes a false conception of the Life-Power, it also indicates the true nature of that Power when we know how to interpret the symbols. For it is written, "The Devil is God as He is misunderstood by the wicked," and God misunderstood is not the less divine because men see His image upside down. Hence the wise men who invented the Tarot assigned the number XV to this picture, because the number 15 is the number of the divine name I H, Jah, which is attributed to Chokmah.

Reference to the Qabalistic dictionary in the lesson on the Literal Qabalah will give you an opportunity to trace the connections between various words corresponding to the number 15. Each refers to some aspect of the Astral Light, and you should endeavor to work out the hidden meanings from this point-of-view. Particularly should you observe that 15 is the number of הוד Hod, the sphere of Mercury, because Hod is the Sephirah completing the 26th path עין on the Way of Descent, as it is also the Sephirah whence the same path rises on the Way of Return. Observe, too, that even the number of this path hints at the divine nature of the activity manifest in it, because the number 26 is the number of IHVH, the Tetragrammaton.

The faculty assigned to the 26th path and to the letter עין is Mirth. The Hebrew noun is שחוק (414),

which is 9, the number of Teth, the coiled serpent, and also the number of YESOD, the Foundation). Work out the deeper meanings of this Qabalistic term with the help of the Tarot cards. The first letter is that of the Fire (the Fire of the Divine Breath, remember, because ש=300=אלהים רוח, Life-Breath of the gods) which leads to the birth of the regenerated personality (Key 20). The second letter is that which suggests the circumscribed field of human activity, and its card is the one that shows the true relation of the Divine I AM to Its vehicle. The third letter refers to the revelation of the arcana of the Ageless Wisdom when we listen in silence to the Revealer within, and it also shows the operation of the power which is the conjunctive and mediating principle in the universe. The last letter, through the Tarot, calls up a picture of the Way which leads out of the delusions of this world into the Beyond of the higher consciousness that is our Goal.

But apart from these and other meanings of שחוק which the Tarot will enable you to evoke from your inner consciousness, please do not overlook the obvious implication of this Qabalistic marriage of the idea of laughter with that suggested by the name of the 26th path, Renewing Intelligence. A sense of humor is indispensable to the practical occultist. Laughter is a cleansing activity, and the ability to use it is one sign whereby you may always distinguish a person who is really an occultist from the crank who merely supposes himself to be one.

When we think of an Egyptian priest, most of us call up an image of an austere, grim being. This is a false image, and fortunately we have indisputable evidence that it is so. Let me quote an old Egyptian hymn to the sun-god Ra, from Robert Silliman Hillyer's metrical version, to be found in his anthology of Egyptian hymns, entitled <u>The Coming Forth By Day</u>:

> "Homage to thee, O Ra, at they tremendous rising.
> Thou risest. Thou shinest. The heavens are rolled aside.
> Thou art the King of Gods, thou art the All-comprising,
> From thee we come, in thee are deified.
> Thy priests go forth at dawn; they wash their hearts with laughter;
> Divine winds move in music across thy golden strings.
> At sunset they embrace thee, as every cloudy rafter
> Flames with reflected color from thy wings."

Laughter is a prophylactic. A sense of humor is one of the best protections against the sense of separateness. No egotist is ever a humorist, and no egotist ever succeeded in accomplishing the Great Work. For the egotist is encased in the impenetrable shell of his sense of personal importance, and just that sense is what the Great Work seeks to overcome.

We have learned to laugh at the devil, but we are just a little afraid, perhaps, to laugh at the equally demoniac idea of God which theologians have tried their best to impose upon the race-consciousness. If you can understand that this grotesque figure in the 15th Key of the Tarot represents what sages have thought in all times and ages concerning the notion of God advanced by esoteric teachers you will be well on the way to realizing that the aim of practical occultism really is. The DEVIL is an image of man's silly imaginings about God.

For even those silly imaginings are the outworking of the Life-Power through unripened minds. Remember the words of <u>The Book of Tokens</u>: "Into every state of knowledge do I enter, into false knowledge as well as into true, so that I am not less the ignorance of the deluded than the wisdom of the sage. For what thou callest ignorance and folly is my pure knowing, imperfectly expressed through an uncompleted image of my divine perfection" (ALEPH; par. 6)

Concerning the Astral Light Levi says also that "man, in the image of the Deity, modifies and apparently multiplies it in the reproduction of his species." This is the force of the earthy sign, Capricorn, the sign of the goat. It is the power ruled by Saturn, and Saturn is the force of limitation, the force which gives concreteness, or definite shape and form, to all things. The Astral Light as manifested in Capricorn is also the means of the exaltation or lifting-up of the fiery activity of the Mars-force.

This aspect of the One Force is the tempter in the allegory of Adam and Eve. Its name, Nachash, נחש is by Gematria to the name of the Christos, Messiach, משיח. You remember that נחש is also the spelling of a Hebrew word for copper, the metal of Venus, so that נחש conceals a reference to Love and Beauty. For Love, after all, is the great secret of the Life-Power. Therefore is the Sephirah of Victory called the sphere of Venus, because of the truth which the New Testament writer phrases thus: "Love faileth never."

What has all this to do with concentration? Simply this: You must understand the inner nature of the Astral Light before you begin to direct its currents, unless you are looking for trouble. You must know, too, something concerning the proper emotional mood in which to approach your work. If you look upon concentration as a disagreeable task you will never accomplish much at it. Its real purpose is to intensify, purify, control and set at work the love-force in your whole being. We do not know how to put the matter any plainer than this, yet it may be that not every reader will rightly understand us. Let the words stand. If you do not grasp their full import now, you will when you are riper.

So much for the force, as represented by the DEVIL. Let us now consider the law which enables us to modify that force. This law is pictured in the Tarot by STRENGTH.

The number of the card is one clue. Read the lesson on the meaning of numbers, and you will find that 8 is the symbol of flux and reflux, of evolution, of vibration. This last word is the name of the law which we shall apply in our work of modifying and intensifying the currents of the Astral Light.

What is vibration? It is an alternating activity, a reciprocal ebb and flow of energy between two extremes or poles. The name calls up an image of wave-motion, and in this image are two elements -- the crest of the wave and its trough. We find the same image in the 14th and 18th Keys of the Tarot. In both pictures the Way of Return is shown as a path ascending over rolling ground, so that it rises and falls in its progress, like waves.

Knowledge of the law of vibration, and skill in applying it, are the basis of practical work in every department of occult science. It is a universal law, and because it is at work in all things the path of the letter Teth is called "Intelligence of the Secret of all Spiritual Activities." He who is perfect in his use of this law of vibration is called a Master or a Yogi. His works are what the ignorant call miracles. So well does he understand the art of combining the inertia of Saturn with the energy of Mars, (or as alchemists would say, the fusion of Salt and Sulphur), that he can, if need be, multiply a few loaves and fishes until he has food enough to feed five thousand.

The key to the secret of mastering the Astral Light by using the law of vibration is shown by the attribution of the letter Teth of the sign Leo, which rules the heart. For even as Love is the essential principle of divinity, so that the devil is merely a caricature of love, so is the practical secret of the Great Work a secret of the human heart. This is subtly and beautifully shown in the symbolism of the 8th Tarot trump, where the lion is being led by a chain of roses. Love, beauty, service -- these are the key-words to the art of mastering the currents of the Astral Light.

They have been horribly misunderstood. Fools and charlatans misuse them daily. Cranks of every stripe known to the 57 varieties of pseudo-occultism mouth and mumble these sacred syllables until one who really knows is almost physically nauseated by the sound of holy words emerging from unclean lips. For they are unclean lips, those that besmirch all the beautiful laws of the Divine Life which flows through us, poisoning the wells of existence with their vile imaginings. Would there were other words to use than those which have been so often abused. But no others will serve. Love, beauty, service –understood aright – sum up the whole mystery of the Great Secret.

Love, because its essence is reciprocity, so that it is directly related to the great law of vibration represented by STRENGTH. Beauty, because nothing unbeautiful is strong, nothing inharmonious lovely, nothing ugly serviceable. Service, because no service can be one-sided. We cannot serve you unless you serve us too. We cannot love unless we are loved. I waste my time in efforts to produce a beauty which no eye but mine beholds. Service, too, (and this particularly for students of occultism,) because the ability to master the Astral Light is not to be sought for the sake of being able to astonish your neighbor.

Jesus did not heal to show that he was a Master. He did not multiply the loaves and fishes to convince anybody that he understood the secrets of cosmic law. Again and again he warned the recipients of his favors against vain babbling, saying, "See that thou tell no man."

All this is vitally important to you when you begin to study the practice of concentration, because your success depends largely upon your ability to begin the work in the right mood. The work is hard, and its first stages are disheartening. Days and weeks and months pass before one begins to get any striking results. If you begin in the wrong mood, these difficulties will soon lead you to abandon practice.

If you begin with the idea that you are going to unfold wonderful powers which will raise you above your fellows, or if in any other way your motive for study be a selfish one, it is extremely unlikely that you will persevere long enough to get results. But if you begin with the understanding that this work aims to make you more lovely by making you more lovable, more beautiful by making you stronger, more serviceable by turning all your life-force into constructive action which shall make your world a better one for all its inhabitants, then the power of the ideal thus set before you will carry you through the periods of depression, through the troughs of the waves, on to ultimate success.

Those apparent set-backs, these moments of depression following a period of exaltation, are simply expressions of the great law of alternation or vibration. We warn you of them now so that they may not surprise or disturb you. You cannot maintain yourself at the highest levels of consciousness all the time. Your body could not stand the strain. Neither can you expect to make steady progress in concentration, as if you were walking up a long, gradual incline. You will have your ups and downs. Some days the exercises will be easy, and you will be happy over your success. Other days will come when you will have more breaks than usual, and the more you try to concentrate, the more your thought will wander from the selected image. Curb your elation over a successful day, and be sure not to let yourself become unhappy over an unsuccessful one. Waves gather force for their ascent while they are at the very lowest point of the trough. So it is in mental practice. A "bad day" is one in which you are gathering your forces. The main thing is to keep on.

No matter how many times your attention wanders in the quarter-hour of practice, bring it resolutely back to the selected image. Keep your record just as carefully on bad days as on good ones. Never for a moment trouble your mind about any other member of the class, and do not compare notes as to your progress.

This is most important. You are responsible to no other person in this work but me. Be sure that I shall play no favorites. If you begin to compare notes, you will do yourself and your associates much harm. If you find it easy to concentrate, you will discourage your less-gifted neighbor by a recital of your successes. If concentration is hard for you, you only make it harder by telling other people so. And above all, I wish to avoid the spirit of emulation or competition, which may be the life of trade but is fatal to success in the work we are engaged in.

The force you are learning to control is depicted in the 8th Tarot Key as a lion because the lion, when we think of him as the king of beasts, is a synthesis of all the powers of nature below the human level. In Hebrew the noun for <u>lion</u> and also for the zodiacal sign Leo is Arieh, אריה.

Observe the numeration of this word. It is 216, and is the number of Geburah, גבורה, the sphere of Mars, and of ראיה, sight, the faculty attributed to the letter H, corresponding to Aries, one of the two houses of Mars. Furthermore, the same number, 216, is that of the noun רוגז, anger, wrath, excitement, the faculty corresponding to the letter S, assigned to the sign Sagittarius.

Thus to every one of the three signs of the fiery triplicity in the zodiac the Qabalah gives a name which corresponds by Gematria to the names assigned to the other two signs of the same triplicity, To Aries, Sight, for the perfection of the inner vision is the end of concentration, and he who attains to it restores the Emperor of creation to his throne. To Leo, the lion, because this beast is a symbol of all the forms of force which must be controlled before the higher vision may be experienced. To Sagittarius, excitement or intense activity of the desire-nature, because this is what gives us courage to persist, and supports us (S) like a staff in our progress toward liberation.

What is this fiery power? It is the Mars-force, ruling in Aries where it has its highest throne, and active in Leo and Sagittarius because these signs partake of its own essential quality. It is the force exalted in Capricorn, the sign symbolized by the DEVIL, and represented in that picture by the demon's inverted torch, as well as by the inverted pentagram upon his forehead. It is the force, again, whose most occult aspects are those connected with the letter Nun, with the sign Scorpio, and with the symbolism of the 13th Key. Finally, it is the force whose sphere of action is the fifth Sephirah, Geburah. Consider it in all these aspects until you know what it is that you are learning to master when you set out to learn how to concentrate. It seems to us that more open exposition of the nature of this force has never been given. Certainly we would not make it any clearer if we could, for if any reader of these pages remains in ignorance after this plain exposition of a secret long kept hidden, that ignorance betrays him as one who has heard and read, but who has done no work.

A word further concerning the number 216. It has something to do with the number of beads whereby you are to record the breaks in your practice. Even as the color and the substance of the beads were not chosen at random, so has their number several hidden meanings, which are really suggestions to your subconsciousness.

The number 108 is half of 216, so that the beads in your rosary symbolize the synthesis of the opposite or polar manifestations of the Mars-force in a higher mode of expression. That is, because 108 is half of 216, it suggests a drawing together or concentration of the forces of Geburah. Thus your beads symbolize that transcending of the pairs of opposites which the sages recommend. He who transcends the pairs of opposites is on the Middle Way, and the Hebrew noun for "middle" is חצי (108). The first letter of this noun signifies Speech, the second corresponds to the faculty of Meditation, and the function attributed to the third is that of Coition. Control of speech through meditation leads to the perfect marriage of the consciousness with the subconsciousness. That perfect union is the occult significance of Coition, and it is the uniting of subject and object which results in the experience of superconsciousness.

The numbers 216 and 108 have the same least number, 9, so that both refer to the force of cosmic electricity, the FOHAT of the Theosophical teaching, which H.P. Blavatsky tells us is represented by the letter Teth. And because 9 is also the number of the Sephirah Yesod, the root of that power is the activity centered in that Sephirah.

Your beads, then, because the least number of their total is 9, symbolize the cosmic force of FOHAT, the serpent-fire of the letter Teth, and relate also to the center where that force is most active in human life. Their color is that of the Saturnine influence of limitation dominant in Capricorn, the DEVIL in the Tarot. Their material, wood, is chosen for two reasons: 1st, because wood is an organic substance, which absorbs personal emanations of the Astral Light, so that your bead-string will eventually be a reservoir of your personal forces; 2nd, because "wood" is ὕλη in Greek, and Hyle was the Gnostic name for the Astral Light.

Thus your rosary symbolizes the force you are learning to control, and it also represents the means you will use in order to control that serpent-power.

The number of beads has yet another meaning. It is composed of the symbols 1, 0 and 8. Let 8 serve to remind you of the law of vibration symbolized by STRENGTH. Let 0 recall the fact that the goal of concentration is union with that One which is neither Aught nor Naught, whose Tarot symbol is the FOOL. Let 1 bring to your recollection the MAGICIAN, for this Key shows exactly what happens when you concentrate.

You remember that we interpret this Key as a symbol of attention. It shows an adept in the act of concentration. The power he uses is being brought down from above. Here is a subtlety, for one result of concentration is the raising of the Mars-force from lower to higher centers of the sympathetic nervous system. This is what the Hindus mean when they say that concentration raises the Kundalini. What they do not say, for no Hindu occultist ever makes a complete statement concerning any phase of practical work, is that the serpent-power rises in response to the descent of the undifferentiated Prana from above. In concentration we do not try to lift up the Kundalini by main force, as if we were trying to raise ourselves by our boot-straps. We simply open ourselves to the descending current of light which flows down from Kether, and that current, when it returns, raises the serpent-fire from chakra to chakra. For it must never be forgotten that the Astral Light is cosmic electricity, and every electrician knows that no matter what the application we make of that force, it must always pass from a higher to a lower potential.

Begin every period of concentration, therefore, by reciting the affirmations, beginning with the first. During the recitation picture the white light of Kether descending through the course of the lightning-flash on the Tree of Life, changing color as it passes from Sephirah to Sephirah – from the white of Kether to the opalescent gray of Chokmah, from this to the black of Binah, and so on, until you reach Malkuth, where you should visualize the color-cross of the four elements: Citrine, Russet, Slate and Black. Thus you will set up in the sphere of your personality the vibrations of every aspect of the One L.V.X., and so prepare yourself for the work that follows. DO NOT USE THE COLORS IN THE MORNING AND EVENING USE OF THE AFFIRMATIONS, OR AT ANY OTHER TIME EXCEPT AS A PRELIMINARY TO CONCENTRATION PRACTICE.

This exercise should not be explained to affiliates of the Builders who have not advanced into the second Section, and it should never be mentioned to outsiders. It is by no means "all imagination." You really set up the vibratory action of these forces when you recite the affirmations and visualize the colors at the same time.

Another thing to notice about the MAGICIAN is that his left hand makes a gesture indicating definite purpose. He is directing his power to a plane below that of his own existence, for a specific reason. The plane below him is shown as a garden, which typifies the subconscious. In concentration remember always that you seek to impress some definite images upon the subconscious. You do not draw down the power from Kether without any particular object. You aim to accomplish some concrete modification of the subconscious field of activity.

What the purpose may be will vary from day to day, according to the circumstances. It will always have certain characteristics. You will use the force either to promote the culture of a desire image (roses), or also to develop some seed of intellectual perception (lilies). Again, whatever the exercise may be, it will necessarily partake of the dominant quality of one of the implements symbolizing the elements. For in each path on the Tree of Life one of the elements predominates, except in the 10th, Malkuth, the 3rd, Binah, the 2nd, Chokmah, and the 1st, Kether -- these four being synthetic paths, in which the operation of all four elements is mingled, without any one element predominating.

The garments of the MAGICIAN show that the outer aspect of the One Force utilized in concentration is Rajas, Sulphur, or the fiery desire-nature (red), while the inner reality is Sattva, Mercury, or the white brilliance of Kether. For it is really the descent of power from Kether which does the work, although the manifestation of power takes the Rajasic form of the ascent of Kundalini. The MAGICIAN'S serpent girdle symbolizes the Tamasic limitation imposed upon the white light of Kether in all concentration practice.

The exercises to be practiced in connection with this lesson are connected with the 32nd path of Tau, the 31st path of Shin, and the 30th path of Resh. In the exercises for the 32nd path, imagine yourself also to be in Malkuth, but projecting your consciousness upward to Yesod. In the practice of concentration connected with the 30th path, however, you must imagine yourself as being placed in Hod, and as drawing power up from Yesod to Hod, along the channel of that path. Observe these directions carefully, even though the reasons therefore may not be evident at a first reading.

Place your watch where you can see it without having to alter your position to look at it, and practice five minutes of your fifteen-minute period on each path. By so doing you avoid strain in these first exercises, because the shifting of attention at the end of five minutes from one path to another is a kind of rest.

On the first day of practice confine yourself to the color of the path. Begin with the color-cross of Malkuth, and then picture a ray of deep indigo force passing upward from the citrine segment of Malkuth toward Yesod. See yourself projecting that force upward and inward. Whenever the image wavers, slip a bead on your string. At first this action of slipping the beads will interfere with concentration, but eventually it will become automatic, as will the noting of the passage of time. (In passing I may say that this work will ultimately provide you with a sort of interior clock, so that you will be able to estimate the passage of time automatically.)

After the first five minutes, change to the path of Shin, picturing a red ray projected upward from the russet segment of Malkuth. Then, after five minutes of this, place yourself in Hod, seeing yourself surrounded by a sphere of orange light, and see a ray of the same light being drawn upward to your from the sphere of Yesod. (This imagined activity is in actual correspondence when one succeeds in this particular exercise.)

On the second day, concentrate on the planetary symbols and elementary symbol. Begin with Saturn, and visualize the symbol in color, holding it firmly before your mental gaze, and recording as a break each variation in shape or color. Next take the path of Shin, and imagine an upright red triangle. Finish this series of concentrations with the path of Resh and use a sun-symbol in orange.

The third day, use the Hebrew letters, visualizing each in its proper color. The fourth day, using your pitch-pipe or the piano (which is not nearly so good) to give you the tone, sound the names of the three letters, one during each five minutes, at first audibly, and then internally. The fifth day picture the corresponding Tarot Keys. The sixth day use this formula: "I am the Administrative Intelligence, uniting the Kingdom of Light to its Foundation," during the first five minutes; in the succeeding five minutes say, "I am the Perpetual Intelligence, which rules the two great lights of consciousness"; and in the last five minutes say, "I am the Collecting Intelligence, gathering up the force of the Foundation, and concentrating it in the sphere of Splendor." The seventh day you should do no practices.

At the end of the period make a brief record of the following things:

1. Time practice began.
2. Number of breaks in each five-minute period.
3. Easiest part of exercise.
4. Hardest part of exercise.
5. Any unusual impressions.

This record is essential, and I shall wish to examine it from time to time. A good record contains few words, and one that describes a lot of marvelous psychic experiences is a very, very bad one.

The Power of the Mind

The purpose of these lessons on concentration and meditation is really two fold. Primarily they are intended to give you some first-hand knowledge of what happens when one attempts to control mental imagery. This is the object of the exercises at the end of each lesson. Secondarily, they aim to condense into a comparatively small compass the substance of the many books that have been written on the subject, so that at the end of the course you may have in your possession a practical working manual on the practice of this phase of occult training.

By this time your experiences with the exercises already given should have convinced you that those teachers who come periodically to our great cities with the message, "You can have anything you want if only you will hold the thought," are telling only part of the secret. What they say is true so far as it goes. The "catch" is that not one person in ten thousand can even begin to "hold" a thought. We do not expect that you will have attained any startling degree of skill in this art by the time you have completed these lessons, but we do hope that your experiences with the exercises will have interested you sufficiently to induce you to keep on with the practice for the rest of your life.

You must not suppose that the fifteen minutes practice-period suggested is a <u>maximum</u>. On the contrary, it is the <u>minimum</u>. The more time you can find to devote to this work, the better. The only reason that a period of fifteen minutes is mentioned is that many students of these lessons are busy people who are more or less obsessed by the illusion that they cannot spare time for lengthy practice. We say "obsessed with the illusion" because a person who really understands the need for concentration will give up almost anything to practice it. Until that understanding comes, however, it seems best to give you a small task, which you <u>can</u> perform, so that you may not be tricked by your brain-cells into neglecting it.

For it is your brain-cells that trick you. Like all other living beings, they hate to change their habits, and you have been letting them do as they please so long that now they will try to wheedle you out of sticking regularly to the practice-period. It is on this account that we ask you to keep a record, and to note the days you do not practice as faithfully as those that you do. In time this will act as an incentive which will help you to overcome the inertia of your lazy brain-cells, if for no other reason that you will be ashamed to send me a report which says repeatedly, "Did not practice today." (Of course, shame is the very worst of reasons for being faithful in practice, but it is better than no reason at all.)

What we have just said about the task being primarily one of getting your brain-cells into a habit of industry and obedience goes to the root of the whole matter. It all goes back to the teaching of that master of concentration, the Hindu sage, Patanjali, who begins the Fourth Book of his <u>Yoga Sutras</u> with this declaration:

> "Psychic and spiritual powers may be inborn, or they may be gained by the use of drugs, or by incantations, or by fervor, or by meditation."

So Charles Johnston translates it. In some respects the version given by Swami Vivekananda seems to me to be clearer:

> "The Siddhis (powers) are attained by birth, chemical means, power of words, mortification or concentration."

This is Vivekananda's commentary on this aphorism:

"Sometimes a man is born with the Siddhis, powers, of course from the exercise of powers he had in his previous birth. In this birth he is born, as it were, to enjoy the fruits of them. It is said of Kapila, the great father of the Sankhya Philosophy, that he was a Siddha, which means, literally, a man who has attained to success. The Yogis claim that these powers can be gained by chemical means. All of you know that chemistry originally began as alchemy; men went in search of the philosopher's stone, and elixirs of life, and so forth. In India there was a sect called the Rasayanas. Their idea was that ideality, knowledge, spirituality and religion, were all very right, but that the body was the only instrument by which to attain to all these. If the body broke now and then it would take so much more time to attain to the goal. For instance, a man wants to practice Yoga, or wants to become spiritual. Before he has advanced very far he dies. Then he takes another body and begins again, then dies, and so on, and in this way much time will be lost in dying and being born again. If the body could be made strong and perfect, so that it would get rid of birth and death, we should have so much more time to become spiritual. So these Rasayanas say, first make the body very strong, and they claim that this body can be made immortal. Their idea is that if the mind is manufacturing the body, and if it be true that each mind is only one particular outlet to that infinite energy, and that there is no limit to each particular outlet getting any amount of power from outside, why is it impossible that we should keep our bodies all the time? We shall have to manufacture all the bodies that we shall ever have. As soon as this body dies we shall have to manufacture another. If we can do that why cannot we do it just here and now, without getting out? The theory is perfectly correct. If it is possible that we live after death, and make other bodies, why is it impossible that we should have the power of making bodies here, without dissolving this body, simply changing it continually? They also thought that in mercury and in sulphur was hidden the most wonderful power, and that by certain preparations of these a man could keep the body as long as he liked. Others believed that certain drugs could bring powers, such as flying through the air, etc. Many of the most wonderful medicines of the present day we owe to the Rasayanas, notably the use of metals in medicine. Certain sects of the Yogis claim that many of their principal teachers are still living in their old bodies. Patanjali, the great authority on Yoga, does not deny this. The power of words. There are certain sacred words called Mantrams, which have power, when repeated under proper conditions, to produce these extraordinary powers. We are living in the midst of such a mass of miracles, day and night, that we do not think anything of them. There is no limit to man's power, the power of words and the power of mind. Mortification. You find that in every religion, mortifications and asceticism have been practiced. In these religious conceptions the Hindus always go to the extremes. You will find men standing with their hands up all their lives, until their hands wither and die. Men sleep standing, day and night, until their feet swell, and, if they live, their legs become so stiff in this position that they can no more bend them, but have to stand all their lives. I once saw a man who had raised his hands in this way, and I asked him how it felt when he did it at first. He said it was awful torture. It was such torture that he had to go to a river and put himself in water, and that allayed the pain a little. After a month he did not suffer much. Through such practices powers (Siddhis) can be attained. Concentration. The concentration is Samadhi, and that is Yoga proper; that is the principal theme of this science, and it is the highest means. The preceding ones are only secondary, and we cannot attain to the highest through them. Samadhi is the means through which we can gain anything and everything, mental, moral or spiritual."

There once lived in our little New York village a woman of sixty who was the most thoroughly disliked person in the community. Of all the "ingrowing" dispositions that ever one encountered, hers was the worst. Her tongue was like a dagger, and both old and young had suffered from the poison of her envenomed words.

She was a regular attendant at the Baptist Church, but her religion seemed to be limited to occupying a pew twice on Sunday. And her voice! Who could forget its piercing tones as she yelled, "El-mer-r-r!" to call her nephew into the house -- usually in order to give him a thorough tongue-lashing for some trifling misdeed.

Now it chanced that the poor old lady had to have two teeth extracted, and the dentist gave her laughing-gas. And as she was coming out the anesthetic she has a vision. We don't know just what she saw. She never could be induced to say much about it, and it is probable that she could find no words. But she used to testify that the Lord had come to her to give her a "look into things." Whatever it was that she saw, the experience changed her life.

At first, of course, people didn't notice the change; but after a while they began to wonder what had "come over Mrs. Watson" (We hide her identity under a fictitious name, for good reasons.) One of the things that struck us all was the change in Mrs. Watson's voice. Then Elmer began to tell us boys what a difference he found in her.

Little by little she began to make friends. The young people who used to cross the street to avoid her began to look forward to her appearance. More than that, they began to go to her for advice, for when the Lord gave her "a look into things". He also gave her the priceless power of looking with understanding into the hearts of men. For twenty years she was an incarnate blessing to that village – and all because she had two teeth pulled.

For the change in Mrs. Watson was brought about by the laughing-gas. She didn't know it, of course, and neither did anybody else in the village. We found it out years afterward when reading William James's, The Varieties of Religious Experience. In that book James describes the experiments of a little group somewhere here in America, who published some pamphlets concerning what they called "The Anaesthetic Revelation." The sum-total of their discovery was that the superconscious experience can be induced by inhaling laughing-gas. In the same way the experiences of people who have experimented with hashish bear internal evidence that they were temporarily raised to the superconscious plane. Let it be definitely understood that I am not even hinting that to take any of these drugs is a good way to develop the superconscious state. On the contrary, it is a very bad way, because it is like breaking an egg-shell to help the chicken get out, or opening the cocoon to release a butterfly. The superconscious powers ought properly to be unfolded from within, and neither the use of drugs, nor the practices of those who "develop passives" by some variation of hypnotism can be defended by any one who knows the law.

Our reason for dwelling upon this phase of the subject is to make you see that the superconscious state is a brain-state, a body-state, a condition of the blood-chemistry which makes the body able to register the higher, finer, more rapid vibrations of the consciousness beyond thought. The various means enumerated by Patanjali all bring about this change in the physical body, and until that change is made, there is no experience of superconsciousness. For what is called "the law of parsimony" is at work throughout nature. One principle takes form in manifold effects. In the case now under examination, the established fact that superconsciousness may be induced by taking a drug shows that every example of superconsciousness must involve a change in the body-chemistry similar to that induced by the drug. But the disadvantage of the drug is that it produces other changes, as well as those which temporarily enable certain organs in the brain to register these high vibrations; and it is the reaction from these other chemical activities which has so disastrous a result in the long run.

This danger is obviated when we use the other means that are mentioned by Patanjali – and in spite of the concluding remarks in Vivekananda's comment on the aphorism, also in spite of much that we hear today from people who really ought to know better, it is impossible to succeed in meditation until one has also used the other means. Incantations, or the power of words, must be employed. Mortification is indispensable. Without these there can be no concentration, and we shall now proceed to outline the Builders teaching concerning these two important details.

We make a great deal of use of the power of words. From the very beginning of our work we ask our affiliates to learn the affirmations which state the truth about the Self of man, and these affirmations are what Vivekananda calls <u>mantrams</u>, written in English. There is more to them than the words, as you know by this time. In these ten sentences there is a sound-value and a rhythm-value, and the sound and rhythm play their part in making the affirmations effective. The English language, however, is not so good a medium for making "words-of-power" as are some other tongues.

Latin, for example, lends itself very well to this kind of thing, and the sentences of the Roman Catholic liturgy have a very strong <u>mantric</u> power. Sanskrit is also well-adapted to making powerful combinations of sound and meaning, and whole books on this subject are to be found in the occult literature of India. It is because of the sound-value in certain words that we find this injunction in <u>The Chaldean Oracles</u>:

"Change not barbarous names in evocation, for they are names divine, having power ineffable in the mysteries."

One principle, however, that we try to adhere to is that nothing shall be used in practice that is not understood by the person who is doing the work. It is on this account that we prefer the Hebrew words of power. For we know the sound-value and the color-value of every Hebrew letter, so that every technical term in the Secret Wisdom of Israel can be expressed for us as either a sequence of colors or as a sequence of tones. And all our study of the Qabalah is designed to make us familiar with the realities corresponding to these colors and tones.

A member of this class came to us with the objection that it seemed to her that in our concentration work we were only getting reflections of our previous studies -- that after all this work only sets the mind to echoing, as it were, the forms implanted therein by learning the various attributions of the letters, the Tree of Life and its paths, and so on. There is merit in such an objection, and to be able to make it shows the right mental attitude to have toward all occult work. But the student overlooked one important detail. <u>Symbolism is the universal language of the race-consciousness</u>. When you learn the First Year work you are not putting anything into your mind except convenient tags or labels for the ideas your mind already contains. Because the Qabalah is built up scientifically, because the correspondences are true ones, because, at bottom, all these attributions were derived by introspection, this work will ultimately put you in possession of details of the Ageless Wisdom which never can be written in books.

Perhaps the most important thing of all is the fact that this Qabalistic symbolism is a product of the self-examination of men trained in introspection. Concerning the value of introspection we shall write at some length in the next lesson. Just now it need only be said that the Secret Wisdom is the truth which the wise have found by looking within. That truth is always within. It is within you even at this moment -- all of it, and every one of its details. The practice of concentration and meditation simply assists you in bringing it to the surface.

And this brings me to the other part of the student's objection. "It all comes from yourself, doesn't it?" she asked. "Nothing comes from outside." And this seemed to her to indicate that something must be wrong with the work. As a matter of fact it is just what is right with concentration and meditation. We are never so much on the wrong track as when we try to get anything from outside. Even so careful a writer as Vivekananda made a slip in the very quotation given at the beginning of this lesson when he said, "there is no limit to each particular outlet getting any amount of power from outside."

Power is always <u>inside</u>. Whatever the heights you may attain, the power that takes you there will come from within. For the only place where anybody can contact the infinite and eternal energy whence all things proceed is at the very heart of being. Some metaphysicians even go so far as to say that really there isn't any "outside" at all. We are not prepared to argue with them, although at present it seems otherwise to us. But the Builders hold, in agreement with every teaching of the Ageless Wisdom, that the whole process of occult training and development is the <u>externalization</u> of powers already latent within the heart of man.

This, indeed, is one potent reason why the use of drugs is inadvisable. To take a drug to make you superconscious is to fasten the more firmly upon yourself the delusion that you can get power from outside. As a matter of fact the drug only provides a condition, a fulcrum for the lever of your internal power.

To get back to the subject of words-of-power, let us sum up the whole matter by saying that we use the Hebrew names because they are the ones which we can most conveniently explain, because their number is relatively small, and because we can turn every letter into a color and sound. Let us say further that when these names are intoned in the sound-sequences indicated by the letters, an actual vibration is set up which affects everything in correspondence with it.

We need to remember always that our slightest physical activities modify all the matter in space. This is a tremendous fact, determined by the researches of physical scientists. What it means has been well put by Allan Bennett in one of his lectures on <u>The Wisdom of the Aryas</u>:

"I strike my hand on the table, and the action, in that same indivisible instant of time, shifts – by a tiny space, of course, but still shifts – the center of gravity of the earth. Simultaneously, also, the

27

great Sun swerves in his vast march through space, carrying with him his retinue of servient planets. And, you must remember this: that, minute although that alteration in his path may be, it is, if you give it time enough, by no means inappreciable in its results; for, since it involves a change from the path he would otherwise have gone, the distance goes on increasing forever. And not even at our Sun, at our whole family of planets, does the effect of that action – of every action of every living thing – come to an end. Far otherwise, for in the same indivisible moment of time, if the velocity of propagation (of gravitation) be but infinite, great distant Sirius, mightier than a thousand of our own Sun rolled into one huge orb, is likewise set recoiling at a slightly different angle; and yet again, in that same instant, every sun and star that shines; aye, and countless long-dead suns as well, are similarly affected. There is no tiniest speck of cosmic dust but is changed in its direction because of that my action; however remote or tiny; however near or large. All the great universe thrills in answer to every movement of each living thing in each of all these countless islets of its life; until we come to understand how, even in this purely material sense, all Life is One indeed; for force is indestructible, and the effect continues for eternity. Thus, in a sense, we come to see how somehow every atom of matter has a certain part in every other atom; is in a manner present in it; inalienably affecting it each moment of its life."

Because of this Eliphas Levi wrote, "There are no solitary actions." Because of this, too, there is a meaning within a meaning in Jesus' words, "Of myself I can do nothing." For he meant not only that the One Life personified in His teaching as the "Father" is the Eternal Worker in all human activities, but He registered also His knowledge that not even the least of human actions is confined to the personal vehicle through which the One Life performs that action.

For us the time has come when our knowledge of this truth makes it intolerable for us to be unskillful in action. We begin to see the tremendous importance to the Great Work of even our lightest words and thoughts. Either we mar the Work and delay it a little, or else we aid it, and help to speed it to completion. So when we sit in meditation in the seeming solitude of our own rooms, we are really changing even the physical course of worlds, because we are making slight, but nevertheless actual, rearrangements of the atoms in our brains. And when we say a mantram, whether in English, or in some other tongue, the sound and color vibrations which we set up make themselves felt to the outermost reaches of space.

Yet must we remember always that all this is done in and through us by the One Life. It has brought us together to study Its own finer laws. It will ripen us – perhaps by putting obstacles in our way. The illusion of separateness makes it seem to us that we make personal efforts to gain skill and precision, and we cannot say too often that we must act just as if this illusion were true. At the same time we must KNOW THAT IT IS AN ILLUSION, and so escape being deluded by it. Not illusion, the necessary fiction which makes existence possible, but delusion, the forgetting of the truth back of the fiction, is what we all must learn sooner or later to escape from. Complete escape is Moksha, liberation, cosmic consciousness.

Mortification goes to extremes among certain types of religious fanatics, but dare we sit in judgment upon our brothers and sisters because they follow ways which seem to us to be painful and unnecessary? We do not know. We advocate no such extremes as those cited by Vivekananda. At the same time we know that physical control is necessary, and we refuse to be stampeded by the fears of people who do not know that what the Hindus call Hatha Yoga is not regarded, even by its most enthusiastic devotees, as an end in itself. Thus we find the Gheranda Sanhita, one of the Hindu classics on Hatha Yoga, saying: "I salute that First Lord who taught first the science of Hatha Yoga. This is a ladder for climbing to the higher heights of Raja Yoga." Even the most rabid of these who denounce Hatha Yoga will recommend the Bhagavad-Gita, and yet the Gita gives precise directions as to posture and breathing, and posture and breathing are part of Hatha Yoga. So is keeping the body clean, inside and out. Vivekananda says, "A dirty man cannot be a Yogi." If you want to learn to concentrate, first learn to be scrupulously clean. All this is Hatha Yoga.

We give no rules for hygiene and diet. They are too well known in these days. A freak diet will not help you, unless you happen to be very suggestible, when your belief in the virtues of this or that kind of food may be of some assistance. You will find out from experience what agrees with you and what does not. The main thing is not to eat too much. An old rule is: Eat half what can conveniently be taken.

As to posture, the Hindu teachers differ considerably in their directions, but their meaning is one. The Gheranda Sanhita describes 32 postures (as many as there are paths on the Tree of Life). Some are very difficult, and some seem at first to be comparatively easy. Patanjali says, "Posture is that which is firm and pleasant." Sankhya's directions are equally concise, "Posture is that which is steady and easy." Be on your guard here. The meaning is not, "Take any posture which is comfortable." No posture is comfortable after a few minutes. To be "firm and pleasant" or "steady and easy," a posture must be practiced, and the practice will take you through a door of pain.

Choose a position that keeps the head and back erect and in a straight line. Do not cross the knees. Be careful to sit neither too high nor too low, because in either instance you will put pressure on the nerves behind the knees. When you have decided how you shall sit, be neither relaxed nor tense. The idea is to maintain perfect balance of the flexor and extensor muscles, so that the muscular pull and push shall be equilibrated all over the body. This is very difficult and painful at first. If this part of your practice does not hurt, it is because you are unconsciously easing your muscles by little movements. Watch for these. They are bad "breaks". Other distractions will come, too. You will develop itching and tickling sensations in the most unexpected places, yet you must endeavor to keep still in spite of them.

Above all things, do not abandon one posture to try another. Stick to the one you begin with. One day, just as you are ready to believe that steadiness and comfort will never come, you will suddenly find that all sense of body is lost. You won't know you have a body, and from that time on your chosen posture will be the most comfortable attitude you can assume.

Besides posture there is also the matter of breath-control, which the Hindus call Pranayama. If you have had any special training in Pranayama, you need not change your accustomed breath-rhythms. If not, practice rhythmic breathing as follows:

Breathe in through the nostrils slowly, while you count four pulse-beats; hold the breath for sixteen pulse-beats; breathe out through the mouth during eight pulse-beats. In the out-breathing pucker your lips as if your intention was to whistle. Let all this breathing be done slowly and evenly, and use ten of these cycles of breathing before you begin to practice.

The exercises for this lesson have to do with the 29th, 28th and 27th paths. They complete the lower triangle of the Sephiroth. This has at its center YESOD, the Sephirah which corresponds to the cell-consciousness, or automatic consciousness of the physical organism. (Consider well the various attributions of YESOD as given in the First Year Course.) This Sephirah is the center of the triangle whose points are Malkuth, Hod and Netzach. YESOD, the foundation, is manifested in all three of these other Sephiroth. In Malkuth the power of YESOD takes form as sensation. In Hod the same power is the root of intellectual activities. In Netzach it takes form in emotions and desires. Thus when you have completed this lower triangle of Sephiroth, with Yesod at the center, you have symbolically formulated an equilibration of sensation, intellect and feeling.

Following the same order of attributions as you used in the exercises given in the preceding lesson, practice five minutes (or more) on each path. Project the light from Malkuth to Netzach through the 29th path. Project it from Yesod to Netzach through the 28th path. Draw it across the Tree of Life from Hod to Netzach along the 27th path. Use colors one session, letters another, Tarot cards another, in the same order that you followed in the exercise with the 32nd, 31st and 30th paths. Rest, as before, the seventh day from the day on which you began.

KEEP YOUR RECORD CAREFULLY. If a day comes when you hate the work, say so. These first exercises have deeper meaning than you may now perceive. Don't make the mistake of trying to write a record which you think will please us, the framers of this work. Write exactly what happens. The thing you think not so very important may be the key to your whole problem, and what bulks large in your imagination may not really amount to much. The ways of this world have a tendency to make unconscious liars of all men. Strive to let this account of your work be the undecorated and unvarnished truth.

When you have completed the exercises up to this point you will have passed symbolically through four grades of the Invisible Rosicrucian Order. That is to say, you will have furnished yourself with the pass-words and with certain signs by which members of that Order know each other on the Inner Planes. More than this, you will have attracted by your practice the attention of certain wise ones who are ahead of you on the Path. But do not practice to attract their attention. Practice because you recognize the need for gaining skill, in order that you may be fit to serve.

Among the members of the Invisible Order, or Inner School, when they have attained to a certain degree of conscious perception that such a School really exists, there is regular communication of thought and ideas. You will find a very interesting description of this whole matter in The Cloud Upon the Sanctuary, by Eckhartshausen, especially in Chapter II. As this book is now somewhat difficult to procure, we shall make extracts from it for the use of our affiliates, and these extracts will be issued as a supplement to this course.

The first grade of the Invisible Order is that of Zelator, and it corresponds to the Sephirah Malkuth. The work of the Zelator has to do with the right classification of the four elements, as shown in the color-cross in Malkuth. His, too, is the work of mastering the senses, of refining them, of purifying them. (Do not forget that to purify is to free from adulteration or mixture. Be on your guard against false interpretations of "purification.")

The Hebrew mantram corresponding to this Sephirah and to the Grade of Zelator is the divine name Adonai Melek, which means "Lord King" or "Divine Royalty." It is pronounced Ah-doh-nah-ee Meh-lek, and the tonal sequence indicated by its letters is as follows:

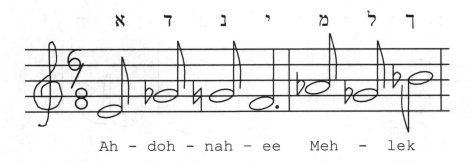

Ah - doh - nah - ee   Meh - lek

The Sephirah Yesod corresponds to the Grade of Theoricus, which means one versed in the theory of the Great Work. This is an intimation that the whole theory of the Work is somehow connected with the mystery of this 9th Path. So it is, for the basis of the work is the equilibration and sublimation of the power of Yesod. Ponder the attributions of this Sephirah, ask for light from within, and you will begin to realize what it is that you are trying to accomplish.

The mantram for this Grade of Theoricus is the divine name Shaddai El Chai, which means literally "The Almighty Strength of Life", the tonal sequence with the pronunciation:

Shah - dah - ee   Ay - yil   Ch'ah - ee

To the Sephirah of Intellectual Activity, the sphere of Reason, corresponds the Grade of Practicus, the grade of those who have passed from study of theory to the experimental work upon which all valid inductive reasoning must be established. The practice of the Builders is founded upon reason. Its method is the scientific method, the method of observation, inference and trial. The mantram of this Grade is Elohim Tzabaoth, "The Powers of the Hosts," and it is intoned as follows:

Ay - yil - oh he - eem Tsah - bah - oo - ooth

The fourth Grade is the Grade of Philosophus, in which, after experiment, observation and intellectual examination have determined the laws of the Work, the advancing seeker for light begins to grasp somewhat of the meaning behind the laws, something of the philosophy behind the facts. The mantram of this grade is as follows:

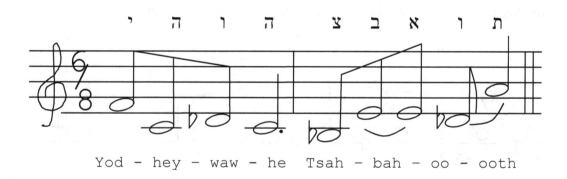

Yod - hey - waw - he Tsah - bah - oo - ooth

CAUTION: Do not use these mantrams thoughtlessly, or "just to see what will happen." They are given at this point for the sake of completeness, and because it is necessary now that you should know what they are. Do not forget that these tone-sequences are color-sequences also. Rightly performed, these names are seen as well as heard.

On the next page you will find a summary of your progress on the Path of Return up to this point. Do not attempt to go beyond this lesson until you have every detail of this portion of the work.

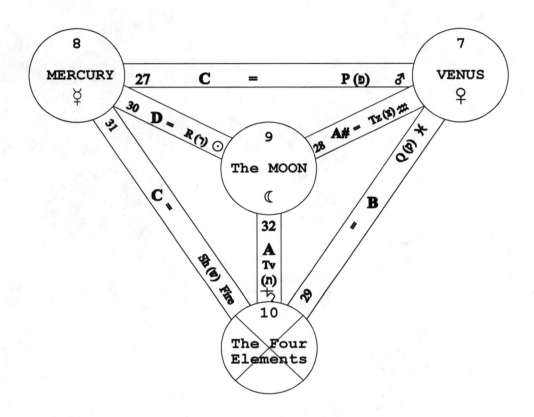

Watchful Introspection

Ideal Suggestion Through Mental Photography is the ponderous title of a good book by the New Thought-pioneer, Henry Wood, in which he begins a chapter (or perhaps it was a chapter in his The New Thought Simplified) with an anecdote about a boy who answered, when admonished not to whistle, "I ain't whistlin'. It whistles itself." So it is with the activity of the brain-cells in most of us. "It thinks itself" is a pretty accurate description of what happens to us all day long.

One evening at dinner with one of our affiliates who has begun these concentration exercises, various points on concentration came up. Among other thoughts, he said, "The most astonishing thing that I have learned is that we do not think. We are thought. I begin to hold an image, and perhaps two minutes later find myself thinking about the potatoes I had for dinner, and this without any realization of the moment when my attention began to wander."

To be able to recognize this is encouraging. Many practice a long time without noticing their "breaks." Some pupils have assured us that they only made ten or eleven breaks in the course of five minutes. This means simply that they haven't learned how to watch. Ten breaks in five minutes would be an average of one every thirty seconds, and if you can really hold a selected image steady for thirty seconds you do not need this course at all. For the Yogis teach that when the thinking principle can be restrained from taking any but a selected form for twelve seconds, that is Dharana, or concentration. And Dharana prolonged becomes Dhyana, or meditation, which is defined by Patanjali in the third chapter of the Yoga Sutras: "A prolonged holding of the receiving consciousness in that region is meditation" (that is, in the region selected as a focal point of concentration.)

What really happens to many people who suppose themselves to be concentrating is that they disconnect attention altogether from the associative processes of the mind. This is what is done when we follow any of those directions for "going into the silence" which bid us make the mind passive, and try to think of nothing. DON'T TRY TO MAKE YOUR MIND A BLANK. To do so is to invite anarchy in the brain-cells. Not only anarchy in your own brain-cells, but susceptibility to every vagrant thought-form that may be in your neighborhood. Remember that your personality exists on more planes than one, and that within and above the physical (in the sense that the finer rates of vibration are higher, just as the more rapidly vibrating notes of the musical scale are "higher") there are forms of Life which seek externalization through physical vehicles. Some of these forms are beneficent, some are hostile, some are best described as "sprites." If you relinquish command of your brain-cells by becoming passive and making your mind a blank, you give up all power of selection. Remarkable phenomena may result from this kind of "development," but you never can tell what will happen, nor can you ever be sure that the same "forces" will come twice in succession. You will be played upon, but you yourself will not gain the least bit of added control over your brain-activities, or over the finer forces of your being.

That some people who make themselves passive perform works of healing, speak in strange tongues, describe distant scenes, get apparently authentic messages from the departed, and deliver wonderful inspirational addresses is true. But these people are puppets of forces they do not understand, and they do not ripen with the passage of time. Their spiritual stature is not increased, their own latent forces are not unfolded, their store of wisdom is not tapped. Such people have performed a great service to the world, for they have forced upon a materialistic age the realization that besides the forces perceived by the senses there are other subtler modes of the One Life in which we all share. We believe that in the long run they will be compensated for this work, because it is a tremendous sacrifice. For theirs is not the way of mastery, and in taking it they impose upon themselves the necessity of a greater number of incarnations, in order to restore the balance which is disturbed by passive surrender to the elemental vibrations of the etheric and astral planes. We look upon them as self-immolated victims, but we would not have you among their number.

For the time has passed when the world needs to be convinced at such tremendous cost. And there is great need for skilled workers in another field. The Great Work now demands adepts in the conscious direction of these forces to which the passive must needs blindly surrender. The call has gone forth from Those Beyond for those trained by patient practice in the command of these groups of living beings which our physiologists call "brain-centers" and "sympathetic ganglia." Such command is not to be achieved by the person who practices making his mind a blank, who endeavors to think about nothing.

Concentration is not this. It is, says Patanjali, the restraint of the thinking principle from taking various forms. Psychologists would call it the restraint of the tendency of the mind to make associations of ideas. Not one person in ten thousand has sufficient command of this associative activity even to direct it in a predetermined course. Not one in fifty thousand is able to check it altogether. hat one in fifty thousand who can really stop the association of ideas has not gained his power by becoming passive. On the contrary, his adeptship (for such a man is deserving the title of adept) is the fruit of long and patient, and watchful training.

When we first begin we do not notice the breaks, because we do not really see what goes on in the mental field at all. We really have some moments of oblivion, and do not notice when the image chosen slips out of range, nor when it comes back. The result is that we think we have been attending to it much longer than we really have. Be on your guard against this. Almost everybody experiences it when such practice as this is first begun.

In the preceding lesson we said we should have something to say about introspection. All that you have just read is by way of preparation. For the essence of introspection is watchfulness, and this intense, alert observation of what is happening in your mental field is just the opposite from the passivity of the person who is trying "to think of nothing."

Introspection, called Pratyahara in the Yoga Sutras begins as mere attentive observation of the current of images flowing through the mental field. Before beginning this practice you should understand that there is a sense in which the production of these images may be thought of as being almost automatic. If you keep this in mind you will escape the horror which assails some people the moment they find out what is really going on just below the surface of consciousness.

To understand what is happening you must remember that the subconsciousness contains a great deal of experience that you have absorbed without knowing anything whatever about it. The most respectable spinster in New York, for instance, undoubtedly has tucked away in her memory a complete vocabulary of slang, profanity and obscenity. For we are all exposed daily to the language of the gutters, and although we refuse to attend to the filth which assails our ears, we hear it just the same, and our brain-cells record everything. In like manner there are stored away in our brains hundreds of phrases in foreign tongues, thousands of facts and names and faces, thousands of impressions of scenes of which we have no conscious recollection. And from this tremendous mass of images -- some beautiful, some horrible -- the process of association brings up all sorts of things. And not only does it bring up the duplicates of long-forgotten and partly never-realized experience, but it brings up, too, fantastic combinations of these elements -- strange beasts like the Snark, the Jabberwock and the Mock Turtle in the Alice stories.

You must not hold yourself responsible for this. Some people have been driven almost to desperation when they found their minds echoing with phrases like those we see chalked up on blank walls everywhere. They have come to us, convinced that they were either going insane, or that they must be terribly depraved. Nothing of the sort. It is all perfectly natural, and all the working of a law that you can utilize to produce marvelous results, once you learn to command it.

Begin, then, by watching the mental images as they rise. They will be as varied as a crowd of people passing in the street. As you sit by your mental window you will see all sorts and conditions of thoughts go past. Some will be clean and beautiful. Some will be dirty, and unspeakably ugly. Let them pass. Be careful not to detain any of them at this point in your practice. There will be a temptation to do so, when some lovely image comes along. Resist it for the present. Just watch, until you learn the first lesson from introspection which is: unless controlled, the process of association is purely automatic, and is not in any sense to be regarded as a self-conscious function.

If we could go no farther than this, however, our case would be hopeless indeed. The second exercise in Pratyahara gives us encouragement. Simply by intending that the flow of the images past your mental observation-post shall be slower, you will find that it really does slacken in speed. Do not make the mistake of trying to check the images one by one by holding onto any of them. Simply will the procession to move more slowly, and you will find that it does. "Will," perhaps, is not quite the right word. Probably "expect" is better. Calmly expect the slackening of the speed of association, and wait patiently but confidently. What you expect will happen, and then you will have learned your second lesson: the speed of association can be modified by expectant attention.

Perfection in slowing down the associations will not come all at once. This is what Vivekananda has to tell us on this subject:

"How hard it is to control the mind. Well has it been compared to the maddened monkey. There was a monkey, restless by his own nature, as all monkeys are. As if that were not enough someone made him drink freely of wine, so that he became still more restless. Then a scorpion stung him. When a man is stung by a scorpion he jumps about for a whole day, so the poor monkey found his condition worse than ever. To complete this misery a demon entered into him. What language can describe the uncontrollable restlessness of that monkey? The human mind is like that monkey; incessantly active by its own nature, then it becomes drunk with the wine of desire, thus increasing its turbulence. After desire takes possession comes the sting of the scorpion of jealousy of others whose desires meet with fulfillment, and last of all the demon of pride takes possession of the mind, making it think itself of all importance. How hard to control such a mind."

"The first lesson, then, is to sit for some time and let the mind run on. The mind is bubbling up all the time. It is like that monkey jumping about. Let the monkey jump as much as he can; you simply wait and watch. Knowledge is power says the proverb, and that is true. Until you know what the mind is doing you cannot control it. Give it the full length of the reins; many most hideous thoughts may come into it; you will be astonished that it was possible for you to think such thoughts. But you will find that each day the mind's vagaries are becoming less and less violent, that each day it is becoming calmer. In the first few months you will find that the mind will have a thousand thoughts, later you will find that it is toned down to perhaps seven hundred, and after a few more months it will have fewer and fewer, until at last it will be under perfect control, but we must patiently practice every day. As soon as the steam is turned on the engine must run, and as soon as things are before us we must perceive; so a man, to prove that he is not a machine, must demonstrate that he is under the control of nothing. This controlling of the mind, and not allowing it to join itself to the centres, is Pratyahara. How is this practiced? It is a long work, not to be done in a day. Only after a patient, continuous struggle for years can we succeed."

It takes years, that is, to gain perfect mastery; but long before perfection comes we may experience the benefits of introspection. The beginner at music has to play little pieces to parlor audiences before he makes his appearance on the concert stage. Does he refuse to practice because he cannot be a Rubinstein the first year? This thirst for immediate results -- any thirst for results, indeed, -- has a touch of indecency about it. It drives people who like to call themselves "occult students" from teacher to teacher, sets them to playing Indian in one "Order" after another, and provides an endless supply of gulls for the exploiters of "easy methods." Can you give me a better reason for practicing concentration than the one advanced by Vivekananda?: "A man, to prove that he is not a machine, must demonstrate that he is under the control of nothing."

Assertion is not demonstration. Affirmations are not demonstrations. Going about saying, "I believe every human being has free-will" won't help you a bit to demonstrate that you aren't just a puppet on the strings of the currents of thought and emotion which impinge upon your brain-cells from all points of the compass. Practice is the only thing that will enable you to demonstrate that while your whole personality -- your body, your emotions, your mind or consciousness in all of its three planes -- is incontestably a machine, YOU. The Self behind it all, the MAN behind the personality, the GOD behind the human mask, are really a center of Free Will, controlling the whole of this complex vehicle of your self-expression.

We echo my friend and teacher (though I knew him not in the flesh), that great Seer, Jacob Boehme: "It is not I who write these things. This that you see is but a simple-minded and foolish old man. These things are of the love of God." It is not Paul Case telling you to practice. It is not Paul Case sounding the call to make yourself fit for service. It is the God in you, speaking to you from this page, announcing to you the miracle of His mastery of your life, laying before you the perfect beauty of His law of mastery. Will you answer that one with a whine about practical benefits, or are you ripe enough to give the only answer that is an honest one, the answer of hard work?

Three paths lie before you now on the Way of Return, and as best we can we shall try to let the light that has come down to us from those who have gone before illuminate them, so that you may the better understand the real purport of your practice for this lesson.

All of them are paths of projection. On the Tree of Life they are the 26th, the 25th and the 24th, the paths of OIN, SAMEKH and NUN.

The first is the path of the Dweller on the Threshold, and this is that Terror which we have tried to mitigate a little for you by telling you beforehand of the horrors you will encounter when you begin the practice of introspection. It is the path of THE DEVIL in the Tarot, and what says the Scripture? "Resist the devil, and he will flee." And how shall we resist him? Not as so many have tried to do, only to find themselves in worse bondage than ever. Not by repression, not by shuddering aversion which imputes to the phantom a power he does not possess, not by looking some other way, and pretending that he is not there. None of these is the prophylactic method. None of these is the way of the priests of old Egypt, who washed their hearts with laughter.

That is what is behind Vivekananda's comparison of the mind to the antics of a monkey. We all laugh at monkeys. So should we laugh at the devil. And the devil is only a personification of the unrestrained activity of the subconscious power of the association. It is a personification developed in the animistic ages when there was no science of psychology, and when men misunderstood the voices and the visions which come sometimes so sharp and definite that they seem like objective realities. All the demons that tempt us are nothing but the results of unrestrained associations rising from the subconsciousness. We must learn to laugh at them, as we would laugh at a monkey.

Approach your introspection exercises, therefore, prepared to be amused, not frightened, at the monsters that will appear before your astonished gaze. Remember that all this is merely the automatism of an uncurbed mind. Observe it with cool, impassive interest, and you cannot fail to be amused.

Just take a look at the picture of the DEVIL in the Tarot. Isn't he laughable? The essence of mirth, we are told, is incongruity, and this whole picture is a mass of incongruous details. It is as ridiculous as the theological idea that a God of love could permit the existence of a devil, as mirth-provoking to anybody with a sense of humor as the notion of hell.

Remember, too, that this is the path of the Renewing Intelligence, of which it is written: "Thereby God -- blessed be He! -- reneweth all which is capable of renovation in the creation of the world." In Lesson 2 of this Section. I have written at length about THE DEVIL, and now let me add something to confirm what I said about the number of the path (26) and the number of the card (XV) showing that this is really a picture of the Life-Power.

The name of the path is the clue. "Renewing" in Hebrew is spelt מחודש, and its numeration is 358, the numeration alike to נחש, the tempter, and of משיח, the Redeemer. Truly our Elder Brethren in the Secret Wisdom have blazed here a trail so plain that he who runs may read! And consider one by one the Tarot Keys corresponding to the letters of מחודש.

First comes the HANGED MAN (מ), the symbol of the path which, on the Way of Return has its beginning in HOD and leads upward to GEBURAH. "I look forward with confidence to the perfect realization of the Eternal Splendor of the Limitless Light," we say, and so saying, take a position which is exactly the inversion of that held by the masses of humanity, who look forward with fear and terror to all sorts of evils which they imagine to be hid by the veil of the Future. Because we look forward with such confidence, we expect a day when not only we ourselves shall be at one with the perfect Law of the cosmic life. We anticipate a time when our full surrender to that Law will change it from PACHAD, the inspirer of fear, to GEBURAH the source of our strength, and DIN, the clear-eyed recognition of the undeviating Justice of the perfect law. This is not the outlook of the world, and he in whom it has become vital and compelling lives as Boehme advises us to live: "In all things walk thou contrary to the world." He who so walks does nothing of himself, is in all things as one suspended from the Tree of Life, seeing always that not his personality, but the One Life, is the performer of all action, the speaker of all words, the thinker of all thoughts. Thus, in the midst of action he does nothing, in the midst of speech he is silent, and in the midst of the thinking of which his brain is the vehicle he remains unmoved. Such is the beginning of the renewal of the mind.

The next Key is the CHARIOT, and this Key represents the perfection of what the Hindus call Kriya Yoga, "working towards Yoga." Vivekananda gives an almost perfect description of this Key in his commentary on the first sutra in the second chapter of Patanjali's book:

"The organs are the horses, the mind is the reins, the intellect is the charioteer, and this body is the chariot. The master of the household, the King, the Self of man is sitting in this chariot." In the Tarot the King and the Charioteer are one, and that one is the Warrior, the Conqueror of Whom it is written: "Stand aside in the coming battle, and though thou fightest, be not thou the warrior." He is the Nike, too, of the Apocalypse, concerning whom it is written, "To him that overcometh I will give a crown of life." When the personality has become as the HANGED MAN, then is it transformed into the CHARIOT of the Divine Self, and all that makes up the personality becomes a vehicle for the ONE. This is the second step of renewal.

The third Key is the HIEROPHANT (ו). When the personality has become the vehicle of the One Life, then the VOICE of that Life speaks in the silence which follows the hurly-burly of our identification with personality, and the revelation of the mysteries begins. Then is the inner ear opened, and we hear the secret word which unites us to the ONE. The beginning of this way is in the mental attitude expressed by our fourth affirmation, which corresponds to Chesed, for the path of the HIEROPHANT leads up from Chesed to Chokmah. When we say "From the exhaustless riches of its limitless substance I draw all things needful, both spiritual and material," we are turning to the only source of instruction open to any man. The illusion of separateness makes us look to books and teachers for light, but they set nothing before us but symbols, and unless the Interpreter within the Temple expounds the meaning of those symbols we learn nothing from what we read or hear. And until we silence the clamor of personality we cannot hear His voice, for it is a voice that must be listened for, even as Elijah found it, a still, small voice. And the listening is the third stage of our renewal.

The fourth KEY is the EMPRESS (ד). And this is the Key of the path which leads us back from Understanding to Wisdom. And the Understanding is knowledge of the limitations imposed upon all things and creatures in the Without by the working of the perfect Law. It is understanding of the great truth that even as fences keep cattle from straying out of fields where they may feed, and losing themselves in desert places, so do the obstacles which seem to hedge us about prevent us from leaving the field marked out for each of us to cultivate. For the Sephirah of Understanding is the sphere of Saturn, and the last Key of the Tarot shows us that Saturn, Lord of Limitation, is really the world-consciousness which gives meaning and definition to the dance of life. It is the law that Life, to express itself, must take on form, and when form is understood it is seen to be our opportunity. So from Understanding springs the path of LOVE, and that Love, remember, is what the alchemists called Venus, or Copper, the metal whose name in Hebrew is also the name of the serpent of temptation, N Ch Sh. Love, sprung from Understanding, the perfect Love which casts

40

out fear, the unfailing Love whose sphere on the Tree of Life is VICTORY, is the fourth stage of our renewal.

The fifth and last Key is JUDGMENT (ש), and this is the Key of that transmuting Fire which is identical with the Life-Breath assigned to the path of Aleph. For Sh=300, and 300=RVCh ALHIM, Ruach Elohim, the Life-Breath of the gods (who so long imagine themselves to be but mortal men), and that same RVCh is the keen, sharp air of superconsciousness which takes us up the path of Aleph back to the Crown. Yet the pat of Aleph and the path of Shin are really one, and this is why our Brother, Eliphas Levi, sworn to conceal the mystery of the Tarot, did nevertheless reveal it by attributing the FOOL to the path of Shin. For the FOOL and JUDGMENT are two aspects on one thing, even as the AIR which is assigned to Kether as its sphere of action and the Mercury which is assigned to Hod are also one. In JUDGMENT we see the regenerated soul ascending as a little child, and the sphere into which he ascends is that of which we say "I look forward to the perfect realization of the Eternal Splendor of the Limitless Light." The Child and the Fool are One, and the regenerating fire of the Path of Shin is the Life-Breath of the path of Aleph. For the Child is the Christ, and the Fool is the Christ as well, the Messiah, the anointed one, even as Waite says, "a prince of another world."

And in the Fire of the letter Shin the DEVIL is cast, becoming one with that fire, and ceasing forevermore to scare the Child with his gargoyle visage. For the Devil is God misunderstood, and when misunderstanding ceases the Devil ceases too, and we see that the grinning monster of the 26th Path, the terrible Dweller on the Threshold, is only the purifying fire of the Great Divine Life-Breath.

So, this grinning ape that we watch, this bubbling witches' caldron of subconscious cerebration that we must learn to laugh at, is really the power that shall finally set us free. For it is the very same power of association that gets us into trouble now, which will enable us to find the way to union with the Self. That is why I have given you a whole year's work at learning the wonderful language in which the sages have set down the directions for the wayfarer on the path of Return. All this Qabalah and all this symbolism in the Tarot give the necessary materials for subconscious association to work upon. But you will not be able to use these materials, as I have used them in these last few pages, until you have had some practice in the stilling of the mind. For until you can stop activity you cannot master it, and to stop this dancing monkey there is just one way, the one outlined early in this lesson.

The 25th path corresponds to the Key of TEMPERANCE. It is the path of testing, the path of trial, wherein one fails who has not done the work of the 25th path. For this is the path of Samekh, remember, and its essential meaning is shown in the significance of that letter's name -- a prop, a support. The tests that come to us in the path are such as we may not meet unless we are truly resting our lives upon the firm foundation of Eternal Being. And so this path leads upward from YESOD to Tiphareth, and its color shows us that it is essentially the same as the path which leads upward from Tiphareth to Kether. For both paths are blue, and thus both correspond to the Moon.

This correspondence escapes those who cannot correlate symbols. Why is Sagittarius, ruled by Jupiter, assigned to a path that shows its essential nature is that of the Moon? We hear this question often. But consider. One aspect of the sign Sagittarius we have learned to identify with Iris, the goddess of the rainbow. Yet Iris, like all feminine deities is but one phase of the great

Mother-principle, the Moon. Nor must we forget that one aspect of the Moon-goddess is Diana, the huntress, whose silver bow is the crescent-moon. Both Iris and Diana, then, are goddesses of the BOW, and the bow which speeds the arrow of concentrated Astral Light is actually the driving-power of the subconsciousness, symbolized by the Moon. More than this, that driving power comes from the very roots of <u>physical existence,</u> is the power which is expressed in those primal instincts of subconsciousness, the instinct of self-perpetuation and its fruit, the instinct of self-reproduction. So long as our lives do not rest upon the foundation of Eternal Being, so long as we have not passed the Dweller on the Threshold, so long as we have not cast the delusion of the Devil into the liberating Fire, we cannot meet the tests of the 25th path, for those are tests of our skill in tempering and modifying the power by which man seemingly multiplies the power of the Astral Light in reproduction. I repeat, we cannot meet these tests so long as we are deluded by separateness, for every test is a test of USE, and <u>right use</u> is impossible unless we know beforehand that not the personality, but the SELF is the User, and know, too, that nowhere in the universe is there any Adversary or any Genius of Limitation that can bring harm from right use, that is, use free from personal limitations, free from the lie of possessiveness, free from all the chains that bind us down to earth. These are two-edged words that we write. This teaching is a sword. Beware lest you grasp it by the blade instead of the handle. Here is no proclamation of sottish license, no intimation that the way of life is the way of lust. Read, and then read again, until the clean, pure inner meaning flashes on your mind.

The last of the three paths that lead to Tiphareth is the path of Death, the path of the letter Nun. Observe that the name of that path is דמיוני = 120 = סמך, so that here is a Qabalistic hint that the path of Samekh and the path of Nun are essentially the same. This number 120 is said in the Bible to be the number of the years of man, a symbolic way of saying that 120 signifies the full perfection of human life. And 120 is also the product of the multiplication of the numbers from 1 to 5 (1x2x3x4x5), which implies the perfect synthesis of all sensory activities in the sixth sense, superconsciousness. Again, the extension of the number XV, which is that of the Tarot Key corresponding to the 26th path, is also 120, so that this path, too, corresponds in a way to the same ideas. Finally, since, as we have just seen, 120 is the number which represents the extension of 15, it is also the secret number of the 15th path on the Tree of Life, and this 15th path is that of the letter Heh, the path of VISION, the path of the Emperor, who is the symbol of that Creator concerning whom it is written in the Sepher Yetzirah that he who understands the mystery of the Ten Sephiroth restores Him to His throne.

All this probably seems very involved. Let us boil it down. All these cross-correspondences point to different aspects of one thing, and that thing is the attainment of superconsciousness. That attainment is the result of introspection, which casts out the devil. It is not perfected until we have passed the tests of the 25th path. Its result is the banishing also of the delusion that we are mortals, and with the banishing of this delusion comes right understanding of the mystery of death. He who has entered even for a moment into superconsciousness, he who has synthesized sensation into that Existence-Knowledge-Bliss Absolute, sees that as the skeleton is the basis of all the movements of the body, so is what we call "death" the very framework of the continual mutations of existence. He who sees this has attained to the full measure of a man. With Paul he says, "I die daily," and with him exults, "O, Death, where is thy sting?" For when we have restored the Creator to his throne, when the VISION that leads upward from the contemplation of the Beauty of the Divine Order to grasp of the Wisdom behind that Order (the Path of Heh leading up from Tiphareth to Chokmah) has been granted to us, then we know ourselves for what we really are, not mortals condemned to death at some unknown date in the future, but immortals existing for a little while in this world of name and form, and existing by means of a never-ending death. Death then becomes familiar, and ceases to inspire fear, because it is seen to be the process whereby the One Life provides itself with a never-ending series of vestments of Name and Form.

The goal of these three paths is one, the Sephirah Tiphareth, called BN, Ben, the Son. For in the mystical inner Grade to which this Sephirah corresponds, we come to know our unity with the Solar Logos, to experience His consciousness of the Beauty of the Cosmos. And because that Son is indeed "one with the Father," that is, "One with AB, "which is the Qabalistic name of the Sephirah of Wisdom, entrance into this Grade of the Inner School, although it bears only Adeptus Minor, or Lesser Adept, for its title, gives us the means of union with each of the Three Supernals. For from Tiphareth three paths lead upward -- one to Binah, one to Chokmah, and one to Kether, and from Tiphareth alone may we cross the Abyss that separates the Supernals from Chesed. Here is the solution of a difficulty which has puzzled more than one student of the Tree of Life, and which has led at least one earnest seeker for light far from the Ancient Way marked out by the Builders who have passed on before us.

I make no doubt that a great deal in this lesson will seem vague and mystical to you when first you read it; but there is nothing that can be changed. Here if you can grasp what lies behind the words, is a clear statement of the Great Secret of the Way of the Return.

The name of the Grade, as said, is Adeptus Minor, or Lesser Adept. The key to its whole significance is the word תפארת, which we commend you to ponder upon, with the help of the Tarot. The Divine Name is יהוה אלוה ודעת, and may be translated, "Everlasting Existence (IHVH), Power (ALVH) and Insight (VDOTh). The pronunciation and the tonal sequence are:

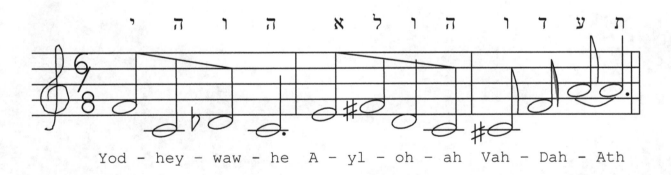

Note the close correspondence of this Hebrew name to the Sat-Chit-Ananda, "Existence-Knowledge-Bliss, of the Hindu Yogis, who use this term to describe the experience of union with the Solar Logos.

The paths corresponding to this lesson are:

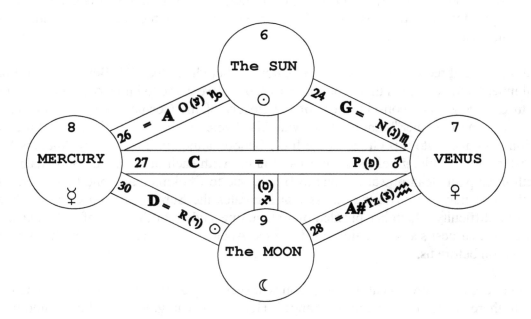

Use the same general method in your daily exercises, but remember that each of these is a path of projection upward to Tiphareth.

Contemplations of the Adepti

Are you beginning to see the real purpose of these ten lessons? Has a glimmer of their real meaning entered your mind? Do you realize that their object is not so much to develop any "powers" which you may have as to bring you, by actual experiment, to a point where you know, from having put your own feet upon the stones of the Path, just how rugged is the Way of Return?

It has come to us that some think our Work has too little love in it -- is too intellectual. We hope there's no mawkish sentimentality on any page that we write, for if any has crept in unawares we have failed in the work that has been entrusted to us. But no love in this work? What is love? Is it a tickling sensation somewhere around your fifth rib? Is it an emotional compensation for what you have missed because you have been too selfish to dare to live? No, love is the gift of one's all to the service of life. It is not just a throb in a speaker's voice that brings tears to your eyes, nor a rhythm and cadence in his words that makes your heart beat faster for a moment. Love has its roots in feeling, we grant you, but it is a barren fig-tree unless it bring forth the fruit of action. And action demands skill and training. You cannot <u>feel</u> your way into the Kingdom of God. There is no substitution for the agony of hard work.

Why does a mother love here child so dearly, if not for the pains it cost her? Why does the artist love his work, if it is not for the agony he must pass through in bringing it to completion? Why does a mighty stream of love flow without cessation from the Heart of Life to us? Why else but that the One Life suffers with, and through, and because of us? He who refuses to drink from the cup of pain is unfit for love, does not know what love means, brings a smile of pity to the lips of Those Who Know. For they, the Workers, know how many weary years and lives must be spent in fruitless questing by the soft sentimentalist who refuses to go through the gate of pain.

So we have given you a touch of Their suffering during this last month, in order to arouse you to a realization of the wonder of their love. Every Master of the Wisdom has passed along this very road. Not one of those who have attained the heights of liberation but has first passed through the valley of the shadow of the death of the old, false, deluded notion of the meaning of personality. Not one but has endured the torments of mind and body that attend the early stages of the path of concentration. We all regard the Masters with what we call reverence, but few of us realize that their own declaration that they are adepts of the Patanjali school means nothing else but that they began, in one of their incarnations, the very kind of work that you have been trying to do. Began it, and continued it to the end, to the glorious end of being <u>fit</u> for service, of being conscious of immortality, of having power to renew their bodies moment by moment, so that they might through centuries hold up the light for wayfarers toiling up the Narrow Way. Once they were as we are, deluded by the sense of separateness, filled with petty jealousies and place-seekings, thirsting for the joys of this world and an extra-special crown in the world to come. But a day came when they heard the call, and when they had set their hands to the plough, they turned not back.

Theirs is no easy way. In the old versions of the Tarot we see it represented in the picture of THE MOON, the XVIIIth KEY, and drops of blood are falling from the Moon upon the path. Even so <u>Light on the Path</u> tells us: "Before the soul can stand in the presence of the Masters its feet must be washed in the blood of the heart." Notice the correspondence between this saying and the XVIIIth

Key, which represents Pisces, the zodiacal sign that governs the feet. It is only another proof that the wise have one language.

Well, we know that many who begin our Work will not persevere in it until the completion, even, of those first steps upon the Way. Sometimes the burden of that knowledge is not easy to bear. These are tests for us, too, tests of our patience, of our forbearance, of our ability to keep on with the work in spite of misunderstanding, in spite of false reports, in spite of small harvesting from so much scattering of seed.

So, if the path of concentration has cut your feet, remember that every one of those whom you think of as being Masters of the Wisdom has suffered the same pains, in order to be fit to serve the World, in order to be ready to do his part in the great enterprise.

Remember, too, that the Path of Return is what Lao-Tze called TAO, and of which he wrote:

> "The path of Tao is backward.
>
> The characteristic of TAO is gentleness.
>
> Everything in the universe comes from existence, and existence from non-existence."

Now, the name of this three-sentence chapter in the <u>Tao-Teh-King</u> is, "Resigning Work," and it may seem strange that we should quote it to you just after saying so much about action. But to resign work is not to attempt to stop working. Look closely at the word "resign." You will get a new thought if you think of it as meaning "to sign again." We have all of us been signing our names to our work, and it not seldom happens that the signature is more prominent than the work itself. We have to rub out this flamboyant personal signature, and learn how to let our work become so perfect an expression of the One Artist that it will sign itself.

For if everything comes from existence, and existence from non-existence, the true Source of all action is the Unmanifested Limitless Light, and if we would be in harmony with the rhythms of the cosmos it's about time we began to stop scribbling our names on the masterpieces of Life, like travelers scrawling their names on the walls of a temple.

This is what is meant by <u>The Book of Tokens</u> (Meditation on Mem, 10 to 12):

10. "Absorb thyself in this Great Sea of the Waters of Life. Dive deep in it until thou hast lost thyself. And having lost thyself, then shalt thou find thyself again, and shalt be one with me, thy Lord and King.

11. Thus shalt thou learn the secret of the restoration of the King unto his throne.

12. And in this path of Stability shall my knowledge of the Roots of Being be united to the glorious Splendor of the Perfect Knowledge which is established in the mirror of the clear waters of HOD. For when the surface of those waters is disturbed by no slightest ripple of thought, then shall the glory of my Self, which is thy true Self, be mirrored unto thee."

This is the secret of the path of the letter MEM, which is the first that you are to traverse mentally in the exercises connected with this lesson. It is the path of re-signing the work that is done through your personality. It is the path of the total loss of the illusive personal self. It is the path of THE HANGED MAN, concerning which I wrote in the preceding lesson.

How men dread to take it! How reluctantly they set foot upon it! For they fear to lose what is really nothing. A delusion like that in the Eastern story makes them think of themselves as being rich in possessions when in truth all that is in the treasure-chest is a handful of dead leaves. One day the truth will flash like lightening before your eyes, and then you will see that all this talk of "sacrifice" is only meaningless noises. Literally and explicitly, you are called upon to give up <u>nothing</u>, but you hang onto that nonentity as if it were a pearl of great price. Do we say "you?" Let us include ourselves in the indictment. For we, were the full realization of this path of the letter Mem at work through us, should be able to stand silent before you, and transform your lives with a single glance.

Who is the King that has to be restored to His throne? He is the true Self, standing patiently waiting at the door, and knocking gently for admittance. But the clamor of a multitude of anarchistic cells, shouting madly, "the voice of the people is the voice of God," drowns the still, small voice, and the Stranger-King must wait outside. He could command their silence, and even hush them forever, because His is the life-power that they depend upon for everything. But He stands and waits until they remember, until they awaken from their dream of separateness.

The path of the letter Mem leads upward from HOD to GEBURAH. It begins in expectation, in aspiration, in an eager, long look upward toward the Source of Life. This is what is expressed in the affirmation, "I look forward with confidence to the perfect realization of the Eternal Splendor of the Limitless Light." Our lips say it now. When our hearts begin to whisper it we shall enter gladly the path of surrender.

We enter it with trepidation now because we still have more or less fear of the undeviating Justice which is at the upper end of this path. We ourselves are just. Most of us are sure of that. But we are a little in doubt about the justice of our neighbor, and one of the main reasons why we find it so hard to give up this illusion of free-will, this sense of separate personality, is that we see that we shall then have no more shadow of excuse for holding another responsible for the seeming evil that is done through him. Yet this was the mind which was in the Master Jesus, as it has been in every other Master of the Wisdom. "Judge not," is the admonition of them all, and this implies, "Do not presume to fix the measure of another's responsibility." All the world's law, all the world's customs, all the habits of a billion life-time pull against us when we try to stop this judging of our neighbors. That is why the church has to confuse the issues, concealing the humanity of Jesus behind the lie of his special divinity, and making acceptance of that lie the test of salvation. The reason Fundamentalists are so set upon their dogmas is that they feel the utter impossibility of conforming to this world and at the same time trying to live the teachings of Him to whom they cry, "Lord! Lord!" For He summed up His whole message in this: "Do the will of the Father. I do nothing of myself. The Father working in me doeth the works. Follow me." The fundamentalists and formalists of every age know instinctively that he who practices the teachings of the Masters must walk contrary to the world, so they dodge the issue by saying that belief is the one thing needful, and go on judging their fellows and condemning to eternal torment all who do not conform to the standards of their creeds. They are not ready for the Kingdom of Light, and their time for entrance into the Inner School has not arrived.

Jesus, like the Masters K. H., M. and R., and all the others of whom we have heard so much in recent years, came with the message that personality originates nothing, that the Primal Will of the Source of Life is the only real Will, that men, (and this is the most important message that He left us), can become wide-open channels of that Will once they get themselves out of the way. Theologians tell us we shall go to hell if we don't believe that Jesus was the only Son of God. We tell you that you'll pass through hell over and over again until you realize that the theologians are mistaken, that Jesus set an example we can follow, that He was a Son of God, as we are all sons and daughters of the One Divine Life. The Masters have lived to show us what we are able to do. The way they took is open to us, just as soon as we summon courage to brave its terrors.

This we cannot do until we have become at least Lesser Adepts. The path of the Hanged Man is not for beginners on the Way of Return. For it is the path of what the Hindus term Samadhi, the path of perfect concentration, long continued, which brings a man into conscious union with the essence of the Law of Life, and makes him see the exquisite adjustment everywhere that we express in our fifth affirmation.

Such a man, having been a Lesser Adept, faithful in the lighter tasks of the Inner School, now becomes a Greater Adept, who knows himself as a channel for the operation of the unfailing law of the cosmos. He ceases to regard his actions in any personal light. He not only feels the One Law working through him, but also knows just how it is at work in every specific instance. He perceives both the seeds and the fruit of all that is done through him, and he becomes a reader of the hearts of men.

For Samadhi is not just going into a trance. It is a trance, to be sure, but Samadhi is known by its results. As Vivekananda writes:

"Whenever we hear a man say 'I am inspired,' and then talk the most irrational nonsense, simply reject it. Why? Because these three states of the mind -- instinct, reason, and superconsciousness, or the unconscious, conscious and superconscious states -- belong to one and the same mind. There are not three minds in one man, but one develops into the other. Instinct develops into reason, and reason into the transcendental consciousness; therefore one never contradicts the other. So. whenever you meet with wild statements which contradict human reason and common sense, reject them without fear, because the real inspiration will never contradict, but will fulfill. Just as you find the great prophets saying, "I come not to destroy but to fulfill," so this inspiration always comes to fulfill reason, and is in direct harmony with reason, and whenever it contradicts reason you must know that it is not inspiration.

Now, just because the superconscious state does not contradict reason is why we say so much about training the intellect, and about the truth that the only reasonable interpretation of the discoveries of modern science is this doctrine of determinism. The world's leading thinkers accept it. Superconsciousness completes it, and shows its meaning by pointing out what is the true nature of the principle of Will at work in man. The lie is that we have a free-will by means of which, somehow, we may be able to circumvent the laws of the cosmos -- a lie invented to give mankind an excuse for thinking ill of the neighbors, and condemning the other fellow to perdition.

Samadhi is a hard path to follow, but it does away with all this delusion. Notice that nobody can go this way who has not passed the trials of the path of DEATH. For this is more than the death of the physical body. It is the extinction of the illusion (while Samadhi lasts) that there are TWO in the sphere of being. It is the extinction of the candle-light in the blaze of noon-day, the vanishing of the stars before the sun. It does not last for long, but it is another man who comes out of Samadhi from him who went in. He has become what Will Comfort calls, "one of those who know and cannot tell." And that one is a Major Adept, for thenceforth he participates consciously in the administration of cosmic laws. Having given up all delusions of personality he has done as Lao-Tze advised: "Having emptied yourself, remain where you are." He is an open channel for the One Life, and because he takes great care not to yield to the illusion of separateness, not to believe in it, although it still surrounds him, when such a man says, "Thy sins be forgiven thee," he voices the knowledge of the One Life that that man's failures to hit the mark shall no more count against him. It is the Greater Adept who seems to perform miracles, but he does them all by getting himself wholly out of the way. And the way to his Grade begins in intellect, in the sphere of Mercury, for until the lesser delusions of faulty logic are overcome a man is not ready for the last great surrender.

From this point on, as the pictures in the Tarot show, the nature of the paths changes. The terrors are past. The last illusion of "me and mine" -- that great barrier to love -- is dissolved in the path of the HANGED MAN, and thereafter the initiate identifies himself, one by one, with the ascending scale of perfections represented by the remaining paths and Keys.

We have just said that the Elder Brothers who have reached the grade of Greater Adepts are those who participate consciously in the administration of cosmic laws. In this our first preliminary survey of that Way of Return, we can only faintly image the meaning of this. Yet we should try the best we can to see what the adept sees fully on the 22nd path, the path of Lamed.

Even the Greater Adepts must traverse this path before they can advance to the next Grade. It is not enough to be conscious of participation in the government of all things. One must know, but one must also be able to instruct. It is not enough to be consciously immortal, so that one may say, "Before Abraham was, I am." One must recognize the truth that he is the incarnate Law, and this is what the Tarot means by the picture of JUSTICE, when we seek the meaning of this picture as a symbol of one state of the Way of Return.

As always, the meaning of the letter-name is one clue. The Greater Adepts prefect themselves by becoming Teachers, or rather, by becoming mouth-pieces of the one Teacher. That is why we call anybody who holds the teaching office a "Prolocutor," which means "One who speaks for."

Now, right here, long before we actually become eligible in the inner grade of Greater Adept, we may prepare ourselves by remembering that each of us stands as an image of the One Teacher. Somebody, somewhere, takes us for an instructor now, even though we may not be aware of it. Be careful lest you be taken as an instructor in what to avoid! Try to be like the Masters by watching yourself moment by moment, to the end that you may be a faithful likeness of the One Life, so far as you see the beauty of that life now. To do this is to teach, and one of the things it will help to teach a great many people is that one may be an occultist without being a freak, without neglecting the niceties of appearance, without compensating for an inferiority complex by doing or saying anything in order to seem unusual.

Some years ago I met a man whom I believe to be one of the Greater Adepts. He made no claim to that effect, and in fact, made no claim at all. But I have good reasons for my belief, for like another

Teacher, this man told me all the things that ever I did. You would not turn to look at him on Fifth Avenue. He could sit unnoticed in the lobby of any New York hotel. His clothes conformed to the ancient Rosicrucian rule, "Adopt the customs of the country." And I believe the number of such men is far greater than we have been led to suppose. They conceal themselves in order to teach the better. And they may be known by this: they are faithful to the ideal of Beauty in all things. For this man's dress was beautiful, his voice was beautiful, his choice of words was beautiful, his outlook on life was a perpetual recognition of the beauty that is in everything, and the lesson he taught me -- a lesson I shall never forget -- was a lesson of beauty, too.

To Beauty, moreover, the whole system of the Qabalah is dedicated. That is why it seems so strange to us that any who have heard us say this, as we have said it, over and over again, should think of this as a cold, intellectual teaching, with not enough love in it. We wonder what some people mean by love? No, we don't wonder, we know. Thank life for having brought us through that phase! You'll get clearer instruction through us because of those early ignorances.

The Book of Tokens has some words about this 22nd path which may help you in your meditations. It says:

"Before this have I declared myself to be the Teacher of teachers, and now I say to thee, O Israel, that my instruction is like unto a goad, which guideth thee through the long circuit of existence, until thou returnest to myself.

"I am the root of all action. No work is anywhere performed whereof I am not the doer.

"By action are all things determined, and every action proceedeth from my grasp of every condition of my self-manifestation.

"No man accomplisheth anything of himself. They are deluded who think otherwise.

"'Have I not free will'? saith the fool; but the wise knoweth that in all the chains of worlds there is no creature that hath any will apart from my One Will.

"My Will is free indeed, and he who knoweth it as the wellspring of his willing remaineth free from error.

"Let thy meditation bring thee to rest in that Will. Then in the midst of action shalt thou be at peace, and in thy busiest hours shalt find the Eternal Worker doing all things well in thee.

"Lo, I guide thee all the way. Rest thou in me."

When this perfect rest in the Will of the One Life is a vivid daily experience, the Greater Adept is ready to progress to a still higher stage of the Path, to the Grade corresponding to Chesed or Gedulah, Mercy or Majesty. And the name of this Grade is "Exempt Adept." Exempt from what? From the delusion of personal participation in anything, or in any action, perfect freedom from the least tinge of the error that comes from belief in separateness.

He who has reached this Grade is more than an open channel for the Law which cannot be broken, more than a Teacher of that law. He is a channel of the exhaustless Mercy of the Life-Power, and even his outward appearance shows that in Mercy there is a higher majesty even than in Justice. Some readers of these pages may have seen pictures of two of the Masters whose names are connected with the revival of the Eastern Wisdom here in the West. One is of rather stern appearance, the other is of kindlier mien. We have never been given any direct assurance on the matter, but we believe the one is in the Grade of Greater Adept, and the other in the Grade of Exempt Adept. For not only their faces, but the letters from them which are now available, show the characteristic differences in the inner quality of the two Grades. And the kindly Master is, to my mind, a more majestic figure than his fellow.

Whether this surmise of ours be founded in fact or not, there is truly a higher majesty in Mercy than in Justice. And Mercy, strange as it may seem, at first, is more impersonal than Justice. Justice keeps a balance, and so long as there is the idea of balance there is the shadow of separateness. But Mercy gives without sting, even though the Qabalah hints that this beneficence is in accordance with measured rhythms, since it calls Sephirah Chesed the Path of Measuring Intelligence.

It is because of this unifying quality of sympathy in all expressions of Mercy, because of this highest aspect of love, Compassion, that the path to the Grade of Exempt Adept is one which leads upward from Netzach to Chesed, upward from the emotional plane of the desire nature, the sphere of Venus, to the plane of the cosmic self-impartation. The path begins in love (Venus), and ends in compassion (Chesed).

The name of the 21st Path, which leads upward from Netzach to Chesed, is, you will recall, "Intelligence of Desire," and Qabalists say it is the Rewarding Intelligence of those who seek. It is by the sublimation of the desire-nature that we attain to union with the Divine Beneficence, and in that union all sense of separateness is lost. This attainment is the Great Reward, and in it all opposites are reconciled. On this account the 21st Path is also called Intelligence of Conciliation.

This, too, is why it is pictured in the Tarot as a Wheel, for every point in a circle is equidistant from the center, so that there is nowhere the slightest irregularity, and as opposition is suggested by the two extremes of a line, so the circle, and the wheel, because they symbolize an endless line, are emblems of non-separateness.

The Exempt Adept is in the state represented by the Sphinx at the top of the Wheel of Fortune. Mr. Waite tells us in his <u>Pictorial Key to the Tarot</u> that the Sphinx stands for the equilibrium in the perpetual motion of a fluidic universe, for stability in the midst of movement. So the Exempt Adept remains unmoved, for he is as that one of whom we read in the Bhagavad-Gita: "He who knows the divine truth thinketh 'I am doing nothing' if seeing, breathing; even when speaking, letting go or taking, opening or closing his eyes, he saith, 'the senses and organs move by natural impulse to their appropriate objects.'"

This is the meaning of the Grade of Exempt Adept, for he who has really attained to this Grade has lost all sense of "my-ness" in the performance of action. In the 21st Path, which is the first leading to this Grade, this sense of "my-ness" is overcome by constant meditation upon the One Self as being, like the Sphinx, unmoved in the midst of the flux of cosmic activity, and by constant dwelling upon the thought that all the actions of the body, all the actions of the nervous currents, all the actions of the finer bodies, all states of feeling and emotion, are really part of the outflow of the

Cosmic Life, and in no sense limited to personality.

Something of this consciousness you may begin to experience, even now, and one way to this is to identify yourself with the inexhaustible current of Love which flows from the Heart of Life to all the world.

The Divine Name which is the pass-word of the Grade of Greater Adept is allied in root-meaning to the name of the Sephirah to which this Grade corresponds, that of Strength, G B V R H, because it is A L H I M   G B V R, literally "The gods of power." The tonal values and pronunciation are:

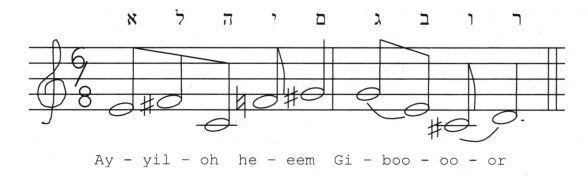

Ay - yil - oh he - eem Gi - boo - oo - or

The Divine Name of the Grade of Exempt Adept is A L, "the strong one." Its tonality and pronunciation are:

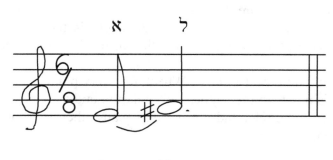

Ay - yil

The first of these names is the number 297, which has for its first reduction 18, the number of the key-word חי, Chai, life, which is the clue to the significance of all other terms corresponding to 18. Thus אלהים גבור, "the gods of power" are Qabalistically shown to be gods of the power of life, and their name, when they are considered as being especially active in Geburah, is מאדים, the plural of מאד, power, strength, might. They represent the force-aspect of life, which is indicated by the fact that Geburah is the sphere of Mars. Note that the final reduction, or least number of 297 is 9, number of the letter Teth, symbol of the serpent-force, FOHAT. Apply these keys to the words אעפיר, Ophir, the place where Solomon got gold; אוצרר, a treasure-house, a place for storing gold and silver, treasure; ארמון, a citadel, a fortified house; כורסיא, the Throne, a name of Briah, the creative world; צואר, the neck. In the comparison of these words, and in the attempt to find the thread of meaning which connects them, you will sooner or later discover one secret of the work of transmutation -- a secret which cannot be communicated except by some such obscure terminology as this. Remember, it is a secret of life, חי and its essence is to be sought in the path which corresponds to the letter Teth. That path you will traverse in the next lesson.

The Divine Name אל is especially important because the reversal of its letters is לא, which means NOT. The Exempt Adept lives this from day to day. "I am doing nothing," he declares. And his declaration is even subtler than it seems to be. For he does not for a moment stop action, since he is wise, and as it is written in the Bhagavad-Gita, "Children only and not the wise speak of renunciation of action and of right performance of action as being different. He who perfectly practices the one receives the fruits of both, and the place which is gained by the renouncer of action is also attained by him who is devoted in action." The Exempt Adept knows that all his actions are the expressions of that One Reality which is No-Thing, which is "described as NOT this, NOT that, and so on, by negatives only." For him "doing nothing" is synonymous with free and unhampered expression of that power, and because for all men the natural symbol of such expression is the Path of Return, לא "not" is the Qabalistic equivalent of הווך to go. For all going is but the turning of the Wheel of the self-manifestation of "that which is NOT." Furthermore, the Exempt Adept has come to the point where his whole life is a satisfactory answer to every problem, to every question that troubles the minds of those who are yet in the grip of the delusion of separateness. He knows <u>how</u> to act without attachment, <u>how</u> to keep himself perpetually adjusted to the rhythms of the cosmic self-expression. And this the Qabalists hint for us when they point to the numerical identity between AL, LA, HVK, and AIK, for איך means "How?"

It all comes back to Lao-Tze's teaching, "Having emptied yourself, remain where you are." And then what happens? Let the same Master of the Wisdom tell us. In the chapter of the <u>Tao-Teh-King</u> entitled "Locking Abroad" he says:

"A man may know the world without leaving his own home.
Through his windows he can see the supreme TAO.
The further afield he goes the less likely is he to find it.
Therefore the wise man knows without traveling, names things without seeing them, and accomplishes everything without action."

In the next chapter, "The Distress of Knowledge," he makes clear the folly of the supposition that there is any need for <u>getting</u> knowledge. The reason, of course, is that <u>getting</u> is a quest for something not possessed, for something outside, whereas the way of wisdom is the expression of THAT which is eternally within. He says:

"Bodily and mental distress is increased every day in the effort to get knowledge.
But this distress is daily diminished by the getting of TAO.
Do you continually curtail your effort till there be nothing of it left?
By non-action there is nothing which cannot be effected.
A man might, without the least distress, undertake the government of the world.
But those who distress themselves about governing the world are not fit for it."

Evolution of Homo Spiritualis

The first of the two paths which you will traverse in the exercises connected with this lesson is the 20th. It is the path of the letter YOD, and in traversing it, the impulse is directed upward from Tiphareth to Chesed. One places himself in Tiphareth, sees himself surrounded by a sphere of yellow light, and then projects the yellow-green ray diagonally upward into the blue sphere of Chesed. In all these projections consciousness should be identified as much as possible with the color employed. First you will feel yourself surrounded with yellow light, then three will be a feeling of flowing movement, taking you upward through a yellow-green stream or current, and finally you will find yourself in a sphere of intense, living blue.

What you are doing, remember, is to set in motion, for the time being, the vibrations of etheric and higher planes which correspond to these imagined physical colors. Do not fall into the error of supposing that nothing happens just because you are "only imagining." When your consciousness takes a particular color-vibration as the result of this practice, even your physical body is slightly modified. The specific result aimed at is the extension of sensation beyond the limits of the physical, the refinement of the senses, and one of the results of this work should be to make you more keenly alive to subtle distinctions of shade and tint in the world around you. A similar result will be effected by your work with tones.

The name of this 20th Path merits considerable attention. It is "Intelligence of Will," and the Hebrew word translated "Will" is רצון (=346). It has many connotations in the Hebrew language, among them being: delight, acceptance, satisfaction, pleasure, favour. All of these words, you see, imply some degree of the <u>bliss</u> which is inseparable from the consciousness of union with the Primal Will.

By Gematria, רצון corresponds to צנור, a water-pipe, a channel, and to מקור, a well, a spring. For to be in the state of consciousness named "Intelligence of Will" is to be conscious also that personality is but a channel for the outflowing of that Will into the externalizations of the world of Name and Form; and it is to be conscious also that this power which flows out into manifestation through personality is like water. Precisely this was what Jesus had in mind when he talked with the woman of Samaria, and told her that within herself she might find a well of living-water.

That living water is the Water which is attributed to Chesed. It is to this that the fourth of our affirmations refers: "From the exhaustless riches of its Limitless Substance." For the <u>substance</u> aspect of the Life-Power is always symbolized as water. (This, too, is one of the reasons why Chesed, the sphere of Jupiter, is colored blue, although the Jupiter vibration itself is violet.)

Consider, too, the letters of רצון. The first is Resh, corresponding to the XIXth Key of the Tarot, and to the 30th path, leading from YESOD upward to HOD. On the Way of Return this takes us upward from the subconsciousness of YESOD, from the automatic cell-consciousness which is the sphere of the Moon, to the intellectual consciousness which is the sphere of Mercury. You will remember that in our exercises this is a path through which we draw up the influence from below, after having stationed ourselves, so to say, in a superior position. All this means that the beginning of our consciousness of Will comes from taking a definite intellectual point-of-view, which is symbolized in the Tarot by the picture of the little boy riding the white horse, and which may be summarized in the statement: "I am a child of the Sun of Life."

The second letter of רצון is Tzaddi, which corresponds to the 28th path of Natural Intelligence, leading upward from YESOD to NETZACH. This, as you know, is a path of projection, and has to do with Meditation. Through its activities the latent powers of the automatic consciousness, are projected up into the sphere of the desire-nature, and this projection raises us in consciousness to the Grade of Philosophus (Netzach). Netzach, on the Tree of Life, and in consciousness, is the sphere of the activity of the Venus vibration, and the reason why it is connected with the Grade of Philosophus is that Venus is the planet of love and of art. The whole philosophy of the inner school is rooted and grounded in love, and seeks ever to express itself in the artistic arrangement of the conditions of life.

The fact that all these ideas are connected with the second letter of the Hebrew word for Will means this: Our consciousness of that Will begins with the grateful recognition that we are children of the Spiritual Sun, and begins, of necessity, as an intellectual point-of-view, reached by careful inductive reasoning from the facts presented to us in the pages of the Book of Nature. Meditation upon our relationship to that Spiritual Sun cannot but awaken within us a feeling of love and gratitude to the Source of our lives, and will, eventually, bring us to the realization that we are children of the Great Artist Who lavishes beauty upon the whole creation, Who paints the East and West as no earthly colorist has ever been able to do, Who expresses Himself in ravishing loveliness of line and mass and color in everything that our eyes behold. As children of that Artist, we are centers of expression for His will-to-beauty, and occult philosophy is ever the doctrine of what Claude Bragdon calls "The Beautiful Necessity." The more we identify ourselves with the Cosmic Purpose, the more we recognize ourselves to be channels for Its externalization of its powers, the more beautiful will be the results of all our action. The ugliness of this man-made world is all spawned from the sense of separateness, all the ridiculous product of the insane fantasy that any man can do anything of himself.

Something of this is hinted at, too, in the title "Occult Intelligence," assigned to Netzach. The Great Secret is that living is an art, having for its object beautiful expression. A half-knowledge of this truth is a very dangerous thing, and from it comes no end of false aestheticism. Qabalistic doctrine has nothing in common with this. It does not confound weak prettiness with beauty. And that is why Beauty is associated with the Mars-vibration, the vibration of Force and Activity.

This Mars-vibration dominates in the path on the Tree of Life ascribed to the letter Nun, for Nun corresponds to Scorpio, ruled by Mars. And Nun is the first letter of the Hebrew noun נסתור, "Occult," the name of the particular mode of consciousness associated with Netzach. Nun also is the letter of the path of Imaginative Intelligence, because the very beginning of true occult philosophy and practice is vigorous, vital, healthful use of the transforming power of imagination. It is because we are creatures of imagination that we can reduce the world to chaos and transform its face, because we can imagine, and so make patterns, that we can adapt the laws of the Life-Power to produce conditions not spontaneously provided by nature. This, and much more, is suggested by נ, the first letter of Occult.

ס, the second letter, is the letter of the path of Trial, concerning which I have written at length in an earlier lesson of this series. The work of the artist is a continual testing, an endless experimentation, and he who truly merits the Grade of Philosophus in the Inner School has to undergo a long probation. Only those who meet the tests are entrusted with the profounder meanings of the Great Secret.

ת, the third letter of "Occult" is the path of Saturn, because the work of the artist in life necessitates a thorough understanding of the principle of limitation. The work of the artist must have the Saturnine quality of definition, must be specific. And this is the detail overlooked by many who aspire to artistic expression -- a detail which often decides whether a given piece of work is good or bad.

Finally, the last letter of "Occult" is ר, and this is related to something which is vital to all artistic effort. No matter what the medium, the adaptation of life to the expression of beauty demands the childlike mental attitude. Except we become as little children we cannot enter the Kingdom, and the moment we begin to be cocky over our work we are falling into the characteristically adult delusion of separateness.

All this is by no means so great a digression from our main theme as you may be disposed to think, although it has taken us a long way from our starting-point, which was the second letter of רצון. For the consciousness of identity with the One Will includes all the elements that have been considered in the last few paragraphs, because we cannot be aware of that Will without knowing it as a power which works through human action to produce beautiful results, and the better we understand the nature of the Secret associated with Netzach and the sphere of Venus, the better shall we grasp the meaning of the Originating Will.

The better we apprehend this inner meaning, the more shall we be disposed to listen for the Inner Voice which brings us the revelations of the One Teacher. On this account we find that the third letter of רצון is that which the Tarot symbolizes as the HIEROPHANT. Intellectual perception begins our consciousness of Will, and artistic aspiration engendered by meditation continues it, but not until we have opened ourselves to instruction from within, not until we deliberately assume the listening attitude, -- not occasionally, but every day of our lives, and as often during each day as we can -- will we begin to penetrate into the deeper mysteries.

Finally, he who is on the path of Intelligence of Will must have conquered death, must have traversed the path of the letter Nun, and must know the higher aspects of the manifestation of the Mars-force associated with Scorpio. This is the Qabalistic explanation of the final letter of רצון. It is the secret of the transformation of the Scorpion into the Eagle, the secret of giving wings to the Serpent, the secret of the metamorphosis which changes נחש the Tempter into משיח the Redeemer. And what is the secret of that change? נחש and משיח are the same in numeration, but in משיח the number 50 is represented by the letters M and I instead of by the letter N. The consciousness of mortality and separateness associated with DEATH has become the consciousness of immortality which comes to the HANGED MAN in <u>Samadhi</u> plus the consciousness of identity with the One Self, the Self represented by the HERMIT.

In its highest expression, the state of consciousness assigned to the 20th Path is a blissful ecstasy beyond words. This is why the mystics of all periods and of all religions have expressed their experience of superconsciousness in terms which grate on the ears of prudes. For they have not scrupled to describe the bliss of union in terms which are reflections of the keenest ecstasy of the senses. And this is one reason why Qabalists tell us that the path of YOD corresponds to the function of Coition. It is not the only reason, but past experience has taught me the unwisdom of trusting too much in the readiness of occult students to hear some aspects of truth. I have learned, too, that the best instructor on these matters is the One Teacher seated in the hearts of men. So I content myself with suggesting that you look for further information concerning this particular attribution.

Consider, now, the symbolism of the IXth Tarot Key as representing Intelligence of Will. Who is the Hermit? He is your true Self, and that Self is the One Self manifesting in countless personalities. This is He whom the Bible calls the Ancient of Days, He whom Jesus had in mind when he said, "Before Abraham was, I am."

When, in traversing the 20th Path, the Seeker for Light on the Way of Return comes to identify himself with the HERMIT, he has arrived at the state of consciousness which the Yogi philosophers call Kaivalya, isolation. Kaivalya is defined by Vivekananda as "Oneness with Absolute Being." The same writer, commenting on the 55th Sutra in Patanjali's book (Chapter 4) which runs, "By the similarity of purity between the Sattva and the Purusha (the Knower) comes Kaivalya," says:

"When the soul realizes that it depends on nothing in the universe, from gods to the lowest atom, that is called Kaivalya (isolation) and perfection. It is attained when this mixture of purity and impurity called mind has been made as pure as the Purusha Itself; then the Sattva, the mind, reflects only the unqualified essence of purity, which is the Purusha."

At first glance this might seem to contradict the teaching which I have given you concerning the absolute self-surrender symbolized by the HANGED MAN. But it does not. You must remember what Lao-Tze says, "All the teachings of wise men are paradoxical." Personality, so we are taught, is always dependent, can do nothing of itself. But the Real Self, the Purusha, the On-Looker, the I AM, depends upon nothing, for everything depends upon that ONE REALITY. Perfection in meditation raises the mind to the Sattva quality of superconsciousness, in which all sense of personal separateness is extinguished, and there is nothing but the knowledge of union with the One who, like the HERMIT, is the Light-Bearer for the whole universe.

Charles Johnston translates Kaivalya as "pure spiritual life," and this is his rendition of the last of Patanjali's Yoga Sutras:

"Pure spiritual life is, therefore, the inverse resolution of the potencies of Nature, which have emptied themselves of their value for the Spiritual man; or it is the return of the power of pure Consciousness to its essential form."

All the sages, you see, tell us the same thing, because they all speak from the same experience. Whether we say with the Qabalists that the Serpent of Wisdom "climbs the Tree of Life," or with Lao-Tze, "The Path of TAO is backward," or with Boehme, "Walk contrary to the world," we are simply expressing the idea that the Goal and the Source are One, and that the way thereto is a Path of Return.

The HERMIT is a symbol of the Goal, for he is attributed to the letter YOD, and this letter refers not only to the 20th Path, but also to Chokmah, since YOD of יהוה is assigned to Chokmah, and even to Kether, since the upper point of that Yod of I H V H is said to be in Kether. For when we have identified ourselves with the HERMIT we have also found the bliss of union with the Wisdom which Qabalists call the Father, and in our union with that Wisdom we are raised to communion with the Primal Will which is the Originating Principle of the whole self-manifestation of the Life-Power. In these subtler cross-correspondences of the letter Yod we find another reason why the 20th path is called "Intelligence of Will."

Notice, too, that the change from נחש to משיח involves a difference in the Tarot correspondences. When the number 50 is represented in any word by N, its sign in the Tarot is the XIIIth Key, DEATH. But when it is represented by M and I, two Tarot Keys, the HANGED MAN and the HERMIT, are the signs that we must consider. And the numbers of these two Keys are XII and IX, whose sum is XXI, the number of the WORLD, which is the picture of the Dance of Life, the picture of Cosmic Consciousness. For when the absolute surrender of personality symbolized by the HANGED MAN is combined with the realization of identity with the Primal Will for which the HERMIT stands, the result is a state of consciousness in which the meaning of the Saturn quality of limitation is understood, in which it is perceived as that which enables Life to express itself in forms of beauty, and in which, especially, one becomes vividly aware of the truth that every human personality is a vehicle or channel through which flows the self-directive potency of the One Life, so that we are all centers of expression for the governing power, or Administrative Intelligence, of the cosmos, and partakers in its dominion over everything.

The Grade of Exempt Adept, associated with Chesed, is perfected when the power of the sphere of Mars, Geburah, has been drawn along the 19th path back to Chesed. In doing this one places oneself in Chesed, for the knowledge of the Great Arcanum, of the Secret of all spiritual activities, is not open to him who has risen no higher than the Grade of Major Adept That is to say, the 19th Path is not open so long as we are no further along the Way of Return than Geburah, and the power from Geburah must be brought over from the side of Severity on the Tree of Life to the side of Mercy, by a process initiated from the point-of-view afforded by Chesed.

When all the desires of the seeker for Light have been unified in the one desire to be a free, unobstructed vehicle for the manifestation of the cyclic activities of the cosmos, he has traversed the first path leading to the Grade of Exempt Adept, the path of the letter Kaph, corresponding to the Wheel of Fortune in the Tarot. After this, by a supreme effort of imagination, he sees behind the mechanistic expression of the Life-Power in the cosmic cycles the operation of a Living Will, and identifies himself with that Will, so that all sense of personal volition is extinguished. Finally, through the 19th Path he transmutes the activities of the serpent-power, and this transmutation is pictured in the Tarot by the woman taming the lion.

You will remember that אריה, lion, the name of the zodiacal sign Leo, is the number 216, and that this is the number of גבורה, Geburah, one of the names of the sphere of Mars. Note, too, that 216 is 9 by reduction, and 9 is the number of Teth, the letter corresponding to the 19th Path. 216 is also the number of ראיה, Sight, the function assigned to the 15th path, and of רוגז, wrath or excitement, which is the function of the 25th Path, that of Probation or Trial. The path to which Sight ראיה is attributed is that of Aries, ruled by Mars. And the path to which רוגז, excitement, is attributed is that of Sagittarius. It thus becomes evident that all these words, גבורה, strength, אריה, the lion, ראיה, Sight, and רוגז, excitement, are related to the fiery power which we have learned to associate with the Mars-vibration.

This vibration, you will recall, is especially active in self-consciousness, and the feeling of strength which it gives is misinterpreted by people who have not progressed beyond self-consciousness. The misinterpretation arises from the illusion of separateness, which engenders the feeling of "myness," and this feeling is at the root of belief in personal will. This is why the Sephirah Geburah is said to represent personal will, which is merely the misunderstanding of the power of undeviating cosmic law in its manifestation through personal centers of expression.

The Major Adept still feels the illusion, although he has overcome the delusion caused by it. But the Exempt Adept, having in his union with the One Self so identified himself with the cosmic memory that he never forgets his relation to the Sources of All, is almost wholly liberated from even the illusion. Almost, I say, because there are times when even he who perfectly remembers the Self (Chesed is the Sephirah of memory) must identify himself with the relative states of being in order to serve, in order to perform the actions necessary to his part in the Great Work. And at such times he feels the illusion of separateness as much as anybody else.

Only one who has freed himself from the error of personal initiative, one who sees in all his actions the outworking of the inevitable cosmic order, and yet realizes that order to be more than a mere mechanism, may safely be entrusted with the Secret of all Spiritual Activities. It is not enough that he should see his actions as part of the cyclic activity that causes every thing which happens. He must see that activity as proceeding from the Self, must know that it is not simply mathematical and mechanical, must realize it as expressing a Living Purpose. For when he sees this, he sees also that the One Purpose is working through every life, and understands what is said in The Book of Tokens: "Nothing is, or can be, my antagonist." None who have not attained to this understanding, none who have not been united in consciousness with the One Self symbolized by the HERMIT, none who have not see that they, like the HERMIT, are light-bearers and guides for others below them on the path of return, are ready to know the Great Secret.

What is that secret? The very letters of the word so translated, הפעולוט, tell us. The first letter is H, the letter of the Path of Sight, for the beginning of our knowledge of the Great Arcanum is an understanding of the mystery of Vision. I do not pretend to tell you what that mystery is, for to do so would be to make two false assumptions: 1. That I have attained to the Grade of Exempt Adept, and 2. That you have also reached that Grade. No, all that I can do is to tell you that the sages have left us this clue to what sort of a secret the Great Arcanum is. It is a secret which begins with a realization of the full meaning of another passage in the Book of Tokens: "I utter myself by seeing."

The second letter, Peh, is the letter of Mars, and of the path of Exciting Intelligence. In the Tarot it is THE TOWER, and since this Key shows us lightening destroying a house, I take it that the Great Arcanum has something to do with the disruptive and destructive effect of electricity. Indeed, I believe it to be something associated with what modern science has to say about what would happen if a man knew how to release interatomic energy.

The third letter is a contrast to the one which precedes it, because it is ע, the letter corresponding to the sign Capricorn, ruled by Saturn. Yet we should remember that in Capricorn Mars is exalted, so that this letter conveys, by its astrological associations, a suggestion that the Great Secret shows us how to exalt, or sublimate, the Mars-force, and apply it for the establishment of definite, concrete results. Furthermore, since O is the letter represented by THE DEVIL, I take it that the Great Secret has something to do with the control of the subconscious forces which the Devil symbolizes.

The first three letters of הפעולוט, you see, are all related in one way or another to the Mars vibration, Heh through Aries, ruled by Mars, Peh as the letter of Mars, and Ayin as the letter assigned to Capricorn in which sign Mars is exalted. The next three letters are all related to Venus.

Vav is assigned to Taurus, which Venus rules. It corresponds to the Tarot Key of the Hierophant, and may be understood as being in some sense the complement of the Emperor, even as Venus is the complement of the Mars, and as the color of Venus, green, is the complement of the Martian red. In like manner the function assigned to ו, Hearing, is what completes the function assigned to ה, which is Sight. When we have learned the deeper meaning of Vision (ה), have mastered the destructive force of Mars (פ) and have exalted this force through learning how to utilize the limiting power of Saturn which seems at first to be our Adversary (ע), we are ready for the deeper revelations of the mysteries which come to us through the channel of interior Hearing, direct from the One Teacher who is represented in the Tarot by the HIEROPHANT.

Lamed is the letter of the sign Libra, which rules the kidneys, and this suggests that the next stage of our initiation into the Secret of All Spiritual activities is a practical lesson in elimination. I think Lao-Tze gives the gist of this particular lesson when he says, "Having emptied yourself, remain where you are." In this connection we might remember that Saturn, the planet which governs excretion, or the purifying processes which rid our bodies (all of our bodies, understand) of waste, is exalted in Libra. The sword of JUSTICE in the Tarot refers to this excretory or eliminative aspect of Saturn. Note that it has a handle like a T, or Tau, which is Saturn's letter, and that the fact that Libra is ruled by Venus means that every activity of this sign must necessarily excite complementary Mars activities, inasmuch as no planetary vibration can be active without inducing its complement, any more than a color-vibration can exist without arousing the complementary color. Thus the sword of Justice has a Saturn hilt (the T) and a Mars blade (steel or iron, metal of Mars). All this means, I take it, that the knowledge gained by listening to the HIEROPHANT enables us to rid ourselves of everything useless in our personalities, helps us to eliminate all waste, to remove every obstruction to the free outflow of the Life-Power. And by this elimination we attain the balance which is represented by the scales of JUSTICE, the equilibrium which is the basis of the Great Work. Elimination is the active part of the process, and hence the sword is held in the right hand of JUSTICE, where it corresponds to the first clause of Lao-Tze's admonition, "Having emptied yourself." Balance is the result achieved, and because the perfectly balanced scales are symbols of rest and stability, they correspond to the second phrase of the Chinese Master's injunction, "Remain where you are."

Vav is repeated in this word, because, it seems to me, the first instruction of the Inner Teacher has to do with purification and the attainment of balance, after which we are ready to listen again; and it has been said to me that the second revelation is to the effect that the HIEROPHANT is the true Self of the Seeker for Light. We can apprehend this teaching intellectually, but we have no words to express what the experience really is. Yet all the sages who have entered into superconsciousness agree in telling us that they have been granted a vision of the inmost meaning of existence, and at the same time they tell us that they have been One with the Father. And this revelation, it would seem, includes the knowledge that the Adversary, so to say, has only been the Father in disguise, playing the game of existence with His children, in order to help them to unfold their latent powers and possibilities. Thus the HIEROPHANT is not only the complement of the EMPEROR, but he is also closely related to the DEVIL. This correspondence will be evident if you compare the symbols of the Vth and XVth Keys, when it will be clear to you that the DEVIL is just a caricature of the

HIEROPHANT. Thus the DEVIL wears the Pentagram, symbol of the HIEROPHANT'S number, but wears it upside-down, recalling the occult maxim, "The Devil is God upside-down." Then, too, XV, the number of the DEVIL, is the extension of V, the number of the HIEROPHANT, even as the Adversary is our misinterpretation of the Father, when the Father extends Himself, so to say, in the conditions of Name and Form. All our ideas of the demoniac or diabolical are derived from wrong judgment as to the real nature of the seemingly antagonistic forces which surround us. Nothing is more clearly established by the study of psychology in connection with comparative religions than the fact that every devil known to man is an image conjured up to account for something in his environment which makes a man afraid. The Ageless Wisdom tells us that the Adversary is only a human caricature of the Redeemer, and men who have experienced superconsciousness confirm this doctrine by testifying with one voice that in the state of union all consciousness of evil disappears completely. Thus the final revelation of the HIEROPHANT may well be: "Child, long hast thou feared me, and that fear was the beginning of thy wisdom, for it drove thee in quest of refuge from thine Adversary. Now, at the end of thy long quest, thou hast no need for fear. For I was the Adversary, I the opponent without Whom there would have been no game to play. And this, which seemed a game of war thou seest now as but the game of love. Enter into joy, for He with whom thou hast wrestled is none other than thy true Self."

The final letter of הפעולוט is ט, or Teth, and this is STRENGTH in the Tarot. It shows the Lion being mastered by the Woman, who has above her head the symbol which appears also above the head of the MAGICIAN. Thus is intimated the idea that the dominant thing in the picture of STRENGTH is the Mercurial activity which descends through the path of Beth. The MAGICIAN points his left hand downward toward the garden, and roses and lilies spring up in response. STRENGTH shows the hidden law which finds expression in the growth of these flowers. It is the law that all subhuman expressions of the solar energy are under the immediate direction of subconsciousness, while subconsciousness, the Woman of the picture, is ever amenable to control through suggestions formulated in self-consciousness. When self-consciousness, by right intellection, grasps the truth that all the power a man can exercise is a transformation of the One Life-Power, that all the volitions a man feels at work within him are expressions of the One Will, this right knowledge of the relation between personality and the One Life becomes the dominant suggestion to the subconscious. In response to it, the body-building activities of the subconscious plane are all directed to the fashioning of a personal vehicle which shall offer no obstruction to the free outflow of the Life-Power into the externalizations of the objective plane of name and form. Thus, little by little, the bodies of the man are purified, changed day by day into a more truthful likeness and image of the Life above and within. And the end of the process is the radiant, deathless, beautiful body of the Master, concerning which I shall have more to say in the next lesson.

Finally, הפעולוט = 206, and 206 is the number of דבר, Word, concerning which the Sepher Yetzirah says: "Voice, Spirit, and Word: this is the Spirit of the Holy One." (S. Y. I., 9). Notice the planetary attributions of the letters in דבר, Venus-Mercury-Sun. Venus for love and art, Mercury for intellect, merging at its highest sublimation into superconsciousness, the Sun for vitality and light, for the heart-consciousness which astrologers rightly interpret as the direct expression of individuality. (Individuality, remember, is akin to indivisibility, and the only Individual in all the universe is the One Self manifest through countless masks or persons.) Here are some clues to the Secret of the Word. It is the Secret of the Word made flesh, of the Primal Thought which, through vibration begun as Sound, and then raised to the electric potency of FOHAT, clothes Itself with garments of pulsing radiance which our imperfect senses only half-perceive, which our deluded minds belittle and besmirch with lying labels. How long will it be before the world will come to understand the beautiful simplicity of the saying, "This is my body, which is broken for you." These were the words of the One Self, speaking freely through an unobstructed channel. Everything that we call "matter" is the body of Spirit, apparently broken or divided into Many-ness and so concealing the essential unity. Not the man Jesus, but the Self behind that personality, spoke these words, too simply clear in meaning for the muddled minds of theologians. The mystery of the Word made flesh is the secret of all spiritual activities. That Word dwells among us. That is to say, we all share in its presence in this world of name and form. That Word is seated in your heart and mine. When we have learned to listen, as quickly as we are ready, it will make known to us all the mysteries of the Great Arcanum.

And then shall the Severity of the Law be swallowed up in Mercy. Then shall the powers of the Greater Adept, wonderful as they seem, be merged with the exhaustless riches of the self-impartation of the One.

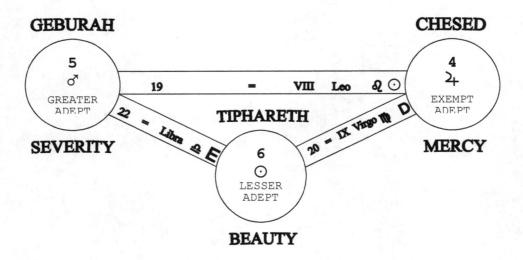

64

Mastership

In the old Rosicrucian texts, the Grade of the Invisible Order corresponding to Binah is called <u>Magister Templi</u>, that is, Master of the Temple. Two paths lead thereto. The first is the 18th, which leads upward from Geburah to Binah. The second is the 17th, which leads upward from Tiphareth to the third Sephirah. In your exercises both are paths of projection, and by this time you understand what this means.

In traversing the 18th path, the starting-point is the Grade of Greater Adept, and the goal is Understanding. But he who travels this path must first have perfected his realization of what it means to be an Exempt Adept. This path to understanding is not open to those who are merely Greater Adepts. For right understanding requires not only that one should realize the universality of Justice. The conception of unchanging Law, unqualified and untempered by Mercy, is not enough to carry us through the 18th path. And great as are the powers of those who have attained to the Grade corresponding to Geburah, it is not until they have become truly exempt from action that they are qualified to follow the course which will make them Masters of the Temple.

You understand, I hope, that anything I can say about these higher Grades can be little more than a faint shadow of the reality. My words are not final. They shed only a tiny gleam of light upon the Great Plan, and this is borrowed light, for all that I can do is to try to make a little clearer some of the directions we have received from Those who have gone on before.

The first of these indications so cleverly "hidden in plain sight" is the letter-name, חית. It is the number 418, and 418 combines 400 with 18.

400 represents, as you know, the totality of manifestation, because there are 400 Sephiroth in the Great Tree of Life. It is also the number of the letter Tau (the Cross), and is thus a number referable to the Saturnine limiting, definitive, concreting vibration associated with Tau. This limiting activity is implied in the meaning of <u>Cheth</u>, a fence, because a fence sets a boundary, marks out a field for cultivation. Note also that the path of Cheth necessarily partakes of the Saturnine quality, because it connects the 3d and 5th Sephiroth, which are the spheres of Saturn and Mars.

18 is the number of חי, <u>Chai</u>, "life," which appears in the divine name attributed to YESOD (Shaddai Al Chai). The digits of 18 are 1 and 8. 1 represents beginning, and is the number of Kether, the Primal Will which is the <u>beginning of whirling motion</u>. 8 is the number of involution and evolution, the number which symbolizes the conception expressed by Ezekiel in the phrase: "And the living creatures (חיים, <u>Chaiim</u>), ran and returned." Yet the number 8 is also the number of Mercury, and the HOD, sphere of Mercury, as if to show us that this involution and evolution is directed rationally. Thus this number, placed horizontally, is over the head of the MAGICIAN in the Tarot, who corresponds to Mercury, and the symbolism of that Key shows the descent of Life through the rational consciousness to the planes below, and the ascent of life from those lower planes back to the rational. For the flowers growing in the Magician's garden are food for his higher sensibilities, even as more homely vegetables are food for his body, and their growth is a type of the ascent of nature up from the subhuman planes, through the human, back to the divine. Finally, the reduction of 18 is 9, the number of the letter Teth, the serpent-power of FOHAT. Thus we see that

חי, life, is numerically defined in esoteric terminology as "the power which enters into manifestation through the whirling motion initiated at the beginning of a cycle by the Primal Will, and involving and evolving itself through the functions of the rational or Mercurial consciousness."

חית, then, as combining the foregoing idea of Life with the idea of limitation associated with Tau, 400, and Saturn, shows us that the 18th Path on the Tree of Life has to do with the self-limitation of the Life-Power.

Observe, too, that חית, as 418, has 13 for its first reduction, and 13 is the number of אחד, Achad, "unity," and of אהבה, Ahebah, "love." The self-limitation of the Life-Power produces the illusion of two antagonistic principles. Esoteric teaching says, "These Two are really One, and that One is Love." We shall find that the other path we study in this lesson has the same connection with the number 13, as has the name of the Sephirah to which each of these paths leads us on the Way of Return.

The name of this path is בית השפע, "House of Influence." It might also be translated "House of Overflowing" or "House of Abundance," for the Hebrew noun שפע means "abundant outpouring." You will see, of course, that the name of this path begins with the letter-name of the second character in the Hebrew alphabet, <u>Beth,</u> and that it conveys to Qabalists the occult significance, "Mercurial outpouring." Look at your Tree of Life, and you will see that on the side of Severity the path of Beth or Mercury leads from Kether to Binah, and that, in consequence, the 18th path, which unites Binah and Geburah must be tinged with the same Mercurial quality. This is the quality of self-consciousness expressed in its highest terms, as shown by the picture of the MAGICIAN. Thus we know that in traversing the 18th path on the Way of Return, we shall be recovering, or remembering, something of the control of external conditions by right use of mental powers which is presented in the symbolism of the MAGICIAN.

Consider the name of the 18th path even more closely. בית השפע. Beth stands for the MAGICIAN. י stands for the HERMIT. Tav is the letter of the WORLD. Put these Keys before you on the table, and consider them attentively. You see the Life-Power descending, for cultural purposes, through the MAGICIAN. That same descent is pictured in the symbolism of the HERMIT. In the WORLD the process is symbolized as the Dance of Life. These are but three aspects of one thing, and that is the process whereby the Life-Power provides itself with an abode, a house, a dwelling-place – a particular field חית of action in Time and Space. The numbers of these Keys are I, IX and XXI, and added together they make 31, which must be reduced, because there are no Key-numbers beyond XXI. The reduction is IV, the number of the EMPEROR. The EMPEROR corresponds to the letter which begins the second part of the title of the 18th path. As used here, Heh is the definite article. The EMPEROR corresponds also to this power of self-definition which is dominant in the creative process. The whole universe is Life's definition of Itself, and this is why it is said that the nature is a book, and we the readers.

The second letter of שפע is Shin, to which Qabalists assign the Fire which is the Life-Breath of the creative powers (Sh=300= רוח אלהים, Ruach Elohim). The third letter is Peh, which is attributed to Mars. The final letter is Ayin, corresponding to the sign Capricorn, wherein Mars is exalted and Saturn is the ruler. Thus the name suggests Qabalistically that the overflowing abundance connected with this 18th path is fiery, Martian, disruptive, yet curbed and directed by means of the Saturnine power of limitation, exerted through the intellectual manifestation of the Life-Power which astrologers associate with Mercury.

I have been at some pains to indicate all these clues, in order to show you how the attribution of the Tarot to the Hebrew alphabet and paths, as given in here, is justified and proven correct by the results we get when we apply it to Qabalistic terminology. In a few words, all that is here indicated may be stated thus: the 18th path is the channel of the abundant outflow of the fiery activity of the Life-Power, taking form as objects (including the objects we call "creatures" as well as those we call "things") by means of the Life-Power's inherent quality of self-limitation, which quality is directed by the intellectual, rational quality called "Mercury" and symbolized by the MAGICIAN.

To travel the 18th path on the Way of Return, therefore, is to overcome the limitations of Saturn by knowing how to utilize them, to master the destructive force of Mars, to awaken in oneself the regenerative potency of the Flame of the Life-Breath, and to restore the creator to his throne. (Each section of the foregoing sentence is suggested by the letters of ע פ ש ה, read backward, or in reverse, as on the WAY of RETURN, thus, ה ש פ ע. Trace out the connections.)

And because this is the path which leads to the Grade named "Magister Templi," or "Master of the Temple," it is symbolized in the Tarot by the CHARIOT. For the chariot is a symbol for the living temple of the Life-Power, and the driver of the car is the I AM. He is master of the positive and negative expressions of the elemental expression of the Astral Light. The positive expression is the white sphinx, the negative is the black one. The sphinxes correspond to the fourfold manifestation of the Astral Light because they are (when drawn correctly, as they are <u>not</u> in Mr. Waite's design) a synthesis of the Man, the Eagle, the Lion and the Bull.

The name of the zodiacal sign corresponding to this path is Cancer, the Crab, spelt סרטן = 319 in Hebrew. The function attributed to the same path is Speech, and this is שוחה =319. A crab is enclosed in a hard, stone-like shell, and it walks backward. The occult idea of Speech is that of a power which can give concrete material embodiment to ideas, can encase thought in the hard shell of material forms. This occult power of speech is implied in the Christian doctrine that all things were made by the Logos, or WORD. And just as a crab grows his shell from within outward, so the occult power of Speech can gradually solidify ideas into things. This, of course, would be called a crazy notion by most people. It is, nevertheless, the basis of all practical magic.

The backward walk of the crab symbolizes the process of retracing the path. It is a symbol of the way of return. Lao-Tze says, "The path of TAO is backward."

Because he walks backward, the crab looks always toward the place whence he has come. In like manner speech is always backward-looking. Even the materials of speech are derived from the past. The growth of a language is like the crustacean's slow progress, and whoever would use words aright must continually turn his mental gaze backward, making himself familiar with roots and derivations, tracing meanings to their sources. Clearness in speech and writing require this backward look. Coherence and consistence demand that we keep our mental gaze upon what we have said or written, as the crab keeps his eyes upon the ground which he has just traversed.

But there is a deeper occult connection between the crab-symbol and the magical use of speech than any I have touched upon. As the crab protects and isolates himself by growing a shell, so may the adept protect and isolate himself from the illusions of his environment by learning the technique of magical speech. By this means he may even build for himself an indestructible body, which will resist every hostile external influence.

This is a work which calls into play the powers which are developed in the Grade of Greater Adept, but because this making of an indestructible body by the power of words would be likely to intensify the delusion of separateness were it attempted before the adept's consciousness had been freed from that delusion, it is only to Exempt Adepts that this path of Cheth is open on the Way of Return.

A person who still labors under the illusion that he has a personal will, that he can do things of himself, is not ripe enough to be entrusted with the secret of building an indestructible body. Only the adept completely liberated from the delusion of separateness can become so free a channel for the outpouring of the Life-Power that none of his thoughts, or words, or actions will do anything but promote the realization of the Will-to-Good which is behind all modes of manifestation. Such a man cannot be selfish, and only one who is wholly unselfish may exercise the powers of a Master of the Temple.

The number 319, which is that of שׁוחה, Speech, and of סרטן, Cancer, when articulated as 300, 10, 9, gives the numbers of the letters שׁ, י, and ט, and these form two Hebrew words. The first, שׁיט, means an <u>oar</u>, and so suggests that by which one drives and steers a boat through water. This is analogous to the symbolism of the little boat in the background of the 13th Tarot Key, a Key also attributed to a sign - Scorpio. The meaning has to do with the artistic adaptation and control of the Water-element associated with this path through the sign Cancer. This Water element has its root in the 3rd Sephirah, בינה, and it is the substance phase of the Life-Power. Binah is called the Great Sea by Qabalists, and in traversing the 18th Path on the Way of Return, the adept learns the secret of adapting the substance-phase, (sometimes called the Astral Fluid) by means of speech. To be more explicit, the occult art of speech consists in such a specific employment of sound-vibrations related to mental images as will tend to materialize those images as physical conditions. By this occult art of speech the Exempt Adept moulds the Astral Fluid into whatsoever shapes he chooses, and the results of his control of substance through the laws of sound enable him to make for himself an indestructible body, and to produce other effects which seem like miracles to the uninitiated.

Another Hebrew word formed from the same letters is יׁשט, which is a verb meaning <u>to stretch out</u>. It hints at the tremendous extension of powers which is the outcome of the adept's command, through occult speech, of the substance phase of the Life-Power. The ordinary circle of human influence is comparatively small. Now and then, in moments of stress, some person is enabled to send his thought over miles of distance, or to project a phantasm of himself into another place. This latent power of human beings, of which you may read accounts in the proceedings of the societies for psychological research, is fully developed in the Master who has passed through the 18th Path.

As Hudson says in his <u>Law of Psychic Phenomena</u>, this power is a function of the subjective or subconscious mind. This is the watery Astral Fluid, or substance phase of the Life-Power, whose symbol is the Moon. The adept is able to utilize it more perfectly than other people, <u>because he has developed a vivid consciousness of the unity of substance</u> and of the illusive nature of time and space. First by reasoning, and then by long practice in creative imagination, he has realized that both Past and Future are summed up in an eternal NOW. He has learned by the same means that there is no such thing as <u>distance</u> to the instantaneous action of the Life-Power. Understand me well. The adept has first perceived these truths intellectually, and then by long practice has developed skill in expressing these truths imaginatively by sound-symbols expressing definite ideas. He is one who has built up by patient practice in concentration and meditation the ability to carry into execution the words of Jesus, "Whatsoever things ye ask and pray for, believe that ye have received them, and ye shall have them." Jesus did not explain to those who listened to his esoteric teaching that a great deal of patient practice is required in order to perfect such a power of belief. He contented himself with an accurate statement of principle, knowing full well that not one person in ten thousand in any generation of mankind is ripe enough to realize that statement to the full.

And upon what is this belief to be established? Upon recognition of the unity of the Life-Power. Thus we find that 319, the number of these words we have been considering, reduces to 13, the number of the word אחד, Achad, Unity, which is also the number of the word אהבה, Ahebah, Love.

To understand the One-ness of All is to see, too, that the One is a principle of Love, which declares itself in The Book of Tokens by the words, "Nothing is, or can be, my antagonist." This is the point-of-view from which the Master of the Temple performs his mighty works. He sees no adversary anywhere in creation. To him there are no enemies. It never enters his mind that there is anything to be subdued, anything to be fought, anything which can possibly set itself up against the realization of the Will-to-Good of which he knows himself to be an open channel. Thus, in the 8th Tarot Key, although the Charioteer is fully armed, he is at rest, and the chariot stands still.

The Master of the Temple realizes to the full the meaning of the affirmation, "Filled with understanding of its perfect law, I am guided moment by moment along the path of liberation." He feels within him the urge of that resistless Will which others not so wise mistake for something of their own. He makes no plans, because he knows that the successful end of the Great Work was determined from the beginning. He has neither anxiety nor curiosity about the future, because he has learned that the great secret is to do as the Hindu sage advises – "live out the present with a smiling heart." He works, as Eliphas Levi puts it, "as if he had all eternity to work in." Here Levi shows the subtlety of his language, for what is really meant is not "as if an endless vista of time lay before him, in which to complete his undertaking," but rather, "as if the medium in which he works were Eternity and not Time." It is by means of this timelessness in his thought and work that the Master of the Temple stretches out the circle of his activities so that it includes points in space far distant from that occupied by his physical body; and by this same freedom from the illusion of Time he produces in an instant results in the way of giving visible form and shape to the substance-phase of the Life-Power which seem miraculous to profane beholders of his works.

The Sephirah בינה, Binah, to which the 18th Path leads, is also the Path of Sanctifying Intelligence. Thus we know that a Master of the Temple is what we sometimes call a saint. And it is important to remember that the "communion of saints" mentioned in the Christian Creed refers to the rapport existing between in the Christian Creed refers to the rapport existing between adepts who have attained to this Grade in the Invisible Order. For these are the ripened fruits of humanity, in whom are developed all the highest powers of the race. Even the Grade of Magus which lies beyond contains no riper souls, for the Magus excels not in ripeness but in practical skill.

"Sanctifying" in Hebrew is מקודש = 450. From the number we are led to see that a saint is a man in whom the full powers of humanity are brought to fruition. 450 is 10 x 45, and 10 is the number of perfection, while 45 is the number of אדם, Adam or Man. Consider the Tarot Keys corresponding to מקודש. A saint is one who has surrendered all personal actions to the direction of the Life-Power (M: HANGED MAN). He has traversed the road of initiation during the sleep of his physical body (Q: THE MOON). He has listened to the Voice of the Inner Teacher (V: HIEROPHANT). By coming to understand the full significance of what it is to be a man, and by denying the false claims of personality, he has restored the Creator to His throne; and all this has been accomplished through the generative power of imagination. For without creative imagination no man ever is able to work out the logical consequences of the Unity of Being, so as to develop a vivid consciousness of the real presence in human life, here and now, of the Originating Principle of the Universe. This creative imagination is the mother, so to say, of the new conception of personality which establishes the Fatherhood of the I AM in our consciousness (ד: THE EMPRESS). This work which makes a saint has its completion in the perfection and unfoldment of a new vehicle for the Life-Power, a liberated and regenerated person, through the operation of the refining fire of the Life-Breath of the Elohim (רוח אלהים, Ruach Elohim=300=ש. The Judgment.) Yet all this may be summed up in the letter Teth, because 450=4+5+0=9=Teth=STRENGTH, so that we may say a saint is one who has succeeded in applying the law pictured in the VIIIth Key. He knows the Secret of All Spiritual Activities, which is the secret of the control of the serpent-power, FOHAT. He has succeeded, as a result of formulating that secret in occult Speech, in learning how to make himself absolute master of the vehicle of personality, and through that vehicle, of the conditions of external nature.

So I put it, because of the limitations of language. But what has the Master of the Temple really learned to do? Simply to "stand aside and let" the I AM work through his personality. He does nothing, not the slightest thing, of himself. This is why everything that he does is so potent. Every thought he thinks, every word he speaks, every action he performs is the direct expression of the one Life which is the Creative Principle of the Universe. The Master of the Temple has attained to Nirvana, and Nirvana means extinction. But what has been extinguished? Nothing that ever had any reality. In this extinction nothing is lost. A delusion ceases to exist, that is all, and with its passing all bondage is forever at an end.

But this liberation is not completely brought about until one has traversed the 17th Path, that of the letter ZAIN, for the delusion of separate personality is really a transposition of Cause and Effect, a mistaking of the instrument for the player, and the correction of this error is what is finally accomplished in the Path of the Sword (Zain). For this is the error against which we are warned in the admonition to "rightly divide the word of God," which has nothing to do with Scriptural interpretations, but everything with the right ordering or classification of the ways in which the Logos, or thought-embodying energy of the Life-Power, makes itself manifest.

Rightly to divide the Word is to have a clear mental perception of the functions of the three modes of consciousness, and the truth of this matter is symbolically set forth in the 6th Tarot Key, which corresponds to the letter ZAIN. For it must be clear to you by this time that no definite creative imagination is possible without a clear-cut intellectual pattern. Intellect has to grasp the principle in order to supply the pattern from which the subconscious generation of mental images results. And since we found, early in this course, that to become superconscious we must have bodies different from those we are using now, the problem is: How may we build these kind of bodies?
Now, we know that the subconsciousness is always amenable to suggestion, and we know that it is the body-builder. Our problem, then, is to set a pattern for the building of a perfect body. Can we do this? Is there any suggestion which will bring about this result?

Yes, there is, but although the self-conscious mind has to give the suggestion, has to set in motion the change in subconscious activities which results at last in the making of the indestructible body of the Master of the Temple, the self-conscious mind does not make the pattern. The pattern is "given in the mount" where are the patterns of the Tabernacle and its furniture.

Why this must be so will be clear to you when you consider the present state of human knowledge concerning the human body. Who knows how to make a pattern of a perfect body? Who among us has seen a Master, so as to know what his body looks like on the outside, let alone what it is like beneath the surface? Nobody. None of us know how to make such a pattern.

What, then, shall we do? The 6th Key shows us. We shall use the law of auto-suggestion to free the subconscious from the domination of the self-conscious, and submit it to the direction of the superconscious. For the superconscious does know -- has always known -- what goes into the making of a perfect vehicle for its self-expression. Thus self-consciousness, the "seed of the woman" who is subconsciousness, shall deliver the woman from the curse. For the curse is that the subconscious shall be subject to the direction of self-consciousness. Yet by right use of that very curse we can turn it into a blessing.

For we can say to subconsciousness:

"Be thou free henceforth from any false idea coming from me. Obey nothing but the real Self. Listen only to it, and act as the vehicle of communication through which I may become aware of its guidance, of its will."

A simple thing to do? Yes. So was washing seven times in the river a simple thing for Naaman, but it cured him of leprosy. So will this simple method cure you, eventually, of the leprosy of separateness. And it can be explained on scientific principles.

If you hypnotize a person and tell him that from that time forth nobody will ever be able to hypnotize him again, your words will be accepted by his subconsciousness, and he will never again be put "under the influence." This is the principle involved in setting the subconsciousness free from self-conscious dominance. Only be sure, be <u>very</u> sure, to make it perfectly clear to the subconsciousness that you are turning it over to the direction of the true Self, to the influx of wisdom from the superconscious plane. Simply to say, in effect, "Henceforth you are free from my control; without specifying that you are merely surrendering the activities of the subconscious to the direction of the I AM, is to invite disaster. For when the subconsciousness is not curbed at all, it simply runs wild, and lunacy is the outcome of its unrestrained activities.

As I said in another lesson, the paths beyond that of the HANGED MAN are paths of realization. This path of ZAIN is the path in which we realize that the superconsciousness, symbolized in the sixth Key by the angel, is at all times the real director of personal activities and destiny. This realization is more than the perception that the I AM is the rider in the chariot of personality. It includes an understanding of the way in which this direction is effected. A man deluded by the sense of separateness supposes that self-consciousness is the plane of initiative, thinks of volition as a power of personality. When he has passed through the path of ZAIN he sees that volition and initiative have their source in superconsciousness, and pass into subconsciousness, where they assume the form of the desires or motives which determine his selection of this or that course of action. <u>Motive</u> always determines volition, and every motive rises from the subconsciousness into the plane of self-consciousness. The Ageless Wisdom teaches that every man is guided, moment by moment, through the whole series of his lives, by the Cosmic Will. This guidance is misunderstood by the unenlightened, who believe that the source of their motives is separate and personal. Sages unite to declare that this is not so -- that the true Self directs the personality through every stage of its unfoldment, and that the Woman of the mental pair is the immediate recipient of this direction.

Eventually the personality reaches a stage of unfoldment where this truth is perceived, and then the personal life is seen to be the direct manifestation of the Cosmic Will. Thenceforth the man acts, speaks and thinks as the conscious instrument of the true Self.

The Grade of Magister Templi, then, is one in which we arrive at understanding (BINAH) of the true order of the Life-Power's manifestation through personality. He who attains to it does not <u>become</u> a Master. The attainment consists in the realization that the SELF is, and has been always, the Lord of His dwelling-place.

Thus Mohini Chatterji, in his introduction to the eighth chapter of the Bhagavad-Gita, says:

"It is true that no one can ever <u>become</u> the Supreme Spirit, for in reality he is never anything else. To know and to become the Supreme Spirit is really the same thing; the difference in expression is due to the difference in the inner peace of the different classes of devotees."

The numbers of the Tarot cards representing the two paths leading to BINAH are 7 and 6. Their sum, 13, is that of the card named DEATH, which corresponds to the path leading from NETZACH to TIPHARETH. He who has passed through the path of DEATH, who has become consciously immortal, knows that the true Self is Master of the Temple. Sooner or later that knowledge ripens into such perfect control of all physiological processes that he is able to prolong the life of the physical body indefinitely.

When the activities of the subconscious plane have been definitely turned over to the direction of the superconscious, no self-conscious interference with the body-building power is possible. I do not mean by this that every person who enters into superconscious experience attains to physical immortality during the same incarnation in which the awakening comes. Boehme was superconscious, Ramakrishna was superconscious, and so were hosts of others who have passed on. Sooner or later, however, the particular line of tendency which the Life-Power expressed through these personalities will descend into incarnation as a human being who lives in a physical body which does not die until he himself sets his higher vehicles free from it. Even then it will not die in the manner that we usually call "death." It will be instantly disintegrated into its component elements, will vanish from the sight of men in the twinkling of an eye.

Moreover, when a man has reached this stage of unfoldment, he is no longer subject to birth. Whenever he needs to use a physical body, he can make one as quickly as he can disintegrate it. I am persuaded that a number of such just men made perfect are at work in physical bodies in our world today. This, of course, is merely my private opinion, which no reader of these pages is expected to accept, unless it appeals to him as reasonable.

We are far from this perfection, yet we may take the first steps in the path which leads to it. We may use our intellect and imagination to build up in our minds the conception of the One Self as being even now the absolute master of its temple, human personality, and day by day we may strive to correct the illusions of our seemingly separate existence by meditation upon this truth.

The True Creative Self

The paths upon which you are to meditate in connection with this lesson are:

1. The path of Triumphant and Eternal Intelligence, corresponding to the letter Vau, to the zodiacal sign Taurus, to the color red-orange, and to the note C-sharp.

2. The path of Constituting Intelligence, corresponding to the letter Heh, to the sign Aries, to the color red, and to the note C.

3. The path of Luminous Intelligence, corresponding to the letter Daleth, to the planet Venus, to the color green, and to the note F-sharp.

The goal of all these paths on the Way of Return is the Sephirah Chokmah, to which is assigned the Grade of Magus in the Rosicrucian Order. What a Magus really is may perhaps be better understood if we quote from our old acquaintance, Eliphas Levi:

"Magic is the divinity of man achieved in union with faith; the true Magi are Men-Gods, in virtue of their intimate union with the divine principle. They are without fears and without desires, dominated by no falsehood, sharing no error, loving without illusion, suffering without impatience, reposing in the quietude of eternal thought... A Magus cannot be ignorant, for magic implies superiority, mastership, majority, and majority signifies emancipation by knowledge... The Man-God has neither rights nor duties; he has science, will and power. He is more than free, he is master, he does not command, he creates; he does not obey, because no one can possibly command him. What others term duty, he names his good pleasure; he does good because he wishes to, and never wills anything else; he co-operates freely in everything that forwards the cause of justice, and for him sacrifice is the luxury of the moral life and the magnificence of the heart. He is implacable toward evil because he is without a trace of hatred for the wicked. He regards reparatory chastisement as a benefit and does not comprehend the meaning of vengeance."

That such a man is truly, to use a Rosicrucian phrase, "more than man," we must all concede. That none of us is able to form more than a vague conception of such a character must as freely be admitted. Yet we altogether miss the point of the Wisdom Teaching behind these lessons if we do not see that this is no ideal picture of what we may sometime become. On the contrary, it is the barest of outlines of what the true Man in every human being really IS.

Levi hints as much in the fifteenth chapter of the third book of his Le Grand Arcane, where he tells us:

"The serpent had said: 'Ye shall be as gods.' Jesus Christ, crushing the head of the serpent under the charming foot of his mother, dares to say: 'Ye shall not be as gods, nor as God, but ye shall be God.'"

"Ye shall be God, for God is my Father, my Father and I are but one, and I will it that you and I shall be as one also."

Remember that Levi writes this as an occultist and Qabalist. Superficial readers of his works may believe, with A. E. Waite, that he stultifies himself by pretending to accept the dogmas of the Roman Church. They who can read him in the original French must be struck by the exquisite care with which he chose his words. He did not <u>pretend</u> to accept. He did really accept, as do all occultists, the very dogmas which orthodox theologians believe that they hold. He accepted these dogmas because he understood that they are magical formulae, embodying much of the wisdom of the ages. He did not accept, nor do we, the naive and childish interpretations of the ordinary churchman. He must have known, as we do, that the very name "Jesus Christ" is an occult formula, indicating the exact process, or method, whereby the true Self of man frees itself from the bondage of delusion. For reasons of his own doubtless good ones Levi kept his peace with the theologians of his day by an apparent agreement which was really a profound dissent from their opinions. Perhaps we might be wiser if we adopted a similar course.

At all events, what he has written concerning the Grade of Magus will help us to form a conception of what is meant by reaching this stage on the Way of Return.

The first of the three paths leading thereto is the 16th, and as we travel upward on the Tree of Life, it begins in Chesed, the Sephirah to which was assigned the Grade of Exempt Adept. This path remains closed until the aspirant has attained to the Grade of Magister Templi. One cannot enter into the state of consciousness which Qabalists call "Triumphant and Eternal Intelligence" until all the vehicles of personality have been cleansed and mastered. Indeed, only a Master of the Temple can possibly experience this degree of consciousness.

What we know about it we must perforce gather from the descriptions of the sages, since we are not by any means even at the portals of this Grade. Yet we may profit by an examination of the name of the path.

In Hebrew it is נצחי=158, formed from the noun נצח, Netzach, with the letter Yod added as a suffix. Netzach is the name of the Sephirah to which the Grade of Philosophus is assigned. Qabalistically, the addition of the letter Yod to this noun is the addition of the <u>hand</u>, suggesting the practical application of a ripened philosophy. To make this practical application, one must be master of his own personal instrument. To be serviceable in order to perform service -- that is the idea. A hard lesson but one that we all must learn thoroughly, sooner or later.

The Qabalistic dictionary says that 158 is represented by the words חיצים, arrows; חנק, to strangle; and מאזנים (Aramaic)[1], balances. We find little difficulty with "arrows," because an arrow suggests the penetrating directness of the concentrated magical will. Nor does the word "balances" puzzle us to any great extent, since we know by this time that equilibrium is the basis of the Great Work. But "to strangle"? At first glance this appears to have little connection with the idea of a state of consciousness described as "triumphant". Yet further consideration will remind us that in every ancient symbolic initiation the candidate had to simulate death. More than this, strangulation is death by constriction of the throat, and this path that we are studying is connected with the letter Vau, and with the sign Taurus, which rules the throat. What it really means is the total eradication of the sense of separate personality. The false belief in "self" must be strangled before the true Self can be made manifest.

---

[1] The numeric value of this word is actually 148 (Ed.)

Consider this word חנק in connection with the Tarot keys. Cheth is represented by the CHARIOT, Nun by DEATH, and Qoph by THE MOON. Add the numbers of the keys together and you have 38, by reduction 11, the number of JUSTICE. Lay these cards on the table before you, and seek their significance in this connection, making notes as in other lessons. The CHARIOT represents mastery of the vehicle of personality. DEATH indicates the transforming agency whereby that mastery is made effective. THE MOON is a picture of the slow process of unfoldment. JUSTICE sums up the whole matter. The equilibrium of the balances is unattainable if the bias of the false personality tips the scales. To direct the arrows of volition to their mark is impossible while the aim is spoilt by personal considerations. While yet we speak of rights and duties something of the old error of separateness remains to be killed out, and there is something yet of the lie of division to be strangled.

This is the first step toward the Grade of Magus. Until it is taken, the Eternal Intelligence cannot be known. To be conscious of eternity instead of time is to leave behind every vestige of the old, false "self." It is to affect the great conjunction indicated by the grammatical use in Hebrew of the letter Vau. This is what is indicated in the lines which H.P.B. culled from the Book of the Golden Precepts:

> "The Mind is the great Slayer of the Real.
> Let the disciple slay the Slayer.
> For --
> When to himself his form appears unreal, as do on waking all the
> forms he sees in dreams:
> When he has ceased to hear the many, he may discern the One -- the
> inner sound which kills the outer.
> Then only, not till then, shall he forsake the region of Asat, the false,
> to come into the realm of Sat, the true.
> Before the Soul can see, the harmony within must be attained, and
> fleshly eyes be rendered blind to all illusion.
> Before the Soul can hear, the image (man) has to become as deaf to
> roarings as to whispers, to cries of bellowing elephants as to the
> silvery bussing of the golden firefly.
> Before the Soul can comprehend and may remember, she must unto
> the Silent Speaker be united, just as the form to which the clay is
> modeled is first united with the potter's mind.
> For then the Soul will hear, and will remember.
> And then to the inner ear will speak --
> THE VOICE OF THE SILENCE."

The picture of the Hierophant sums up the whole meaning of the 16th path. He is the Silent Speaker of the foregoing quotation. His voice cannot be heard while the insistent demands of the false personality are clamoring for recognition.

We must not misunderstand this talk about killing. It does not mean suppression. Neither does it mean sacrifice, as men understand sacrifice. When Levi says that sacrifice for the Magus is the luxury of the moral life, he is not indulging in meaningless, high-flown phrases. Would there be any sacrifice in changing a counterfeit bill for genuine money? What loss would follow giving up a paste jewel for a diamond? Even so there is no loss, but a great gain, in ridding oneself of the delusion of separateness. We repeat, this is not suppression, which only submerges the error for the time being in the depths of the subconscious. It is the total eradication of the mistaken opinion. It completely roots up the erroneous conception of personality which results from mistaking illusion for reality. The illusion persists, as we have pointed out before but the belief that it is real, as one might mistake a piece of rope for a snake, is at an end.

Note the result. "Then the Soul will hear, and will <u>remember</u>." Liberation is the result of knowing the truth, and the Greek word for truth means literally "not forgetting." We, immortal, have forgotten our immortality. Essentially divine, we have identified ourselves with the worm of the dust. This delusion we must strangle. Then we shall remember who and what we really are. Our inner ears shall then be opened to the Voice which reveals the mystery of union, which no human language can possibly convey. Then shall we again experience the triumphant consciousness of eternal life. Then shall we be truly "more than free."

This is not all, as Levi shows by saying that the Magus does not command, but creates. This phase of his activity is developed by the state of consciousness symbolized by the fifteenth path. The old Hebrew verb translated "create" in our Bibles means literally "to cut out." Creation is an act of discrimination, and act of definition, and this act is the result of what Qabalists call "Constituting Intelligence."

The Secret Wisdom of Israel says that the fifteenth path bears the name מעמיד (Constituting) because it constitutes the substance of creations in pure darkness. A hint of similar import is in the Gospel of St. John. "That which hath been made was life in him (the Logos); and the life was the light of men. And the light shineth in the darkness; and the darkness overcame it not."

The same L.V.X. appears in Bible symbology under the figure of the Lamb, borrowed from the Hindu symbol of Agni, god of fire. The Lamb refers to the mystery of the cosmic sacrifice. In one sense the wise have always regarded creation as a self-immolation of the Life-Power. In one of his sermons, the Rev. R. J. Campbell expresses the matter thus:

"What one dimly perceives is that God cannot help himself in this matter; it is written deep in the nature of things; it has to be; omnipotence cannot alter it. 'The lamb slain from the foundation of the world' is no figure of speech but the very heart of all reality. The revealing of the glory of God carries with it a cosmic Calvary in which we, his children, are individually called to share."

Thus the first letter of מעמיד is that which the Tarot pictures as the HANGED MAN. Creation is the self-limitation of that which is really limitless. It is the assumption of the illusions of time and space, the apparent differentiation between "I, the Maker" and "That, the Made." But that which hath been made, we are told, was life in the Maker. By reason of its own nature the Life-Power is creative, yet creation involves the appearance of the Not-I. The limitless takes on the form of the limited. The eternal expresses itself in time. The boundless establishes boundaries. The universal enters into existence as the particular. The absolute enters into the conditions of the relative.

Thus we see that limitation, or definition is the basis of the Constituting Intelligence, and this is plainly indicated by the grammatical meaning of Heh, the Hebrew definite article, corresponding to English "the." With the idea of limitation enters the idea of something opposed to the creative power, of something external which is the object of that power's mental contemplation. Thus the second letter of MOMID, Ayin, "the eye," is connected with the restrictive, materialistic influence which astrology associates with Saturn, and this letter is represented in the Tarot by the DEVIL. We point out these correspondences to assist you in your meditation, but the mere enumeration is by no means sufficient. If you hope to penetrate into the profounder mysteries of the occult gnosis, you must ponder these details, earnestly desiring further illumination.

By traversing this path the aspirant to the Grade of Magus associates himself mentally with the cosmic sacrifice. Thus he unifies his being with the current of the cosmic creative impulse. Levi says, you recall, that he who can master the currents of the Astral Light becomes the depositary even of the power of God.

The origin of the fifteenth path is in Tiphareth, so that one must go back to the state of the Lesser Adept to traverse it. That is, one must identify himself with the SON, the Solar Logos (see lesson 4). It is the SON, one with the FATHER, who is the perpetual sacrifice.

In other words, at this stage of initiation the aspirant so identifies himself with the Solar Logos that no shadow, even, of the sense of separateness sullies his consciousness. This is why he must first pass through the sixteenth path, wherein the last vestige of the false personality is eradicated. The least tinge of personal motive vitiates the seeker's endeavor to utilize the cosmic creative energy. To do nothing for self, but all for the Self, is here the test. It involves what the world misinterprets as sacrifice. Thus the third letter of מעמיד, like the first, is explained by the Tarot picture of the HANGED MAN.

Again, to be a conscious channel of the cosmic creative impulse is to know the state which Hindus call Kaivalya, isolation. How lightly, now that Eastern Wisdom has been translated into our daily speech, does one hear this isolation spoken of. How few in any generation can grasp the meaning of the injunction in Light on the Path: "Stand alone and isolated, because nothing that is embodied, nothing that is conscious of separation, nothing that is out of the eternal, can aid you." We have too much glib speech about this high attainment. Even a little real thought about it soon shows us that it should inspire in us a profound awe. Yet he who would really be a conscious creator must so stand. Creation begins at a point where there is nothing other than the creator. All this is set forth in the symbolism of THE HERMIT.

The last letter of מעמיד looks ahead to the path we have yet to consider in this lesson. What it means will be explained in due course. In the meantime let us consider the word מעמיד as a whole, from the point of view afforded by Gematria. Its numeration, 164, corresponds to הדבקים, "ye shall cleave;" חיצון, external; and עמדים, the Pillars (Jachin and Boaz). The suggestion is that the Constituting Intelligence is one of close union with the Life-Power, in which the manifested cosmos is seen as external to the Self, and as proceeding from that Self at the heart of all being. Again, it is a state of perfect equilibrium, understood as the support (pillars) of existence.

To put the matter more explicitly, the aspirant to the Grade of Magus, passing through the fifteenth path, vividly identifies himself with the great Heart of Life, knows himself to be one with the Great Within whence all that is manifested and external proceedings, and realizes in himself the union of positive and negative, of Mercy and Severity, the pillars of the Tree of Life. We who know only a little about this stage of unfoldment can but faintly imagine what the actual experience is like; but even what dim image will prepare us for the time when, instead of knowing about it, we shall truly know it.

Moreover, two Hebrew words are concealed in מעמיד - מים, waters, and עד, eternity. He who has reached the height of the fifteenth path sees himself alone at the center of the Great Sea of Eternal Subsistence. For him there is naught but the true Self, the Self which is ALL. One of the commonest symbols of this state is that of a great ocean. Boundless it extends on every hand, its circumference nowhere, its center everywhere. These words correspond to no actuality of our sense-experience, and are meaningless unless one has known the Presence beyond personality. Yet we believe that to most readers of this lesson they will convey a great deal of significance.

We read a deal of cheerful talk about our being sons and daughters of God, and therefore by birthright creators. Some of it is most plausible. One might almost think he had only to learn the fact in order to be master of the cosmic creative energy. We _are_ creative always, to be sure, because our lives are inseparable from the One Life and share its potencies. Yet most of our creation is negative, because we lack knowledge and skill. We might as well stop deluding ourselves, and face the facts. Not one person in ten thousand even begins to grasp the principles of occult science. Of those who understand the theory, not one in a thousand even begins to grasp the principles of occult science. Of those who understand the theory, not one in a thousand becomes a skilled creator until after a number of incarnations.

To reach the high altitude of attainment represented by the fifteenth path is to have gained knowledge and skill far beyond that of an Einstein, or Edison, or a Steinmetz. Scientists of the physical world are like children playing with toys, in comparison to the initiate ready to enter the Grade of Magus.

Why, then, should we be concerned with these far-off achievements? Simply because we must make a beginning sometime. The Path may seem long and wearisome, but we may look at it in two ways. One way is to cavil at its length and difficulty, thinking of it as something which separates us from the goal. The other is to look upon every step as part of the goal itself. Whenever we try to perform the least action selflessly we are in training for the post of Magus. Every attempt to abstract our attention from the illusions of the external, every endeavor to stand alone, every moment spent in imaging ourselves one with the Heart of Life, is part of the realization which shall some day be ours.

Every human being is destined sooner or later to gain that high eminence. We say this, even though we have been at some pains to show that the true Self in us is even now the Magus of the Eternal. Our poor words cannot convey to you the grandeur of the ultimate realization, yet they may serve to bring you the good news of your certain destiny. This, after all, is one of the main purposes of these lessons.

Coming now to the last of the three paths leading the Grade of Magus, we find that in Hebrew its title is מאיר, Luminous, a rabbinical Hebrew adjective derived from אור, light.

The path joins Binah to Chokmah, the Mother to the Father, the Root of Water to the Root of Fire. It is the only path connecting the Grade of Master to the Temple with the Grade of Magus, and unlike the two paths preceding, is attributed to a planet, Venus.

With the astrological meaning of Venus you are by now thoroughly familiar. You know that its influence is dominant in a nerve-center at the throat, and have learned that it governs the generation of metal images by sub-consciousness in response to impulses and suggestions originating in the self-conscious field. Its activity is summed up n the one word, Imagination.

Here we may again refer to Eliphas Levi. He says:

"Imagination is actually as the eye of the soul, and it is therein that forms are delineated and preserved; by its means we behold the reflections of the invisible world, it is the mirror of visions and the apparatus of magical life. Thereby we cure diseases, modify the seasons, ward off death from the living, and resuscitate those who are dead, because this faculty exalts the will and gives it power over the universal agent.

"Imagination determines the form of the child in its mother's womb, it gives wings to contagion, and points the weapons of warfare. Are you exposed in battle? Believe yourself as invulnerable as Achilles, and you will be so, says Paracelsus. Fear attracts bullets, and courage turns them back on their path.

"Imagination is the instrument of the adaptation of the Logos. In its application to reason it in genius, for reason, like genius, is one amidst the complexity of its operations. Demons, souls, and the rest, can therefore be really and truly be held by means of the imagination; but the imagination of the adept is diaphanous, whilst that of the uninitiated is opaque. The light of truth traverses the one as though a crystal window, and is refracted in the other as in a vitreous mass full of scoriae and foreign matter.

"The things which contribute most to the errors of the vulgar and the extravagances of the insane are the reflections of depraved imaginations in one another. But the seer knows with an absolute knowledge that the things he imagines are true, and experience invariably confirms his visions." (Mysteries of Magic, p. 66 ff)

Eugenius Philalethes (Thomas Vaughan) says that he regards the cosmic imagination as being the cause of the great ocean of primordial substance, the chaos whence all forms proceed. "If it (the chaos) be created," he writes, "I conceive it the effect of the Divine Imagination, acting beyond itself in contemplation of that which was to come, and producing this passive darkness for a subject to work upon in the circumference."

The adept learns to utilize the cosmic imagination by means of his passage through the fourteenth path. It may be employed safely be none who has not surrendered himself to the direction of the Higher Self. The Tarot hints at this, for III, the number of the Empress, is the reduction of XII, the number of the HANGED MAN. Hence, too, the first letter of מאיר is that to which the HANGED MAN is attributed.

What does this mean? Primarily that the only way in which to be sure of suing the cosmic imagination in its purity is to silence the waves of personal consciousness, to hold the personal mind in suspension. Thus we find the books on Yoga defining that art as the subduing of the modifications or waves in the mind-stuff, which they compare to a lake. When the surface is still it gives a clear reflection. Likewise, when we have silenced the tumult of self-consciousness, the

Luminous Intelligence of the cosmic mind can be reflected by and through our personal lives. He who succeeds in this undertaking does so by prolonged practice in concentration and meditation. When he succeeds, he appears to have miraculous powers, and is able to manipulate the chaos, or root-matter, in ways which dumbfound all beholders. Yet such an adept always says, as said Jesus, "Of myself I can do nothing." By stopping the modifications of the personal mind-stuff he lets the light of the Divine Imagination shine through, unobstructed.

That is all, but what can be written in a few words takes several life-times to accomplish, and the beginning of the work is precisely the kind of self-training which has been explained in this course. We may sign, sometimes, at the difficulty of the work; but the truth is, living as do the brutes and the uninitiated is really a thousand times harder. It is easier to live the life of the adept than the life of the profane. Paradoxical as it sounds, this is eternally true.

We find an illustration of this in the art of piano-playing. Hours of practice have made the muscles of the artist obedient to his will. He plays difficult passages with little effort, and actually finds them easier to execute than the five-finger exercises with which he began. An hour of Beethoven and Liszt and Brahms tires him less than the beginner's half-hour of Koehler or Czerny. So it is with an adept. His years and lives of practice have made the most difficult problems easier for him than the ordinary routine of the average man's life.

Do you seek something more immediately applicable to your present problems? Well, it may help you to remember that when you studied the Tree of Life you learned that every Sephirah contains a whole Tree in miniature. You may be far from traversing the fourteenth path in Tiphareth, to say nothing of Kether; but you follow it down here in Malkuth every time you make an effort to stand aside and let the cosmic imagination work through you. If, whenever you have something to do, whatever it is, you will pause a moment to reflect that all the imagination you can put into it is an expression of the universal image-making power, the task will go more smoothly. You will have more confidence in the successful issue of your undertaking, and the event will justify your confidence. Thus you will continually be adding little acts of practice to the store which will eventually bring you to adeptship.

The second letter of מאיר brings out another phase of the state of mind called Luminous. Aleph is the Ox, and its primary significance is derived from the fact that oxen are beasts of burden, symbols of patience. The aspirant for the post of Magus must be more than Master of the Temple. He must be ready consciously to assume his share of the burden of creation. To utilize the Luminous Intelligence, one must become a partner with the cosmic life. In the words of Light on the Path, the attitude of an initiate approaching the Grade of Magus is indicated by the admonition: "Let the darkness within help you to understand the helplessness of those who have seen no light, whose souls are in profound gloom. Blame them not -- shrink not from them, but try to lift a little or the heavy Karma of the world; give your aid to the few strong hands that hold back the powers of darkness from obtaining complete victory. Then do you enter into a partnership of joy, which brings indeed terrible toil and profound sadness, but also a great and ever-increasing delight."

The third letter of מאיר is the same as the fourth of מעמיד, constituting, and has been explained on the preceding pages. Detachment is necessary. Seeking for results, identification with the illusions of appearance -- all that partakes of these must be extirpated from the consciousness of the Magus. Yet this detachment is unselfish. The HERMIT, although he stands alone, far above the others who toil upward, is really actively cooperating with them. He holds up a light for their guidance, and is concerned only with their progress, as one may see from the earnestness of his downward gaze.

The last letter of מאיר sums up all these that have gone before, and is the key to the Luminous Intelligence. It is Resh, letter of the Sun, represented in the Tarot by the 19th Key. "Whosoever shall not receive the kingdom of God as a little child, he shall in no wise enter therein," said Jesus. Childlikeness is the test of mastership. The intensity of the initiate's consciousness that he is truly the Eternal Child of the Eternal Father is the measure of his understanding and the root of his wisdom. We hear a great deal in these days about the Masters of the Wisdom, about their wonderful knowledge and powers, about their moulding of their affairs of nations. From all this we are often led to the conclusion that they must be men of great foresight, in the human sense, great schemers and planners. This conclusion, however, is not according to the teaching of the Ageless Wisdom. All that a Master of the Wisdom endures and practices in his long training has the one object of enabling him to lead the planless life. We have been told again and again that the Masters are of the Patanjali School. It follows that they are unconcerned about results, that they are so perfectly concentrated that neither past nor future enters into their calm consideration of the thing to be done now. Let none misunderstand us. We do not mean to say that the Masters may not see far into the future, may not be prophets among prophets, knowing the outcome of many currents of activity whose end is not perceived by ordinary human beings. What we mean is that they do not make personal plans, that they have no need for plotting out a scheme for future action, because their whole training has made them so exquisitely responsive to the direction of the cosmic superconsciousness that every moment of their lives is a perfect obedience to spiritual law. Obeying perfectly, they achieve perfect results.

This, of course, is true of none but Masters in the highest Grades. Many adepts who are comparatively well known to occultists are, by their own statements, far below this exalted height of attainment, though they are far ahead of us beginners on the way.

The correspondences to מאיר by Gematria are ארן, the noun for a sort of slender fir or cedar from which masts were made, carrying the suggestion of uprightness; and וריהל, one spelling of Uriel. (Compare VRIHL with the <u>Vril</u> of Lytton's "Coming Race.") Qabalists call Uriel the archangel of the North and of the element of Earth, but his name is commonly spelt אוריאל, AVRIAL. Send us your interpretation of VRIHL, worked out with the help of the Tarot.

Let your exercises in general follow the pattern laid down in earlier lessons. The Divine Names of the Grades of Exempt Adept and Lesser Adept may be intoned at the beginning of your meditation on the sixteenth and fifteenth paths, respectively. That of Exempt Adept is אל. That of Lesser Adept is יהוה אלוה ודעת. For the fourteenth path, begin by intoning the name יהוה אלהים (יהוה and אלהים are both pronounced and given their notes on page 33). The conclusion of the meditation on each path may be the intonation of the Divine Name Jah, יה, with the descending cadence from F to C, used in pronouncing יהוה but slurred, thus:

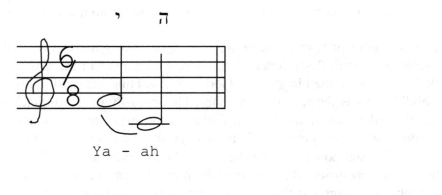

Ya - ah

The Perfect Stone

This lesson deals with a single path, that of the letter Gimel. The beginning of this path, on the Way of Return, is in the Grade of Lesser Adept, in Tiphareth. Its completion is in the Grade of Ipsissimus, in Kether.

As preparation for study, review the attributions to Gimel in Section A, the interpretation of the High Priestess in Section B, and the remarks on the number 108 in Section C.

The name usually given to the thirteenth path, מנהיג, Conductive, is another correspondence to 108. Of the words corresponding by Gematria to this number, חצי, "middle," has been explained in part. It also refers to the position of the thirteenth pat on the Middle Pillar of the Tree of Life, and hints at the secret of equilibration utilized by the Lesser Adept during his journey up this path to Kether.

Another correspondence to 108 is חנן, to favor, to bestow. It suggests an idea often mentioned by the sages, viz., that the supreme attainment is rather by the grace of favor of God than as the result of the aspirant's personal efforts. Yet it must be clearly understood that this grace or favor is not capriciously extended. God does not grant it to some and withhold it from others. It should be realized that his grace inheres in the inmost nature of the Life-power. What is here intended to be conveyed is that this particular aspect of the Life-power, rather than the personal endeavors of the aspirant, is what brings about the final attainment of the Crown.

Finally, חק, "a conclusion, an enactment, a decree," suggests the fulfillment of the Divine Intention by this final stage of the aspirant's journey on the Way of Return to the Supreme Goal.

The full name of the thirteenth path is מנהיג האחות, Conductive Intelligence of Unity. In Hebrew, "Unity" is אחדות = 419 = טית (Serpent), the name of the ninth letter, represented in the Tarot by Strength. The unity here designated is by no means a colorless abstraction. It is the ONE THING "whence all proceed by adaptation, for the performance of the miracles of the One." By letter it is symbolized as the serpent-power, by the symbolism of the Tarot, as a lion, and it is the Fohat of Theosophical writers (See Section B)

מנהיג האחות is the number 532, which may be represented by the following words:

אבן החכמות	Stone of the Wise
אבן הדעת	Stone of Knowledge
חמה החכמות	Sun of Wisdom
חמה הדעת	Sun of Knowledge

(N.B. As a clue to the meaning of alchemy, i.e., אלכמה, observe that חמה, a poetical name for the sun, and אבן, Ehben, Stone are identical by Gematria.)

If you will give a little time to considering the meaning of these four names, you will sooner or later perceive that the work of the thirteenth path must be closely related to the alchemical operation called "sublimation." The completion of that work is the confection of that which may be called either אבן החכמות, Stone of the Wise (i.e. Philosophers' Stone) or אבןהדעת, Stone of Knowledge. In connection with the latter name, note that the place of דעת, Da'ath, Knowledge, on the Tree of Life is on the thirteenth path, at the point where the fourteenth path crosses it -- midway between Chokmah and Binah.

The Short Lexicon of Alchemy appended to A.E. Waite's translation of the Hermetic Writings of Paracelsus, gives this definition of sublimation:

"Sublimation is the purification of the Matter by means of dissolution and reduction of the same into its constituents. It is not the forcing of the Matter to the top of the vessel, and then maintaining it separated from its <u>caput mortuum</u>, but its subtilization and purification from all earthly and heterogeneous parts, imparting to it a degree of perfection not previously possessed, or more correctly, its deliverance from the bonds which bind it, and hinder its operation."

The Matter, as you learned in Lesson 1, Section A, is the Astral Light of Eliphas Levi. Yogis call it Kundalini. It is the serpent-power represented by the letter Teth. Observe that it is not <u>forced</u> to rise, for in this statement is to be found an important key to the whole work. The Matter is simply purified from the adulterations of heterogeneity -- from the semblances of diversity which it presents to us in its ordinary manifestations. In simple truth this means that the Magus performs the Great Work by divesting the serpent-power of all appearances of Many-ness. On this account the thirteenth path is said to be the Conductive Intelligence of UNITY. When the work of this path is completed, the One Energy which presents itself to our senses in the innumerable forms we call "objects" is directly <u>experienced</u> as ONE, ONE and ALONE.

As we know it here on earth, the Matter is solar force. The Stone and the sun are two aspects of one reality. Therefore אבן = חמה. Alchemists agree that the Great Work which results in the perfection of the Stone is an operation of the sun and moon. To this idea the thirteenth path relates, especially as part of the Way of Return. As we climb the Tree of Life, this path begins in Tiphareth, sphere of the sun, and is itself, through its correspondence to Gimel, the path of the moon.

To traverse it, one must be a Magus, having full comprehension of the principles of cyclic motion which are exemplified in astronomy. Hence the Grade of Magus corresponds to Chokmah, which has the name מסלות, Masloth, "highways of the stars."

The principle of cyclic motion is fundamental in the cosmos. To understand it aright is to possess true wisdom. The Ageless Wisdom, applying the Hermetic axiom, "That which is below is as that which is above," teaches that the same law which keeps the stars in place is manifest in all activity, everywhere. The discoveries of modern science confirm this ancient doctrine -- particularly those discoveries, so often referred to in these pages, which have to do with the constitution of atoms.

The true magician and alchemist knows how to apply these laws of cyclic motion. Indeed, many of the seeming marvels accomplished by adepts are based upon control of interatomic energy, in accordance with these laws. The principles of this control, we may say (although it would be extremely unwise to give specific information, even if we dared claim that we possess it), are principles identical with those revealed in the science of astronomy.

To make the Stone of the Wise, so that we may change base metal into gold, we therefore apply the knowledge which Qabalists attribute to Chokmah. And when we speak of this transmutation, we are by no means using purely figurative expressions. True as it is that the Stone of the Wise effects a transmutation of consciousness, so that the base metal of sense-illusion is transformed into the pure gold of spiritual knowing, it is also true that one who has that consciousness gets with it a command of physical forces which enable him to alter the structure of atoms. Such a man can make gold, if he needs to, and the ancient Rosicrucian declaration that the Brothers of the Order have at their disposal "more gold than both the Indies bring to the King of Spain," is far from being an exaggeration. The knowledge whereby this is brought about is represented by the first two letters of אבן, Stone, because אב, Father, is a Qabalistic title of Chokmah.

To make use of these principles of cyclic motion, we must have some specific object. Furthermore, this object must aim at some realization of beauty, so the Qabalists teach, and this they indicate by the last two letters of אבן, which form the word בן, Son, a title of Tiphareth.

This title, בן, is by Gematria equal to אימא, Mother, a name of Binah. אימא, sphere of Saturn, represents concrete, definite applications of the principles of Chokmah, the Father. בן, sphere of the sun, alludes to the idea of beauty which must qualify these concrete aims.

In brief, then, the Great Work makes the Sun of Wisdom rise, perfects the Stone of the Wise. It is a work wherein Chokmah אב supplies the mathematical knowledge of principles, wherein Binah אימא provides the specific understanding of concrete application, and wherein Tiphareth בן contributes the motive of beauty. Thus the powers of a Magus (Chokmah) and a Master of the Temple (Binah) are conjoined in an operation which begins from the level of the seemingly inferior Grade of Lesser Adept (Tiphareth).

The operation must be a Magus, because one who has not attained to that Grade does not know the secret of True Will, nor does he possess a sufficient command of the Life-Force. For True Will and חיה, Chiah, the Life-Force, are both realized in Chokmah.

Jesus expressed the mystery of True Will when He said, "My meat is to do the will of him that sent me, and to accomplish his work." The Will expressed in the thought, word, and action of a Magus is not personal. It is the resistless impulse of the eternal, universal vital energy. In truth, the life-fore in every human being is identical with the energy of the One Life. This is the cosmic Life-force which Jesus personified as "Father," using the very name, AB, which Qabalists attribute to Chokmah, and following the Secret Wisdom also in his saying, "The Father אב hath life חיה in himself." He openly declared that what is hinted at time and again in occult writings, viz.., that when we are actually doing the Will of the Father, by letting the universal life-energy flow freely through a personality cleansed from all sense of separateness, our work is not labor. We are not fatigued by our endeavors, no matter how strenuous they may seem to other people. On the contrary, work that is an expression of True Will vitalizes us, fills us to overflowing with abundance of power, really feeds us. Hence we find Jesus saying, "I have meat to eat ye know not of."

A Magus does not infer this. He does not believe it. He does not hold it as a conviction, as do we. He <u>knows</u> it. His personal consciousness is lost, swallowed up, in complete identification with the One Life. He does nothing of himself. His personality is an unobstructed vehicle for the perfectly regulated operation of the Life-Power.

His least action, therefore, is a conscious expression of the inexhaustible power of the ALL. To human eyes he seems to perform miracles. He seems to have developed a tremendous personal will. He seems to have powers not possessed by other men. To himself it is quite otherwise. He knows that the mightiest of his works are simply demonstrations of unchanging law. He knows that he wills nothing but what the Father wills. He knows that he has not a jot or title of power peculiar to himself. The difference between a Magus and other men is that the All-Power flows through his life into external expression, unchecked by the illusions and ignorance of personal consciousness.

Such a man is Master of the Temple of Spirit -- that sevenfold body, symbolized in ancient architecture by Babylonian temples of seven stories, but the Great Pyramid, which has a vertical axis of seven units, and also by the seven-sided vault, described in the Fama Fraternitatis, the first book issued by the Rosicrucians in 1614.

As Master of the Temple, he is guided moment by moment by the clear direction of true Intuition. Not merely in times of stress and trial is he aware of the Inner Voice. Whether his physical body wakes or sleeps, he hears always, and always obeys. To other men he seems to have extraordinary foresight. When they do not call him a prophet, they imagine that he is a most careful planner. As a matter of fact, he lives a planless life, and his one rule of action is that of Jesus, "As I hear, I judge."

Having, therefore, identified himself with the Pure Source of all life, and so harmonized his least actions that whatever he does he says, "I am doing nothing," because he lives only to express the perfect rhythms of the ALL – guided by an understanding which foresees and forewarns, and keeps his feet upon the true path – the Magus is duly and truly prepared to essay the last stage of the Great Work.

Yet he begins this final operation of placing himself in the Grade of Lesser Adept. The initial processes of his undertaking depend upon mental powers peculiar to that Grade. Not from the point-of-view of a Magus, or from the vantage-ground of a Master of the Temple, but from the relatively simple realization of Sonship does he proceed, in beginning his last advance along the Way of Return.

His starting-point is the mode of consciousness called Intelligence of Mediating Influence. The Hebrew is שפע נבדל. שפע = 450 = פרי עץ, Fruit of the Tree. נבדל = 86 = אלהים, Elohim. The Fruit of the Tree is בן, the Son. Its number, 450, is 10 x 45, suggesting the tenfold expression of אדם =45, Man. נבדל is a formula for the powers of the Elohim. (You should study it, letter by letter, with the aid of the corresponding Tarot Keys.) Thus the title of the sixth path hints Qabalistically that the Sonship of Man makes him heir to the powers of the Elohim. The idea is similar to that suggested by the symbols of the Hanged Man.

Bear in mind, too, that the letter-name, גמל, is by Gematria equivalent to חכמה, Chokmah. This indicates that the thirteenth path has a close correspondence to the specific powers developed in the consciousness of the aspirant of attaining the Grade of Magus.

As corresponding to the High Priestess, the path of Gimel is predominantly a path of recollection, and of the equilibration of the affirmative and negative aspects of the Life-Power represented by the twin pillars depicted in that Key. To traverse the thirteenth path is to read the scroll of cosmic memory.

As the scroll must be read by unrolling it in reverse order, so do the letters of גמל, read in reverse, indicate the steps of the Magus' progress upward along this path.

His faith in his Sonship must be firmly established. He must not only believe himself to be a veritable Son of the Elohim, but he must also have established that faith by works. These are works whereby the power of Ruach (here understood as Imagination) have been controlled and directed. All these practices are aimed at the equilibration of the conflicting elements of personal consciousness, together with the elimination of everything superfluous.

The aspirant must also, as has been said, eliminate all sense of personal action. He must be fixed in union with the One Life. High as are his attainments in comparison with ours, no slightest trace of pride of power can be mixed with his realization that his personality is absolutely and unconditionally dependent upon the ALL. (Mem and the Hanged Man).

In this condition of self-surrender, a state which presents outwardly the aspect of profound trance, the Magus begins his journey upward. In no other way can perfect mastery of the powers of the cosmic subconsciousness be developed.

What this mastery really is cannot be put into intelligible language. Even if this were possible, adequate description would be impossible here, because neither the writer of these pages nor those for whose instruction they are intended have reached the Grade of Magus. We can only do our best to pass on what reports have reached us from Those who have made the journey, knowing full well that what we write will fall short of the truth.

The goal of the thirteenth path is Kether, the Crown. The Rosicrucian Grade corresponding thereto is called "Ipsissimus," which means, "I, my very Self." Thus the Grade title agrees with the Qabalists' attribution of יחידה, the Self (the <u>Atma</u> of Hindu philosophers) to Kether.

The Latin word Ipsissimus indicates by its form what we might call the superlative degree of selfhood. It represents the highest possible realization of the meaning of I AM. Qabalists indicate this realization by יחידה, the feminine form of יחיד, "unity." The feminine construction shows that although the I AM is one and alone, it is also conceived in the Ageless Wisdom as the vehicle for אין סוף אור. As vehicle, or receptacle, it is therefore feminine.

It is said that there are ten degrees of this Grade in each of the four worlds, that is: Kether of Kether, Kether of Chokmah, Kether of Binah, Kether of Chesed, Kether of Geburah, Kether of Tiphareth, Kether of Netzach, Kether of Hod, Kether of Yesod, and Kether of Malkuth -- all in Atziluth; and a like tenfold expression in Briah, Yetzirah and Assiah.

Thus we may reckon forty distinct degrees of this one realization which Rosicrucians call Ipsissimus. It is also said that here on the physical plane (in Asiah, that is) there are, at any one time, just ten human beings in whom this realization of Kether is perfected. One has the perfect realization of Kether in Malkuth, another the realization of Kether in Yesod, and so on, up to Kether in Kether.

These ten human beings are said to be the Secret Chiefs of the ten sections of the True and Invisible

Rosicrucian Order on the physical plane. Each section of the Order corresponds to a Sephirah, and consists of persons whose basic development corresponds to that Sephirah.

This statement, however, should not be interpreted as meaning that only ten persons now incarnate have attained to the Grade of Ipsissimus in the World of Assiah. What has been said is that there are but ten in whom this realization is <u>perfected</u>. These ten are the Heads of the Outer Hierarchy of the Order.

This information, however, can be of little more than academic interest to readers of these pages. It is mentioned merely to give some idea of the constitution of the occult hierarchy. The terms here used differ superficially from those familiar to readers of Theosophical literature, but there is no real difference in the teaching itself.

What, after all, is important is that you yourself may gain a flash of this high perception. For from that august Being Whose consciousness is the יחידה of Kether of Kether in Atziluth, down through the hierarchy, vibrates the "wave-length," so to say, of this supreme realization. If you tune in, you will receive so much of it as you can bear.

Before beginning practice to this end, fix in mind the fact that in meditating on the Great Self you are by no means indulging in a flight of fancy or abstract speculation. The mental result achieved by this exercise is an approximation to the most veritable reality. Now, and always, the true I AM of every human personality is נקדה ראשונה, Nequdah Rashunah, the Primordial Point whence all manifestation proceeds. The wise man sees, as did Jesus, that the true Self, or I AM, is the eternal center of creative activity. With Jesus, therefore, he declares, "Before Abraham was, I AM."

He sees, too, that this Primordial Point is a center of <u>expression</u>. In it is concentrated the limitless expanse of אין סוף אור, the Limitless Light. Hence Kether is also named תת זל, Tath Zal, the Profuse Giver.

Here observe that תת, Tath is 800, equivalent by Gematria to שרש, Sheresh, "root." Tath, however, is written with two Taus, to call attention to the fact that this Rootless Root concentrates the Limitless Light, and in so concentrating, sets up the double activity of that restrictive, boundary-setting phase of the Life-Power symbolized by Saturn. The root of manifestation, in other words, is a self-limitation of the Limitless Light, a specialization of itself.

Again, זל, Zal, is 37. This number has many important connotations in the Ageless Wisdom, but this is not the place to discuss them. The main point to be considered now is that 37 is the number of יחידה, the Self. The I AM is not only a center of expression, It is also the exhaustless root of all ability to give, the Original Source whence comes every supply. Not upon anything else does the Magus ever depend. The more, then, that we train ourselves in realization of the I AM, the more shall we find ourselves able actually to draw upon the illimitable resources of this inexhaustible treasure.

The first step in practice is to meditate upon the three letters of the corresponding word Gimel, גמל in connection with the corresponding Tarot Keys. Begin with the final letter Lamed, and Justice. Then take the letter Mem and the Hanged Man. After this use Gimel and the High Priestess, or rather with the idea she symbolizes. Loose all sense of personal identity in your realization that every element of personal existence is really an expression of the power she symbolizes – the power of cosmic consciousness.

From this meditation you may pass to a similar meditation on the word כתר. Here, too, take the word letter by letter, with the Tarot Keys, beginning with ר and ending with כ.

While you meditate upon ר and the Sun, remember that the force which carries you up to the Crown is the universal electric energy specialized for human beings in the solar radiance. We may always find profit in reminding ourselves that in the Great Work we are by no means dealing with metaphysical abstractions. We are <u>physical</u> children of the sun, and the great Intelligence whose physical body is our day-star has an actual directive power in human life.

In like manner meditate upon Tau and the World, and upon Kaph and the Wheel of Fortune. The latter is a symbol of the whirling motion (Rashith Ha-Galgalim) which begins in Kether.

At the commencement of the period of meditation, intone the Divine Name, יהוה אלוה ודעת, as given earlier in Section C. At the same time see yourself surrounded by the golden radiance of the sphere of the Sun. Remain in this particular phase of the meditation until you feel that your whole being is charged with the electric fire of the sun.

Before meditating upon the letters and Tarot Keys corresponding to Gimel, sound the key-note, and visualize the color of the thirteenth path. Then proceed with the meditation on the letters.

After this, meditate upon the letters and Keys of the word Kether. When you have finished with Kaph and the Wheel of Fortune, continue by intoning the Divine Name, אהיה, Eheyeh, as follows:

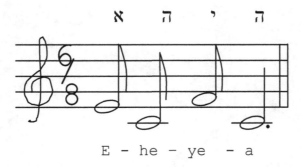

Then see yourself at the center of a sea of white brilliance. We find this difficult to describe. White, cold, fire comes as near the reality as anything. See this white radiance whirling out from the center, which is your real Self, into infinity. Realize also that the center is absolutely still.

Success in this meditation will bring results that cannot be described. The little "self" will be lost for the time in the Great Self. Of the further results it is not lawful to speak, save that they are summed up in the Hindu phrase, "Sat-Chit-Ananda," which means "Existence-Knowledge-Bliss." May your faithful practice bring you speedily to this Supreme goal.

Section D
Esoteric Secrets of Magic

The Secret Force

Webster's dictionary defines magic as "the art, or body of arts, which pretends or is believed to produce effects by the assistance of supernatural beings or departed spirits, or by a mastery of secret forces in nature." This definition reflects common opinion accurately enough, but we must modify if a little before it will serve to define what we mean by Magic. The modification is slight but important. As we understand it, magic is the art which produces effects by mastery of secret forces in nature.

The exact derivation of the noun "magic" is in doubt. It is commonly thought to be of Persian origin, and to have come from the name of the "Magi" & priestly caste of the Zoroastrian religion. Certainly the word comes from Asia and probably it has a close affinity with the Sanskrit terms <u>Mahat</u>, great, and <u>Maya</u>. Max Mueller, at least, identifies <u>Maya</u> with magic, for he translates a passage from the Hindu sacred texts as follows: "Purusha (the SELF) is the Mayin (Magician) and Prakriti (Matter, or Nature) is Maya (Magic)."

Ordinarily Maya means illusion, but Shankara, in expounding the Vedanta, uses this term in several technical senses. Considered as the principle of self-determination, for example, as the power by which the Absolute concentrates itself at a particular point within its own subsistence, the word is used to denote the absolute potentiality of the whole cosmic self-expression that is to be, but is not yet. In this sense Maya is neither a thing nor a being nor a quality. It is nothing that is real, and yet it is not unreal. It is absolutely indescribable. Yet it is completely under the control of the Absolute Subsistence, and this Absolute Subsistence is absolutely free with reference to it.

In other words, this particular sense of the Sanskrit term Maya corresponds exactly to the Hebrew conception denoted by the Qabalistic use of the word אין, No-Thing. It is for this reason that אין is called the first <u>veil</u> of the Absolute.

I may seem to be taking you up to a point where the atmosphere is very thin indeed. Yet I must, if you are to understand what we mean by magic. The whole practice of the art depends upon a knowledge of the force we are using, and that force is precisely the "power of becoming" which the Qabalists call the first veil of the Absolute, echoing their Hindu brothers who call Maya "the veil of illusion which hides the Real." The practice of magic is the art of determining the forms and shapes which shall be taken in the outer world by this veil of Reality, and the ability of human beings to practice this art is derived from the fact that the <u>undifferentiated power which Qabalists call אין is</u> eternally present in every human life. Not only this, but the Absolute Subsistence of which אין is the veil is eternally present, too. In a word, the power which completely controls Maya or אין is NOW, at this very moment, a present reality in your life, and it is now, and always, free to exercise its unlimited creative, preservative and transforming command of the veil of illusion thorough which it makes itself manifest.

Thus the force named אין is the secret force by the mastery of which magical effects are produced. I despair of finding words to make you understand, until the Life-Power Itself has ripened you to understanding, that when I say "are produced," I use the present tense deliberately and with a careful regard for exact expression. I do not say, "By means of which magicians have produced their wonderful results." I do not write, "By means of which you will, when you learn how, be able to produce magical effects." I say that אין which is at this moment a part of your make-up as a human being, IS the secret force by the mastery of which magical effects ARE produced. As I write the words on the typewriter I find myself banging the keys, as if by that means to impress upon the stencil from which these words will be reproduced something of the clear vision of this truth that comes to me as I write. "May the words be as enlightening as the experience they express," would be my prayer, only I know that no word can convey the meaning of that experience. If you have KNOWN that the אין is within you, if you do know it now, you need no words. And the most the words can do is to raise the temperature of your mind from the heat of self-consciousness to the white heat of Superconsciousness. If that happens, you will know what I am only trying to say.

One of the purposes of the our curriculum is to make our affiliates familiar with the teachings of our predecessors on the Way of Return, to set before those who work with us some of the brightest gems out of the treasury of wisdom which has come down from the past. Here is one, from Jacob Boehme's MYSTERIUM PANSOPHICUM, (published in Six Theosophic Points and other Writings, by Jacob Boehme, Alfred Knopf, New York):

THE FIRST TEXT

"The unbound is an eternal nothing, but makes an eternal beginning as a craving. For the nothing is a craving after something. But as there is nothing that can give anything, accordingly the craving itself is the giving of it, which yet also is a nothing, or merely a desirous seeking. And that is the eternal origin of Magic, which makes within itself where there is nothing; which makes something out of nothing, and that in itself only, though this craving is also a nothing, that is, merely a will. It has nothing, and there is nothing that can give it anything; neither has it any place where it can find or repose itself."

The eternal nothing which makes an eternal beginning is making the eternal beginning in you even now. Never is there a time, whether you wake or sleep, that the אין which makes something out of nothing is not a work within you. Its work, indeed, is what you call your life.

Notice that Boehme speaks of the eternal beginning as a <u>craving</u>. Out of this craving is projected the boundless Chaos concerning which another adept, Thomas Vaughn says:

"I am come now to the gross work or mechanics of the Spirit, namely, the separation of several substances from the same mass: but in the first place I shall examine that Limbus or huddle of matter wherein all things were so strangely contained. It is the opinion of some men, and those learned, that this sluggish empty rudiment of the creature was no created thing. I must confess the point is obscure as the thing itself, and to state it with sobriety, except a man were illuminated with the same Light that this Chaos was at first, is altogether impossible. For how can we judge of a nature different from our own, whose species also was so remote from anything now existent that it is impossible for fancy to apprehend, much more for reason to define it. If it be created, I conceive it the effect of the Divine Imagination, acting beyond itself in contemplation of the which was to come, and producing this passive darkness for a subject to work upon in the circumference."

Compare the last sentence of this quotation with what is said on page 2, near the top of the page, concerning Maya. The same thought has been revived within very recent times in the excellent writings of the late judge Troward, who teaches that the beginning of the creative process is the self-contemplation of Spirit.

That self-contemplation includes the idea of the primal activity or Life-Breath which is the One Force of which all others are transformations. And this creative principle is precisely what is represented by the Aleph in the word אין. In the Tarot it is the FOOL, descending into the abyss of existence by the path of Involution.

Knowing itself perfectly, the Life-Power must also contemplate, or look forward to, its evolution. And in the word אין this second aspect of the Divine Imagination is represented by the letter YOD, the HAND. Since the hand is a human member, it is the special sign of MAN among the Hebrew letters, controlling all the others. By the Hand the House (ב) is built, by the Hand the Camel (ג) is driven, by the HAND the Doors (ד) are opened. And MAN of whom the Hand is the symbol is the Life-Power's conception of Itself as evolved from lower forms of manifestation to the stage of self-recognition. Hence in the Tarot the card which represents YOD is a picture of HIM WHO STANDS ALONE, the Ancient of Days Who is the Eternal Light-Bearer for all the evolving begins on the Way of Return.

Finally, the self-contemplation of the Spirit must include its perception of itself as a transforming power. Changeless in itself, it must nevertheless be the principle at work in every change. And this is definitely and unmistakably indicated for us by the Qabalistic meaning of the third letter of אין. For besides meaning "to sprout, to grow," the letter Nun has assigned to it the Qabalistic notion expressed by the word MOTION, which we must understand (on account of the fact that this word comes to use even in English translations from sources several centuries old) as having the now obsolete meaning of "impelling cause, reason, motive." Furthermore, we must not forget to take the hint offered by the attribution of the Path of Imaginative Intelligence to Nun. Again, MOTION in Hebrew is הלוך = 61, and 61 is the numeration of אין. Here it is as if the final letter of אין summed up the whole word, just as the idea of the Divine Imagination (which is the transforming power that works in the "separation of several (particular) substances," as Vaughan says) sums up the whole creative preservative and transformative self-expression of the Life-Power.

What all this metaphysical and Qabalistic discussion of אין has to do with Magic is simply this: אין is the first of the three veils by which Qabalists designate the secret force which is employed in the Magic of Light.

It's number, 61, may be translated as "WILL-to-BEAUTY," because in number symbolism we interpret the figure in the units place as being the origin of whatever process is symbolized by a number, and the figure in the tens place (if the number be one of two digits) as representing the result, or object aimed at. Thus we see that according to this interpretation of the nature of the secret force used in magic, all our practical work in the art must take into account the fundamental fact that the power we are seeking to direct is one whose intrinsic nature is a will, a craving, an urge toward the production of beautiful results. Consequently on the principle that to make Nature obey us we must first obey her laws, it becomes evident that any magical operation which we attempt is foredoomed to failure unless its motive or central purpose be the manifestation of some beautiful result. And to the degree that all the elements in this operation are expressions of the same urge, will each stage of the process be effective.

It matters a great deal, too, that the name of the secret force we use in magic is NO-THING. Due meditation upon this will reveal to you deeper meanings than those I shall set down here. But even here, through my veil of words you may perhaps perceive something of the wonder of the thought. Primarily it signifies that in the practice of the art of magic we cannot in the least be prevented from success by any lack of things. To read some books about magic, one might suppose that before one could begin the practice of the art he must first surround himself by innumerable rare and costly objects. Take, for instance, this passage from the seventh chapter of Eliphas Levi's Ritual of Transcendental Magic:

"The magus who intends undertaking the works of light must operate on a Sunday, from midnight to eight in the morning, or from three in the afternoon to ten in the evening. He should wear a purple vestment, with tiara and bracelets of gold. The altar of perfumes and the tripod of sacred fire must be encircled by wreaths of laurel, heliotrope, and sunflowers; the perfumes are cinnamon, strong incense, saffron, and red sandal; the ring must be of gold, with a chrysolith or ruby; the carpet must be of lion skins, the fans of sparrow-hawk feathers."

And then he continues with equally formidable lists of expensive things which are required for the operations dedicated to the several days of the week. All this is an elaborate blind, characteristic of Levi's ironical genius. If you had to get all these things before you could practice magic, I certainly should not be trying to tell you anything about the art, because I never had a carpet of lion skins in my life, and I couldn't tell you what a sparrow-hawk's feathers look like. Yet I have practiced what Levi calls "works of light," more than once.

It is true that for the more elaborate forms of magical ceremonial certain accessories are used--but none of them is indispensable, and the true magician does not depend upon any of these appurtenances for his results. The more he practices magic in the right way, the nearer does he approach that freedom from material limitations which would make it possible to carry out Eliphas Levi's instructions literally; and it is certainly true that a real magician will surround himself with the most beautiful objects that he can procure. At the same time, he never makes the mistake of supposing that these objects have any intrinsic magic power of their own. If you understand the laws of the art, you can practice it in an empty room, and get results.

For magic includes all the procedures made familiar in these days by Christian Science, Now Thought and Applied Psychology. Whatever the theories of the various schools, and whatever the particular variations of their practice, all these mental methods for healing disease or overcoming the limitations of circumstances are really the practice of magic.

One principle is always at work in these practices. No matter how the different practitioners may think they accomplish their results, the fact is that all of them do the same thing. Whether he knows it or not, every successful giver of "treatments," whether for health or for prosperity, has learned how to form clear, sharp mental images of the effect he desires to produce. These images or thought-forms are the patterns through which the secret force works, and that is why the last letter of the Hebrew word which names this force is N, which Qabalists associate with Imaginative Intelligence and with Change, Growth and Development.

If you will refer to your Qabalistic Dictionary, under the number 61 you will find these words: ADVN, Lord; ALIK, to thee; ANI, the personal pronoun "I"; HVN, wealth. The secret force is thus shown to be the power which every religion personifies as the LORD. It is, by implication, revealed also as a power which enters into human life, which is not afar off, but near by, for ALIK, "to thee," hints at what Jesus expressed more openly when he said: "The kingdom is within you." It is, furthermore, the secret power which you name "I", and which you try vainly to grasp with the self-conscious intellect. This is that of which we are told in the Upanishads: "If thou objectest 'how should I grasp this?' Pray, do not grasp it; for the residuum after all grasping is an end, is none other than thy real Self." (Yet remember that neither ANI nor AIN is that Self, although ANI is the equivalent of the pronoun "I". For whatever has name is not THAT, and "pronoun" means "name used in place of a noun". ANI or "I" is the veil of THAT, is the word that indicates the identity between the No-Thing and what produces in your personal consciousness the feeling of "I". But this, which makes you aware of the Self, is only the veil or power of that Self.) Finally, the secret force, as HVN, is the true wealth, of which external riches are but the materialization or demonstration. And in what does that wealth consist? In VISION, for H is the letter of Sight. In INTUITION and the power of correlation, because V indicates both these ideas. And in IMAGINATION, the basic creative power by which the Self projects from the depths of its eternal Subsistence the Chaos out of which it forms a cosmos.

Let us revert to the number 61, which represents all these words. We have seen that as 1 working through 6 it symbolized with WILL to BEAUTY with which we must harmonize our magical operations, if we wish them to be successful. The consideration of this fact leads to further light concerning the means employed by magicians. All magical operations, whether they consist in the recitation of words and phrases; the use of perfumes or incense; the tracing of combinations of lines and letters in the air, on paper, parchment or metals; the employment of sounds and colors, or whatever else may enter into a ceremonial, are effective to the extent that they formulate the operator's realization of the nature of the force he uses, establish his consciousness that this force is fully able to accomplish the result aimed at, and make clear and vivid the mental image of that result as an accomplished fact.

A well constructed magical ceremonial is therefore an exercise in auto-suggestion. It utilizes all the senses to build a thought-form. It calls into play every kind of mental imagery. Thus its efficacy depends a great deal upon the operator's understanding of what he says and does. Effects are certainly produced when we simply go through the motions of a ceremonial, even if we do not understand it. We all possess a vast fund of subconscious knowledge which includes perception of what many symbols mean. The vibratory effects of sound and rhythmic gesture, moreover, are set up, no matter whether a person knows or does not know the meaning of what he says. Teach a child the correct pronunciation of a magical formula, and with suitable apparatus it is possible to register the vibrations of the words. The result will be just what would happen if an adept spoke them, so far as the lower modes of vibration are concerned. Right here is where the danger of dabbling in magic comes in. If we use a symbol, gesture, or other magical "tool" which we do not understand, we may easily set up activities out of harmony with the result we aim to produce. Hence the repeated injunctions of the wise as to the importance of being well grounded in theory.

A common objection to magical ceremonials is that they are too complicated. "Why go to all this trouble when you can get the same results simply by visualizing, or 'speak the Word'?" is a question I hear often. This is plausible and it appeals to the instinctive dislike of hard work which besets us all. As a matter of fact, the same results are NOT achieved by visualization or by "speaking the WORD." These methods work, to be sure, but their effectiveness is not so great as that of other methods.

Few people are good visualizers. The power to make visual images may be developed to some extent, but if you are a person whose imagery is chiefly auditory, you will never be able to make the vivid mental pictures that so many New Thought teachers believe to be indispensable. The limitations of speech are to be taken into consideration also. To express comparatively simple ideas often requires a long series of phrases, which are by no means sharp and definite. This is why we find illustrations in the dictionary. As the Chinese proverb has it: "One picture is better than 10,000 words."

When a magician traces a circle in the air, or makes some other symbolic gesture, by one brief action he formulates a suggestion which would take three times as long to put into words. When, at the same time, he uses color, sound, perfume and significant words, he makes a mental pattern which is like a painting in full color, whereas the simple visualization or spoken word is like a pencil sketch.

While I am on this subject, perhaps it may be well to add something concerning those great works of magic, the healing miracles of Jesus. For it is often from healing cults which rest their practice upon Jesus' teachings, that we hear these objections to ceremonial. The fact is that Jesus himself used "magic words," which are recorded in the Greek of the New Testament. These words have been studied by T.S. Lea and F.B. Bond, two orthodox English clergymen, and they have discovered that these are words of power like those used by Egyptian and Chaldean magicians. The power of these words consists in their vibratory values and in their numeration. The numeration, by the passage of number into geometry, is a clue to the formation of patterns or figures which are fundamental in the cosmic expression of beauty, and which are fundamental therefore in that particular manifestation of this cosmic expression which we call human art.

The remarkable discoveries of these two clergymen are to be found in their books, "A Preliminary Investigation of the Qabala contained in the Coptic Gnostic Books and of a Similar Gematria in the Greek Text of the New Testament," and "The Apostolic Gnosis." These works afford confirmation, from a source which cannot be suspected of partisanship to occultism, of the teaching which has often been mentioned in these pages. They show that in sacred texts language, number and geometry are always mingled, for some practical purpose. They show, too, that the Gematria of the New Testament works itself out geometrically in the Pentagram, the Hexagram, the Triangle, the Cross and the Cube. Each of these symbols is used in magic, and their magical use and efficacy depends upon the fact that from the circle, the line, the triangle, the square, the pentagram, the hexagram and such figures, as combined in the five Platonic solids, are derived the fundamental principles of proportion which find expression in all beautiful forms, whether those forms be those produced by Nature or by Man. Ceremonial magic is a ritualistic, artistic, conscious use of these basic patterns of the cosmos, aimed at the production of beautiful results. This, whether the magician realizes the full import of what he is doing or not.

Let us take a simple instance for illustration of this point. Suppose you send five dollars to a practitioner for a prosperity treatment, and that your only immediate motive in so doing is a desire for more money. There doesn't seem to be any particular urge to beauty in this, but there is undoubtedly a wish on your part to get a better adjustment of the circumstances which make up your environment. That urge is the cosmic insistence upon symmetry and proportion, pressing out into manifestation as your desire for what you hope will make your personal world more orderly-- less of a chaos. The better you know what you want for money for, the more certain is it that you will formulate a pattern of some specific beautiful result.

Magical ceremonial, then, formulates this urge to the expression in the outer world of the Order and Beauty which the Spirit is in Itself. It works to this and by using precisely the numbers and geometrical figures which the Life-Power itself employs in its cosmic self-expression. The numbers and lines of snow-flakes, the points and angles of crystallization, the curves and ellipses of planetary orbits, the lines of symmetry in plant and animal life - these are the things impressed upon the subconscious mind of the magician as he performs his ritual.

These are the numbers, the points, the lines, the patterns that you are expressing in your everyday life. They determine the formation of your body, they regulate its every movement. You cannot walk across a room, nay, you cannot even digest a meal without the working of the Life-Power through these geometrical expressions of numbers. Thus there is a sense in which your whole life is a magical ritual. Like the man in Moliere's play who was amazed to find that he had been talking prose all his life, you have been practicing magic all your days.

It is well to know this, for then you will find it easy to banish all the fears which may have been implanted in your mind by the silly way that some who delight to call themselves occultists (usually with the accent in the wrong place!) write and talk about magic.

What you will learn in the here concerning magic will not give you any new power. The purpose of all these lessons is to make you realize that living is magical, that the art of living and the art of true magic are one and the same thing. By making it as clear as we can that the principal symbols of formal magical rituals are based upon forms which can be seen or traced in all modes of the cosmic life-expression, we aim to enable you the better to understand how the magic of the Life-Power finds expression in your thought, speech and action.

Our purpose, then, is not so much to teach formulas and rituals, as to awaken our affiliates to a realization of the truly magical processes of life, so that they may take conscious part in those processes. When our begin consciously to realize what the Life-Power is doing through them, they will begin to be practical magicians. For whenever a man finds out how some process in nature operates, it is bound to happen, sooner or later, that this knowledge stimulates his invention, so that he makes novel applications of the laws which he has formulated.

A word or two now about the difference between White Magic and Black Magic: The distinction is in two points only. The first has to do with the magician's idea of what he is doing. The second is concerned with his use of his power. Whatever makes us believe that we are using forces outside of ourselves, whatever makes us think that we depend upon anything but the exhaustless Life-Power of which we are all centers, is black, no matter how altruistic its intention. The use of magic for selfish ends, for gaining ascendancy over the lives of others, for promoting our own good at the expense of anybody else, is also black.

I have known many well-meaning people who have been led astray by the first of these errors. They supposed that when they called upon the names of angels, they summoned celestial beings to do their bidding. Or perhaps they used ceremonials in which evil spirits were bound to carry out their behests. There is more of this sort of thing going on today than most people have any idea of, and its results are invariably destructive. The danger lies in the fact that the longer one practices this sort of magic the more does the auto-suggestion sink in that the operator is not able to do his works by the power of the Life within him, but must depend upon the assistance of other beings. Thus his practice intensifies his sense of separateness instead of overcoming it.

Trying to influence people by occult means "for their own good" is a subtle form of evil magic. It flourishes in these days among people who have found out that thought and feeling can be transferred telepathically, but its ultimate results are always disastrous. The error lies in the supposition that any of us is qualified to judge his brother or sister.

It is hardly necessary to enter into details into selfish uses of magic power. But it seems necessary to say that the use of this power to help ourselves, to improve our circumstances, to extend the circle of our influence is not always black. It is by no means selfish to use magic to make ourselves free from disease, to increase our consciousness of supply so that we shall not fall in debt, or in other ways to increase our ability to be of service to others. More than one sincere and earnest student of the occult has died because he would not use magic for self-healing. These mistaken persons do not see that it is really more selfish to refuse to use every available means to prolong the period of their services to humanity.

The principal danger, however, is the tendency to fall into the error of thinking that a ceremonial itself accomplishes the result. We may avert this danger by reminding ourselves again and again that every operation is effective because it concentrates and directs the One Power whose veil is אין, the No-Thing.

The Qabalistic technical term which denotes the particular aspect of this No-Thing utilized in magic is AVD, Od or Aud. (From this, perhaps, Reichenbach derived his term, Odic Force.)

Examine this word Qabalistically. The first letter is the sign of the Life-Breath. The second is the conjunction "and." The third is the sign of the Venus ray, expressing itself in human consciousness as love and as artistic adaptation of external conditions by action rooted in creative imagination.

From another point of view the first letter stands for the balance of Will and Wisdom, because it is the letter assigned to the 11th Path of the Tree of Life. From the same point of view the second letter, corresponding to the 16th Path, represents the balance between Wisdom and Mercy, while the final letter is that of the path which joins Wisdom and Understanding. Our use of magic, then, must be an expression of the Will-to-Good, must utilize the Wisdom which finds expression in the sphere of the highways of the stars, and must link up that Wisdom with a perception of the working of the self-imparting, beneficent quality of the Life-Power. Finally, it must express our perception of cosmic principled (Wisdom) in some specific way. It must look forward to a definite result. It must include an understanding of the outcome of the principles perceived by Wisdom.

In your Qabalistic dictionary you will find (under the number 11) that AVD corresponds to the following words: AI, where?, BBVA, when?; DHB, (aramaic) gold; and ChG, circularity of form or motion.

AI, where? suggests the inquiry, "Where shall we look for the magic force?" The answer has been given again and again. Even the letters of the word are a clue to it. For A is the symbol of the cosmic Life-Breath, and I is not only the symbol of the constructive and formative powers of Man, but it also represents the Intelligence of Will, or the realization of the true nature of Will. Look to the one Life-Breath, expressed as Will, for your magic power. In other words, look within. "Where shall we find the magic force?" Nowhere else but HERE, right where we are at this very point in space.

BBVA, when? indicates the other question, one that I am asked, in one form or another almost every day. "When shall I find this power?" To this question the answer is, "You have found it now. At this very moment you are making use of it. Awaken to its wonderful possibilities, and there is nothing you cannot achieve." Not in some distant future, but at this moment as you read these lines, you are using the force employed in the magic of light. True, you may be like the farmer's children in Russell Conwell's story - the children in South Africa who were playing with diamonds, but thought they were just ordinary stones. We hope in this course of lessons to change all that.

DChB is an interesting word because it conceals an alchemical secret. The first letter is attributed to Venus, the second to a sign ruled by the Moon, and the third to Mercury. Venus, Luna and Mercury are the alchemical terms for Copper, Silver and Quicksilver. Observe that the first two are the metals which are the best conductors of electricity. And the whole word means gold. Thus it is like HVN, which corresponds to אץ, in that it is a symbol of wealth. It is interesting also because on the Tree of Life it corresponds to Paths which balance those corresponding to the letters AVD. The path of B balances the path of A, and the path of Ch balances the path of V, while the path of D is common to both words. Thus, if you were to diagram these two words by placing them in their proper paths on the Tree, the result would be as follows on the next page:

Finally, ChG, representing circularity of form or motion indicates a most important fact about the magic force. It moves in cycles, it comes back to its starting-point, its <u>wheels</u>, so to say. And for this reason every magical ritual is performed within a circle.

Of this I shall speak at some length in the next lesson, which will be devoted to a consideration of the meaning of the Magic Circle.

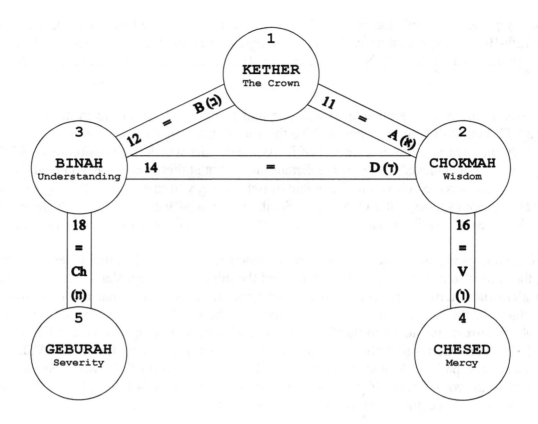

FIGURE 1A

The Magic Circle

Ceremonial magic is always performed within a circle, which is popularly supposed to be a means of protecting the magician against the incursion of hostile forces concentrated outside its limits by his evocations. In the <u>Lemegeton</u>, or <u>Lesser Key of King Solomon</u>, we read:

"This is the form of the magical circle of King Solomon, the which he made that he might preserve himself against the malice of these Evil Spirits. This magical circle is to be made 9 feet across, and the Divine Names are to be written around it, beginning at אהיה, Ehieh, and ending at לבנה, Levanah."

The names referred to are those which are ascribed to the first nine Sephiroth. They are written around the circle from right to left, in Hebrew characters, as shown in the diagram. They are:

Names belonging to 1st Sephira;
1. AHIH, 2. KThR, 3. MTTRVN, 4. ChIVTh HQDSh, 5. RAShITh HGLGLIM

Names of 2nd Sephira;
6. IH, 7. ChKMH, 8. RTzIAL, 9. AVPNIM, 10. MSLVTh

Names of 3rd Sephira;
11. IHVH ALHIM, 12. BINH, 13. TzPQIAL, 14. ARALIM, 15. ShBThAI

Names of 4th Sephira;
16. AL, 17. ChSD, 18. TzDQIAL, 19. ChShMLIM, 20. TzDQ

Names of 5th Sephira;
21. ALHIM GBVR, 22. GBVRH, 23. KMAL, 24. ShRPIM, 25. MADIM

Names of 6th Sephira;
26. IHVH ALVH VDOTh, 27. ThPARTh, 28. RPAL, 29. MLKIM,
30. ShMSh (or ChMCh)

Names of 7th Sephira;
31. IHVH TzBAVTh, 32. NTzCh, 33. HANIAL, 34. ALHIM, 35. NVGH

Names of the 8th Sephira;
36. ALHIM TzBAVTh, 37. HVD, 38. MIKAL, 39. BNI ALHIM, 40. KVKB

Names of the 9th Sephira;
41. ShDI AL ChI, 42. ISVD, 43. GBRIAL, 44. KRVBIM, 45. LBNH.

Most of these names you have encountered in previous lessons. Their total number, 45, is the number of the extension of 9, and it is also the number of אדם, Adam, MAN. But in order to write these 9 x 5 names, more than 45 words are required. The total number is 56 words. This is a number with which you are by this time more or less familiar. It is a Pyramid number. It is related also to the mysteries of Osiris. It is a number, too, which is prominent in the Christian mysteries, as revealed in the New Testament, and as later set forth in the description of the Vault where the Founder of the True and Invisible Rosicrucian Order lay buried. Primarily the meaning of this number is: The expression of Beauty (6) through adaptation (5). It also sums up the totality of existence, for it combines the numbers of the Hexagram (sign of the Macrocosm) and the Pentagram (sign of the Microcosm).

Without going into a detailed account of the numerical symbolism, therefore, we may say that the names written around the magic circle signify:

1. The powers of the Sephiroth from the CROWN to the FOUNDATION.

2. A five-fold manifestation of those powers (since there are five separate names given for each Sephira).

3. The identification of those powers with MAN, inasmuch as the total number of names is the number of ADM.

4. A suggestion that these powers combine the forces of the Macrocosm with those of the Microcosm.

The names, moreover, are written upon a picture of the Serpent of Wisdom. Thus the whole suggestion of this arrangement to an instructed Qabalist Standing within the circle is: "In me, as a center of expression, are concentrated all the powers of the Microcosm. Wisdom is my protection against all appearances of hostility."

Within the circle are drawn four Hexagrams, and in the center of each of these is inscribed a Tau-Cross. Most editions of the <u>Lemegeton</u> say that the name ADONAI should be written in the corners of the Hexagrams, but this is an obvious blind, in as much as ADONAI is spelt אדני in Hebrew. The correct name is a combination of two words, יה, Yah, the Divine Name of Chokmah, and אדני, Adonai, the Divine name of Malkuth. This compound name יה אדני is also particularly associated with Yesod and Malkuth in the creative world, Briah - the world in which every magical operation really begins. The number of this name is 80, the same as that of the letter Peh, and also of the word יסוד, Yesod, the Foundation. Consequently the four Hexagrams, which by themselves signify the fourfold Macrocosmic manifestation of the Life-Power, when inscribed with the letters of this name signify also the fourfold operation of that fundamental energy which is represented in the Hebrew alphabet by the letter Peh.

At the center of the circle is a cubical altar, resting on a square, wherein are inscribed the letters of the Tetragrammaton, IHVH (in Hebrew). The arrangement of these letters is as shown in the diagram at the end of the lesson. This square is the symbol of the number 4 and of the ORDER which every magical operation seeks to realize. It is really a magic square of 4 x 4, the magic square of Jupiter, whose sphere is the fourth Sephira. Upon it is set the cubical alter, to be explained in the next lesson.

The circle is used by magicians in every part of the world. Its name, indeed, is traced by etymologists to the Sanskrit noun <u>chakra</u>, a wheel. From <u>chakra</u>, which has several technical meanings in Hindu occultism, among them being the circle within which are performed the ceremonials of the Tantrik magicians, is derived the Greek noun KYKLOE, whence, through Latin, comes our English word cycle.

Now, in Greek gematria KYKLOE is the number 740, or 20 x 37, and this numbering serves to identify it as a mystery word. The number 740 also represents in Greek Gematria the following words:

> KTIEIE--Creation
> Η ΘΕΡΜΟΤΗΕ--Heat (that is vibratory force)
> ΑΙΘΕΡΟΕΜΕΛΟΕ--Music of the Spheres.

In Hebrew Gematria the same number is represented by the noun יכין (reckoning final N at its value of 700), and this is the name of the Pillar of Mercy on the Tree of Life, the Pillar of the Sephiroth whose numbers, 2, 4 and 7 add to 13, the number of AChD, Unity and AHBH, Love. For the Magic of Light, or theurgy (god-working) proceeds in accordance with the magician's recognition of the One-ness of All, and succeeds in the measure that the ceremonial makes real and vivid the operator's knowledge that the magical force is essentially LOVE.

Magic is KTISIS or Creation. The vibratory force which it controls and directs is rightly named H Thermotes, Heat. The Great Secret of the practical occultist is the secret of the music of the spheres, the secret of sympathetic vibration, whereby impulses of what might be called a certain pitch induce the activity of cosmic forces far beyond the range of the limited powers of the physical man.

The magic circle symbolizes all these ideas, for it is the symbol of the whirling motion whence all the forces available to human use are generated, and it is also the primary geometrical figure which determines the construction of the Triangle, the Square, the Pentagram and the Hexagram, figures whose angles determine FORM throughout creation. The numbers expressed in these geometrical figures are basic in nature, and knowledge of them is the beginning of the science of measurement (geometry) without which no artistic adaptation of cosmic forces can be fully successful--least of all that special adaptation which we call the Magic of L.V.X.

The Greek word KUKLOS, and the other words related to it by Greek Gematria also hint at a mathematical fact about the circle which is of considerable importance. The number 740, besides being 20 x 37, is 11 by reduction, and this is the number of AVD, Aud, the force used in the Magic of L.V.X. and of חג, which means "circularity of form or movement." This number 11 is the number of units in the base-line of the Great Pyramid, whose vertical axis is, in the same proportion, 7 units. Thus the four baselines of the Pyramid total 44 units, and the vertical axis is the radius of a circle whose circumference or perimeter would be 44 units in length.

We arrive at this conclusion by reason of the fact that according to a proportion much employed in occult writings, the perimeter of a circle is regarded as being 3 1/7 times its diameter. Now, the radius of 7 would have a diameter of 14, and 3 1/7 x 14 is 44, the number of units around the base of the Great Pyramid.

I have mentioned these facts about the Pyramid because it, like the magic circle, exemplifies those basic principles of measurement whose application to the control of nature's finer forces constitutes the art of magic. By the proportion here indicated, 11, which is the number of AVD, Aud, the magic force, is the perimeter of a circle whose diameter is 3 1/2 units, because 3 1/7 x 3.5 = 11.

By the same proportion a circle with a diameter of 7 will have a circumference of 22, one with a diameter of 14 will have a circumference of 44, a diameter of 21 will give a circumference of 66, and one of 28 will give a circumference of 88.

In the esoteric teaching whose elements you are receiving in these lessons, the circle having a diameter of 7 and a circumference of 22 is the geometrical symbol of the archetypal world, or ATZILUTH. The duplication or reflection of ATZILUTH is represented by the circle of 14 units diameter, corresponding to BRIAH, the creative world. The formative world, YETZIRAH is represented by the circle having a diameter of 21 units. The circle of ASSIAH, the material world, has a diameter of 28 units.

When we compare these numbers with the Qabalistic words which correspond to them by Gematria, some very curious results are shown. At present they may seem to you to be remote from any practical application to magic; but it should be borne in mind that to be a magician one needs to do more than learn a formula. A magician is a person who has a particular <u>quality of consciousness</u>, and part of the training consists in the tracing out of the ideas which are brought into juxtaposition before the mind's eye by the fact that words whose everyday meanings are sometimes radically opposed to each other are identical in number. When you exercise your ingenuity and patience in study of this kind, moreover, you are reproducing through the agency of your personal brain-cells ideas which have passed through the brains of adepts in the Ageless Wisdom. To think the same thoughts that have passed through the mind of an adept is to become like him. To work them out independently, or with such slight help as is afforded by the suggestions given in these lessons, is really a course in mental gymnastics, by means of which you may develop mental muscles which you will have need of when you attempt the actual practice of magic. I counsel you, therefore, to pay close attention to the paragraphs immediately following, and to develop the hints they contain as much as you can.

Reference to the Qabalistic dictionary will show you that the number 7 is represented by the following words: אבד, to scatter, to disperse; או, desire, either, or; בדא, to invent; גד, good fortune; דאב, to pine; דבא, influx, to flow in, riches; and דג, a fish. These words, then, are related to the number of the diameter of the archetypal world, and since the diameter is what determines the size of a circle, they may be expected to shed some light upon the Qabalistic conception of the characteristic or determining qualities of this plane of cosmic seed-thoughts, which corresponds to the letter YOD of יהוה, and to the element of FIRE.

אבד, to scatter, to disperse, suggests dissemination or sowing. The archetypal world is the great reservoir of seed-forms, these being the Platonic <u>ideas</u>. Its activity is on this account symbolized by YOD, the letter which is the symbol of the male, sperm-giving principle throughout the universe. Other words which are synonyms for dispersion will help you to grasp the fundamental meaning suggested by ABD. Among them are: diffusion, spreading, distribution, apportionment.

או, as meaning desire refers to a conception about the archetypal world which we find taught in all schools of the Ageless Wisdom. According to this conception, the motive power in the Life-Power's self-manifestation is its own desire to actualize its own possibilities. The other meanings of AV--either, and or--imply choice, selection, decision, the shaping of a course, the singling out of particular modes of expression. Thus AV denotes desire combined with decision. It is not mere vague longing which is behind the Life-Power's self-expression, but specific selection. Limitless in its potentialities, the Life-Power, in beginning a cycle of self-expression, centers itself upon some particular possibility which it seeks to realize. Here is a hint for every magician, inasmuch as magic after all is but a personal application of the Life-Power's way of being and doing.

בדא, to invent, brings in the idea of imagination. In the passage from Thomas Vaughan quoted in the first lesson you will find the conception that the archetypal phase of the creative process in imagination. The opening words of Genesis, according to some Rabbis, convey the same thought. For instead of reading BRAShITH as "in principle," or "in the beginning," they understand it to be ב ראשית, Be-Rash-ith, "in the head." Thus they conceive the first step of the creative process to be one of contemplation, by which the Life-Power figures to itself the actualization of some one of its limitless possibilities; thus, too, striking out something new, or inventing a new form of self-expression. Invention, indeed, is practically a synonym for originality, and the archetypal world is held by Qabalists to be the plane of original ideas.

גד, good fortune, is a reminder that although the Life-Power is unlimited in its possibilities of self-expression, so that it may invent new forms of manifestation for itself, it is changeless in its own nature, and must therefore always seek self-expression in ways that are good, in forms that are beneficent.

דאב is a metathesis of אדב, and both words mean "to languish, to pine." The idea here is that which is also expressed by AV. Boehme brings it out when he writes:

"Seeing then there is a craving in the nothing, it makes in itself the will to something. This will is a spirit, as a thought, which goes out of the craving and is the seeker of the craving, for it finds its mother or the craving. Then is this will a Magician in its mother; for it has found in the nothing something, viz. its mother, and so now has a place for its dwelling.

"And herein understand that the will is a spirit, and different from the desirous craving. For the will is an insensitive and incognitive life; but the craving is found by the will, and is in the will a being. Thus the craving is a Magia, and the will a Magus; and the will is greater than its mother which gives it, for it is lord in the mother; and the mother is dumb, but the will is a life without origin. The craving is certainly a cause of the will, but without knowledge or understanding. The will is the understanding of the craving.

"Thus we give you in brief to consider of nature and the spirit of nature, what there has been from eternity without origin. And we find thus that the will, viz. the spirit, has no place for its rest; but the craving is its own place, and the will is a band to it, and yet is not held in check."

Six Theosophic Points

דבא, "influx, to flow in, riches," indicates another detail in our conception of the archetypal world. This world is the sphere of the self-concentration of the Limitless Light, of its entry into the

109

conditions of manifestation. And because the limitless possibilities of that Light are the seeds of all forms whatsoever, this influx, which is the MZLA, Mezla, or <u>influence</u>, is the source of all riches.

Finally, דג, the fish, is occultly a reference to the infinite potency of the archetypal world. The association of ideas is not read into the word by any means. It is part and parcel of the Hebrew language, for the verb דגה, to multiply, to become numerous, to grow is derived from דג, and has for its primary meaning "to spawn, like fish." This verb is used in Genesis 48:16:

"The Angel which redeemed me from all evil, bless the lads; and let my name be named on them, and the name of my fathers Abraham and Isaac; and let them grow into a multitude in the midst of the earth."

In the King James Version of the English Bible a marginal note to the verb "grow" says: Heb. <u>as fishes do increase</u>.

These, then, are the Hebrew words corresponding to the number 7, which represents the diameter of the archetypal world. They show us clearly what is the essential determining characteristic of this plane. It is an eager craving, a disseminating influence, limitless in potency, and able to multiply itself in forms innumerable.

The number 22, which corresponds to the perimeter of a circle whose diameter is 7, is represented in Hebrew by the following words: בידו, with his hand; ביוד, by Yod; חזוא (Aramaic) a magical vision; חטה, wheat; טובה, Good; and יחד, unity.

In the first two of these words some symbolists find a trace of a certain Egyptian idea concerning the beginning of things. Perhaps some readers of these pages may know it, and they will understand me when I say that although I reject all the cruder explanations which writers like Inman, Payne, Knight and others have offered with respect to this particular detail of symbolism, there is, nevertheless, a certain truth (however repellent may be the way it is expressed) in the old Egyptian imagery.

Note that חזוא, a magical vision, designates the mental activity which is the embodiment of desire or longing, that חטה, wheat, a seed-form, is symbolically expressive of the archetypal world, and that טובה declares the goodness of the primogenial ideas, while יחד affirms the unity of their source.

Passing now to the circle of the creative world, בריאה, we find that its diameter corresponds to the following words. (14) אטד, a thron, a spine; דבח, a sacrifice, an offering; דוד, love, beloved (David); הדה, to stretch out, to direct; זהב, gold; יד, hand.

The first of these words, אטד, is from a verb spelt with the same letters, meaning "to pierce, to penetrate, to fasten in." This shows us that the word "thorn" as used in Hebrew implies an idea probably borrowed from primitive custom. In many parts of the world thorns are used as pins or needles, and thus they become the symbols of union, connection, joining, fastening, association, accumulation and aggregation. These ideas are fundamental in relation to the creative world, BRIAH, which corresponds to Water, and to the second letter of Tetragrammaton, the creative letter Heh, assigned to בינה, the Mother. The creative world is the sphere in which the archetypal ideas are combined with each other, so as to make aggregated, conglomerations, accretions. And thus this world is represented by ATD, "the fastening, or the fastener."

דבח, a sacrifice, an offering, refers to the fact that the Life-Power offers Itself in the act of creation. That self-offering is an act of love דוד, and it is also a self-extension (stretching out), or a self-direction, הדה, of which the hand (sometimes spelled יד) is a symbol.

The number corresponding to the creative circumference, 44, has the following words:

אגלי, drops (of fluid); אגם, to gather together; a pool, a pond; דלי, a vessel for drawing water (name of the sign, Aquarius); דם, blood. All these words, as you can see, are directly related to the watery nature of Briah. The noun גולה, captivity, refers to the limitations which are the logical necessities of creation. טלה, a ram (name of the sign Aries) and להט, a flame, are words not only equivalent to each other in number, but also in the letters which form them, and further, in essential meaning, since the sign Aries is a fire-sign. In relation to BRIAH, however, both these words are technical mystery-terms, referring to the same idea that is expressed in the New Testament mention of the Lamb slain from the foundation of the world. The sign Aries, as the beginning of the zodiac, is a symbol of the commencement of the creative activities in BRIAH which result ultimately in the Life-Power's self-expression in the names and forms of the physical world. The Ram and the Lamb are one, and as you have learned, they both correspond to the Hindu deity Agni, Lord of Flame להט.

The formative diameter expressed by the number 21 and the following words: אהיה, Eheieh, EXISTENCE, a Divine name particularly assigned to Kether, which refers to the formative power of the Primal Will; אך, a word having many meanings, but all representing some degree of restriction, such as "only," "this once," "indeed," and "certainly." The restriction is affirmative. It is the restriction of the specific, as opposed to the vagus, of assurance as opposed to doubt; הגיג, deep meditation, which carries out the idea of contemplation we have seen to be related to the archetypal and creative worlds; זח, purity, referring to the unsulliod state of the pattern-forms which exist in the plans of formation; חזו (Aramaic) a vision; יהו, the mystic Name of three letters which, the Sepher Yetzirah tells us, was used in sealing the six directions of space.

The circumference number of the formative world has these correspondences: (66) אכילה, food, victuals, which is of interest to students of magic because it so definitely indicates the source of "daily bread" as being, not in the plane of the material world, but in the pattern-world; ANIH, a ship, which symbolizes the formative world as the connecting medium which carries the powers of the higher worlds down into the external world of physical manifestation (and, conversely, is the means whereby, on the path of return, we may be ferried over from the physical world to those beyond); בחון, a trial, a test, a proof, a word which in its root-meaning is connected with the assaying of metal; גלגל, a wheel, a whirl, which reminds us of the rotary nature of all formative activity (a fact attested to by modern physical science, and symbolized again and again by seers and occultists); all these words being plain hints of the characteristic manifestations or expressions of formative power in Yetzirah.

The diameter number of עשיה, Assiah, the material world, is 28. This, it is to be noted, is the extension of 7 as well as 4 times 7, so that it suggests the complete expression of the archetypal diameter through a four-fold manifestation. The corresponding words are: TIT, clay (but do not fail to study this word letter by letter, and with the help of the corresponding Tarot keys, paths, etc.); יחוד, union, or unity, indicates the fact that the material world, <u>which we misinterpret as the sphere</u>

of many-ness or multiplicity, is fundamentally the ONE expression of ONE reality, in which there is no separation whatever, each of the seemingly separate parts being combined with all the others. This is a conception made understandable by modern rediscoveries concerning the electrical constitution of matter. Finally, 28 is KCh, Kach, power, and this locates for us in no uncertain way the place whence we shall draw the power used in magic and other forms of practical occultism. The power we are to use is, indeed, a physical power. It is not afar off. On the contrary, it is close at hand. We do not have to leave this world to find it. It is here, in plain sight, even as the alchemists tell us again and again when they intimate that the First Matter of the art is procurable everywhere, and without expense.

Does this mean that I am here reversing all that has been said in former lessons about not depending upon external things for supply? By no means. The intention of the closing words of the preceding paragraph is simply this, Do not make the mistake of looking upon the external world as separate from the One Life-Power. Do not think of it as being "material" in opposition to the "spirituality" of metaphysical planes. Understand that the forces you are using in magic are the very same forces which are the subjects of investigation in the laboratories of material science; but understand them as the appearances of the One Power. The external world is not a product of the One Power, different from and separated from its Producer. It IS that Power making Itself known in ways which are perceptible to our bodily senses. This is the inner meaning of what Jesus declared, "He who hath seen me hath seen the Father." It is also what The Book of Tokens teaches in the words:

"All this am I. Therefore, though none may capture me in the net of thought, he shall speak truly who shall say, laying his hand on anything soever (whether men prize it, or scorn it as of no worth), 'Dost ask me to show thee the Lord? Verily, in this shalt thou find Him, if thou hast eyes to see."

The words corresponding to the circumference number of the material world are those representing 88:

חכלל means "colored," and in this connection we may remember that the word "color" is derived from a Latin root, meaning "to conceal." The same implication of concealment is connected with this word חכלל, which suggests that the material world is a veil of color, concealing the real nature of the Life-Power. חכם means "to be hot; to glow, to brood, to hatch." This word is closely related to the old name of Egypt, Khem חם, whence, by an interesting series of linguistic transmutations, we get our modern word chemistry--so that the name of that branch of science which is doing so much to establish the real unity of the material world is, literally, "The Wisdom of Egypt." חסך means "darkness," and suggests the fact that no matter how much we investigate it, the material world remains ever a great field of the Unknown נחל, "something hollowed out, a valley" may serve to remind us of the popular idea that this material world is a vale of tears; but there is a profounder meaning than this, which I trust you will discover for yourself.

In the magic circle, these four circles are implied, even though the actual diameters of 7, 14, 21 and 28 are not indicated. They are implied because within the outer circle of 9 feet is a second circle of seven feet (diameter), so that the figure of the serpent with the divine names is enclosed in a ring one foot wide.

Furthermore, to suggest the presence of the archetypal circle, the square before-mentioned is exactly 27 inches wide, so that it will enclose a circle whose diameter is also 27 inches. The diameter of a circle of 27 inches is to the diameter of a circle of 108 inches, as the diameter of a circle of 7 feet is to the diameter of a circle of 28 feet, that is 27 inches: 108 inches: 84 inches: 336 inches. Consequently, the square at the center of the magic circle implies the presence of a small circle whose proportion to the outer circle is as that of the circle of the archetypal world to the circle of the material world. Of this you will find further mention in the next lesson.

Going back now to the particular form of magic circle described in the Lemegeton, let us consider why it should be 9 feet in diameter, and not some other number. In the first place because 9 is the number of completion, the number whose extension is 45, (the number of ADM, Adam), and the number of the Sephira of FOUNDATION.

But aside from the mathematical fact that 9 feet corresponds to these ideas, this number also conceals another which we discover by expressing the feet of the diameter as inches. 9 feet = 108 inches, and thus the number of units in the diameter of the Magic Circle of ceremonial is the same as the number of units in the string of beads which you used for concentration.

This number 108 has been venerated by occultists for many reasons. It is the product of 2^2 x 3^3, and this fact has mystical interpretations which we need not enter into at present. The gematria of this number in the Hebrew tongue is very rich and suggestive, but this, also, is not the main consideration at present. What is of greater interest and importance for the magician is the fact that 108 is a key-number to the great time-periods which are the basis of the measurements in astronomy. It is, in other words the key-number of the rhythms of the music of the spheres.

In the precession of the equinoxes, 2160 years elapse in each of the twelve periods constituting what is known as the Great Year. One of these periods, then is 108 times 20 years, and the whole Great Year is 108 times 240 years. Again, by the traditional Hindu system of reckoning time, a Manvantara consists of 4,320,000 years, of 108 times 4000 years.

Such are the astronomical meanings of the number 108. But this same number has another important meaning which recurs again and again in nature and in art--especially in the art of magic. Each of the interior angles of a pentagon, or regular five-sided figure, is 108 degrees, so that this is the number which determines the growth of five-petalled flowers, (among which the rose is most prominent in symbolism) which is expressed in the structure of many shells, in the formation of diatoms, and in many other ways throughout the plant and animal kingdoms.

As the pentagon angle, moreover, the angle of 108 degrees determines the construction of that great magical symbol, the Pentagram, to which we shall presently devote considerable attention.

Thus the fact that this number is represented in the Magic Circle by the number of inches in its diameter is an indication that the whole circle is intended to express the basic numeral proportions in astronomy, in the construction of many living organisms, and in the symbolic representation of true magic, or human adaptation of cosmic law to practical results.

On page 41 I said that the Hebrew Gematria of this number is full of valuable indications, but passed it for the time being in order to give first place to the various details just mentioned. Yet I feel that many readers of these pages may profit by a consideration of this Gematria, which is not included in the Qabalistic dictionary in Section A. Here, then, are the Hebrew words corresponding to the number 108: אזנים, the ears; באבי הנחל, the fruit of a deep valley (The "valley" is the Abyss of the <u>Ungrund</u>, or Boundless Subsistence); חיץ, a wall (suggesting protection, as does the Magic Circle); חמס, to be sharp, bold, violent; חנן, to incline, to have mercy, to love; חסם, to close, to shut, to hinder; חזי, the middle, an arrow (compare with Greek <u>kentron</u>, an arrow-point, whence <u>center</u>); חק, that which in inscribed; that which is appointed; revelation, divine (cosmic) law; and, finally, as the most important, MNHIG, conductive (title of the thirteenth path.)

Study of these words will show that they have correspondences to the ideas symbolized by the Magic Circle. Thus Stenring says, in commenting on the thirteenth path:

"No magical work can be accomplished without communication with this path. It is the equilibrating power and the source of volition. It is the spiritual focus of gravitation and the directing force. The Conductive Intelligence is always accompanied by Responsibility. The two ideas stand in direct proportion to each other." - <u>Sepher Yetzirah</u>, page 61.

The Magic Circle, moreover, is a continuous line, having neither end nor beginning. It symbolizes to the instructed operator the fact, which is lost sight of by the uninitiated, that all human activities are expressions of a cosmic process which continues forever. It is a symbol also of perseverance. These two ideas which are represented by the Magic Circle are conveyed in Eliphas Levi's remark that the magician should work as if he had all eternity in which to complete his operation. This means that he should recognize the timelessness of his undertaking. For magic, or theurgy, as god-working aims to enable the operator to express the identical creative power which is the source of all cosmic manifestations. It is, so far as symbol and ceremonial are concerned, an intensive method for impressing upon the subconsciousness the suggestion that man in a center of the Life-Power's creative ideation. It aims to arouse in the subconsciousness an intense conviction of the actual, real presence of the creative power in the operator's life. In short, the purpose of the magic of Light is to establish in the subconsciousness of the operator, by scientific use of symbol, gesture, and other suggestive accessories, that very living faith of which Jesus spoke when he said: "Whatsoever things ye ask and pray for, believe that ye <u>have</u> received them, and ye shall have them." And the circle, which is one form of the zero-sign helps the instructed operator to do this because it reminds him that he is the immediate expression of a Power with which all things ARE possible. ARE, not WILL BE. And we use the present tense, not in blind faith, but because hard intellectual study has enabled us to learn that the limitless potencies of the Life-Power are necessarily potencies existing at the present moment, in all perfection.

Again, the circle is a figure in which every point of the circumference is equidistant from the center. Thus is symbolized equilibrium, poise, adjustment, symmetry, and all such ideas. It is the emblem of the true magical work, which is the confirmation in thought, word and action of the magician's realization that he is a center of expression for the equilibrating power of the cosmos.

And because of this, the circle reminds the magician that his operation cannot possible be any sort of hocus pocus for getting the best of somebody else. Better than most people, the competent magician knows that the Life-Power is no respector of persons - that it cannot be invoked to give any one person an unfair advantage over another. This, indeed, is where the danger of Black Magic comes in. For when, in the presence of, and using, the symbols of cosmic unity, one attempts a magical operation directed against the welfare of another person, the only evil that is effected is the result of the operator's own miserable misinterpretation of the work.

It would be futile to deny that occult forces can be so directed by ill-disposed persons, that other people may be made to suffer temporarily in consequence. But the Ageless Wisdom is very definite in its declaration that no victim of an evil magical operation suffers unjustly, or can possibly be hurt unless that particular experience is, to use the vernacular, "coming to him." And the suffering of the victim of evil magic is nothing in comparison to the suffering which must be endured by the operator. That, too, not in some future life, but invariable in the same incarnation wherein the evil magic is performed. For the occult forces invoked by such operations work swiftly, and quickly return to their source. Hence it is written that he who sows the wind shall reap the whirlwind.

The worst of black magic, as I have said, is the error of consciousness from which the impulse to perform it springs. No operation can possibly be evil when it is undertaken by an operator who recognized the unity of the Life-Power and the impossibility of invoking it to the disadvantage of another. The impossibility, I say, because the suffering caused to the victim is by no means to his real disadvantage, inasmuch as it educates him, and helps him to work off a Karmic debt. And because any seeming ascendancy which the black magician gains over other people is purely illusive, there is certainly no advantage gained by himself. With this let us dismiss black magic.

To summarize this lesson, then, the purpose of the Magic Circle is:

1. To remind the operator that he, as a living expression of the Limitless Light, actually occupies a central position in the cosmos.

2. To affirm symbolically and Qabalistically the idea that his magical operation is part of the eternal cosmic process of IDEATION, or creative imagination, in which manifestation proceeds from the archetypal to the material world by ordered, regular processes.

3. To affirm also the idea that this is a work of equilibrium, whose outcome must be beautiful or symmetrical.

4. To intensify the magician's realization that he works to produce a specific result, as definite, and as accurate as his circle.

5. To remind him, also, that the success of his operation may be expected from the fact that even as he is standing in the center of a circle whose circumference is bounded by the Holy Names, so is he, as a human being, the center of expression for the correlated operation of all the cosmic aspects of the Life-Power symbolized by those names.

The Magical Altar

In Lesson 2 you learned that at the center of the Magic Circle is a square, inscribed with the four letters of the Tetragrammaton, IHVH. This square is 27 x 27 inches, so that one of its sides is equal to one quarter of the diameter of the circle. Consequently its four sides are 4 x 27 inches, or 108 inches, which is the length of the total diameter of that circle.

Upon this square is placed the altar of ceremonial. This is a cube measuring 27 x 27 x 27 inches. Such a great cube would measure 108 inches along one of its boundary lines, so that it would be the cube corresponding to a square, one of whose sides was equal to the diameter of the Magic Circle. The altar cube, as representing one sixty-forth of the entire volume of this great cube, corresponds to the Gnostic-Christian geometrical representation of truth, for the following reason:

In the Greek language, which is like Hebrew in that its letters are numbers, the word for truth is spelt ΑΛΗΘΕΙΑ, in which A=1, Λ=30, H=8, Θ=9, E=5, I=10, and A=1, and A=1, the total number being 64. Now, any square is the symbol of the number 4, but the square of IHVH is a square of 4 x 4, because IHVH represents the Self-Existent One as manifest in 4 elements, and also because there is a correspondence between the JOVE of the Grecian mystery cults and IHVH, which makes the 4 x 4 square, dedicated to Jupiter the one which properly represents the powers of the name יהוה.

This magic square of Jupiter, whose proportions are the basis of the cube containing 64 small cubes, is given below, with the numbers properly arranged. Horizontally, vertically or diagonally, each column adds invariably to 34, and the total number of the square is 136, or S:16.

15	10	3	6
4	5	16	9
14	11	2	7
1	8	13	12

Magic Square of 4

The numbers of this particular square, therefore, are 4, the number on which it is based, signifying ORDER, system, regulation, command, etc., and relating particularly to the fourth path of the Tree of Life, which is named MEASURING INTELLIGENCE. 16, the number of cells in the magic square, corresponding to the Hebrew words אזוב, hyssop, (symbolizing the cleansing which comes with regulation), אחז, to apprehend, to lay hold of (referring to the grasp of cosmic laws which is based upon measurement), גבוה, elevated, exalted, high (referring to the idea of dominion and authority derived from grasp of cosmic law), הוה, to live, to be (originally to breathe), היא, the personal pronoun, she (reminding us that existence is the state of the Life-Power's manifestation through Prakriti, personified in Egypt as ISIS, or Nature, and represented in the Pythagorean triangle by the base line of 4 units), זוג, to enclose, or, like, equal to (words which refer to the essential identity of all manifestations of the One Life); 34, corresponding to the Hebrew words AL, אב, God the Father, a name associated with Jupiter and Chesed, גאל, to ransom, and גלא, to reveal; and 136, corresponding to the words הסמאל, Hismael, Spirit of Jupiter, יהפיאל, Yophiel, Intelligence of Jupiter, מלאך הגואל, the angel of vengeance, and קול, a voice. Furthermore, the square adds to 34 in 4 vertical, 4 horizontal, and 2 diagonal columns, or 10 in all, and 10 x 34 is 340, the value of ספר, a book and שם, the Name.

Thus the magic square on which the altar is based is one that is particularly related to the ideas of ORDER, of DOMINION, of MEASUREMENT, and of the powers of the planet Jupiter. Careful study of the various Hebrew words corresponding to the numbers related to this square will show that all of them refer either to measurement or to powers active in the sphere of Chesed. These powers, so far as human consciousness is concerned, are rooted in Memory, which is the special phase of mental activity associated with Chesed. Memory, too, is the function of consciousness most closely identified with the Jupiterian vibration. Hence Jupiter is said to be the planet which rules priests and lawyers, whose work is based upon precedent.

Now, when each of the 16 squares in this magic square of Jupiter is raised into a cube, the result is a plinth containing 16 cubes, and upon this foundation is built the great cube of 64 small cubes whose number represents in Greek Gematria the word Aletheia, or Truth. The literal meaning of Aletheia is "not forgetting," so that it is evidently a word suggesting perfect memory.

Our altar of ceremonial, therefore, is primarily intended to remind us that our work is founded upon the self-impartation of the Life-Power which is represented by Chesed. It stands before us in the magic circle as a symbol of truth, as an emblem of power and control derived from our grasp of the basic measurements of the cosmos. Thus it brings ever to our recollection the fact that our magical work is never at any time intended to set aside natural processes, is never to be thought of as a means for circumventing the regularity of the cosmic order.

The sides of the altar, as squares, remind us that we are dependent for success upon the classifying activity of self-consciousness, which regulates all the products of imagination.

The number of points or corners of the cube is 8, and this serves to remind us that every undertaking of man is part of the cosmic process of involution and evolution. It tells us also that the support of all our work (as the altar supports our implements) is the rhythm of the Life-Power's vibratory activity. When we grasp the full purport of this word "rhythm" so as to be able to apply it, tremendous power is available for our use. As a simple illustration of this let me remind you of a laboratory experiment in elementary physics.

A weight so heavy that a man may not move it as it hangs suspended may be set in motion, like a pendulum, by a little child. All that is required to produce this result is to strike the weight gently with a mallet, and in a little while the effect of these gentle impulses (which must, of course, be regular) will set the weight swinging.

Again, a member of this Section has noticed that in one of our leading New York cinema houses, a large statue of Diana in the balcony sways perceptibly when certain pedal notes are sounded on the organ of the theater. The motion is distinctly visible--nearly a half-inch displacement from the perpendicular.

The 12 boundary lines of the cube remind us of the 12 signs of the zodiac. Thus they carry our thoughts, as instructed Qabalists, back to Chokmah, the sphere of the zodiac, and remind us that our magic, as practical Cabalah, is founded upon the laws of planetary influence. We must take account of these laws in choosing suitable times for our various operations, and thus no success in the practice of magic is possible for the person who ignores astrology. For every magical operation has its own particular characteristics, as may be seen from the following quotation from Eliphas Levi:

"Magical works are seven in number:

1. Works of light and wealth under the patronage of the Sun.
2. Works of divination and mysteries, under the invocation of the Moon.
3. Works of skill, science, and eloquence, under the protection of Mercury.
4. Works of wrath and chastisement, consecrated to Mars.
5. Works of love, favored by Venus.
6. Works of ambition and policy, under the auspices of Jupiter.
7. Works of malediction and death, under the care of Saturn."

It will not escape the attentive reader that every magical work therefore calls into play the special activities of one of the seven chakras or nerve-centers which the alchemists disguised as "metals," named after the seven celestial bodies. The nerve-currents working in these centers are modified by the revolutions of the heavenly bodies. Hence it is important to choose a correct time for working, and this means, of course, that one must be able to make an election for the work according to astrological rules. This detail, lost sight of in the hit-or-miss procedure of the average New Thought practitioner, is sufficient to account for many failures. All magicians may with profit consider the words of the Preacher:

"To everything there is a season, and a time to every purpose under the heaven: a time to be born, and a time to die; a time to plant, and a time to pluck up that which is planted; a time to kill, and a time to heal; a time to break down, and a time to build up; a time to weep, and a time to laugh; a time to mourn, and a time to dance; a time to cast away stones, and a time to gather stones together; a time to embrace, and a time to refrain from embracing; a time to seek, and a time to lose; a time to keep, and a time to cast away; a time to rend, and a time to sew; a time to keep silence, and a time to speak; a time to love, and a time to hate; a time for war, and a time for peace." – Ecclesiastes, 3: 1 to 9.

Some people, confused by the doctrine of the actual, real presence of the omnipotent Life-Power in human life, and mistaking the meaning of words, "Now is the acceptable time," are of the opinion that the philosophy of times and seasons runs counter to the higher aspects of metaphysical truth. Their error consists in their notion of what constitutes the "salvation" or liberation concerning which it is written that NOW is the acceptable time. The freedom of the wise is not freedom to do whatever they please at any given moment. Rather is it the freedom which is indicated by the name of the 12th path on the Tree of Life, the path which, in the Tarot, is definitely associated with magic, because it corresponds to the picture of the Magician.

That path is called INTELLIGENCE OF TRANSPARENCY, and the freedom it confers is the freedom which comes to those through whom the cosmic life-currents have unobstructed passage.

Hence, in the picture of the Magician we see that he is attentively considering the symbols of the four elements on his table, and that his task is evidently that of arranging them in their proper order. NOW is always the time of liberation, but the truly free man is he whose life from moment to moment is so well-adjusted to cosmic rhythms that in a period ruled by Venus, say, he is not vainly attempting to perform a work of Saturn.

Thus the altar's twelve boundary lines serve to remind us that we are at all times centers of expression for the vibrations of planetary forces, and that by adapting our working to the cycles of those forces we may be sure that what we undertake will be brought to a successful conclusion.

Another consideration which must be taken into account is indicated by the correspondence of the altar to the name of I H V H (because the numbers that represent the points, lines and faces of a cube are 8, 12 and 6, whose sum, 26=IHVH). The Tetragrammaton means "The Self-Existent." It is a name which is attributed on the Tree of Life to Binah, to Tiphareth and to Netzach (See list of names on the Magic Circle, Lesson 2D. Thus it is a name referring to Intuition (Binah), to imagination (Tiphareth) and to Desire (Netzach). Intuition, Imagination and Desire are the basis of all magical working. Intuition as to the real nature of Self-Existence, and its relation to man. Imagination which pictures definite beautiful results as the logical outcome of that relation. Desire so trained and directed that it is a steady aspiration towards the realization of these beautiful results. In other words, a magician engaged in theurgy, or god-working, is a man who listens attentively to the Inner Voice which reveals the presence of Self-Existence, who pictures clearly and definitely some particular beautiful expression of the power made known to him by intuition, and who keeps the flame of desire burning clear and bright to illuminate that picture. Intuition shows him what the Self-Existent One is and can do. Imagination makes a slide for his mental magic lantern by deducing particular applications of what intuition makes known. The flame of desire lights up the picture and projects it upon the screen of space.

Furthermore, since the altar represents יהוה, or the Self-Existent Reality, it serves to remind the magician that the basis of his operation is the constitution of the cosmos as it is. This point may seem to be so obvious that it requires no elaboration, but it is ignored more often than one might think. For example, take the magical operation called "mental healing." We have Christian Science healers, Divine Science healers, Unity healers, healers belonging to any number of religious denominations. Then we have mental healers who assert that religion has nothing to do with the work. All of these healers attribute their successes to various causes. Many of them deny that the curative works of those who hold a different belief are genuine. But the fact remains that they all have just about the same percentage of successes.

What does this mean? This, that a healer's theories may be merest moonshine, but he will cure his patients is his <u>practice</u> conforms to the cosmic order. The basis of the work, in other words, is <u>existence as it is</u>, not the pet theory of the practitioner. And this holds true of all magical working. The basis of the work is not theory but fact, not opinion but reality. Magic, therefore, is not an attempt to escape from things as they are. It succeeds because it gets the magician into harmonic rapport with the Life-Power's ways of self-expression.

This, of course, is implicit in the correspondence between the cubical altar and the Greek word <u>Aletheia</u>. For truth is defined as "conformity to fact or reality; exact accordance with that which is, or has been, or shall be." The magician opposes reality to appearance, fact to fancy, order to disorder. Seeming to do things which are miracles, or departures from the established order, he really accomplishes these marvels by a strict conformity to the workings of the cosmic process. The successful outcome of his undertakings is merely the fulfillment of the promise, "Ye shall know the truth, and the truth shall make you free."

The six sides of the magical altar represent six of the planetary vibrations. The top corresponds to Mercury. The bottom is dedicated to the Moon. The side facing East is attributed to Venus. The southern side corresponds to the Sun. To the western side Jupiter is assigned. Mars corresponds to the Northern face. The point at the center of the altar is attributed to Saturn. (The point, that is, within the cube, at its heart.)

Some magical rituals say that the faces of the cube should be covered with plates of the metals corresponding to the planets (Mercury being represented by an amalgam of quicksilver with silver). When expense is no consideration, this may be done. Quite as effective, however, is the alplan of painting the sides of the cube in the proper colors. The top is bright, deep yellow, for Mercury. The bottom is blue, for the moon. The eastern face is green, the southern face orange, the western face violet, and the northern face red.

The planetary and color attributions are in accordance with the Yetziratic attributions of the seven double letters to the six directions of space. Thus the altar is the synthesis of the seven planetary forces, the representation of the balanced activity of the alchemical metals, the symbol of the orderly manifestations and coordination of the powers of the seven chakras, or nerve-centers.

Its eight points give the number of Hermes, who represents intellect. The cube itself was also sacred to Hermes, who, as the god of science, astrology, magic and medicine, personifies the perception of truth, the knowledge of cosmic cycles, the practical application of the cosmic L.V.X., and the purification and perfection of man. The cube also typifies geometrically the Hermetic axiom, "That which is below is that which is above, and that which is above is as that which is below," because its upper and lower faces are identical in their measurement. Observe that the upper face corresponds through its color to the letter Beth, and so to the Magician, while the lower face corresponds in the same way to the letter Gimel and the High Priestess.

Thus the surface of the cube upon which the operator places the implements of his work represents the plane of self-consciousness and intellect, while the base of the altar represents subconsciousness and memory. This base is placed upon the square in the Magic Circle, upon which the name יהוה is written. Thus the side of the altar symbolizing subconsciousness is in juxtaposition with the square which represents the archetypal manifestation of Self-Existence. That square is colored red, in accordance with the attribution of the element of Fire to the archetypal world.

What this means is that it is through the powers of subconsciousness that the magician makes his direct contact with the archetypal aspects of self-existence. This is precisely what is implied in the symbolism of the sixth Tarot Key, where it is Eve, or the Woman, who looks toward the angel. And the powers of the subconscious plane are indeed those which establish the basis of every magical operation. Yet the ordering and regulation of his implements is accomplished on the top of the altar. In like manner it is in the plane of self-consciousness that the magician exercises the powers which effect the magical results. He finds out where he stands in the cosmos by exercising his ability to make inferences from facts. He formulates his mental patterns in this plane, too. The six faces of the cube are also symbols of the numerical occultism of the number 6. They serve to remind the magician that his work is simply a correlation or arrangement of existing forces, that he produces his results because he stands in a reciprocal relation to the Life-Power, that the success of his work is evidence of his harmony with the urge of the Life-Power to self-expression, and that urge is ever a tendency toward the establishment in the external world of the symmetry and beauty which the Spirit is in itself.

The Hebrew word for "altar" is מזבח, a noun derived from the verb זבח, to slaughter, to sacrifice. Thus the altar, in addition to the various meanings which we have derived from its geometrical proportions, must also be regarded as that upon which something is destroyed or sacrificed. What this is we should have no difficulty in deciding when we remember that the altar represents truth and conformity to the cosmic order. What we sacrifice or destroy is the sense of personal separateness. What we kill out is the illusion that we do anything of ourselves.

By Gematria מזבח (=57) corresponds to אבדן, destruction; אוכל, consuming; און, to breathe, to effect by work, to take pains; אנו, the pronoun "we"; בנה, to build; and מחבוא, making secret.

Most of these words so obviously correspond to the basic idea of destruction or sacrifice that they need no explanation. Note, however, the connection between breath and working, and the implication of the pronoun אנו, which suggests that in getting rid of the illusion of separateness there is effected a realization that all the spiritual powers of the cosmos are finding expression in the magical operation.

Let it be understood, however, that although the altar is a symbol of sacrifice and atonement, it must not be thought of as representing propitiation. There is no angry deity to be appeased, no hostile force to be won over by the giving up of something dear. This old false conception of sacrifice still taints the thought of the world. What one gives up is really nothing. The atonement is better understood as at-one-ment.

True, the illusion of separateness often seems hard to part with, and it assumes protean forms, which we cherish as our dearest possessions while the illusion persists. That is why there are so few real magicians in the world. That, too, is the reason why anyone who promises to teach the art of developing the powers of personality can always find plenty of pupils. Children are not the only ones who hope to find a way to have their cake and eat it too.

But if we are to become magicians, we must follow the path that the other magicians have taken. We must know the truth that no power whatever originates in personality, and we must live in accordance with our knowledge.

Moment by moment, hour by hour, day by day, we must correct the illusion of separateness by the clear intellectual vision of the truth that each of us is a center of expression for the One Power which appears in the myriad transformations of the cosmos. To that vision we must hold until what is at first a mere intellectual apprehension is transferred to subconsciousness and begins to have its effect as an auto-suggestion. All this time it will seem to us that we are making an effort of our own wills, yet we must continually remind ourselves that the seeming is not reality.

It would be futile, and dishonest, to pretend that this is easy. It is anything but that. But where in our lessons have you found any intimation that you would be shown an easy way? The magician cannot be a weakling. He has to develop his spiritual muscles by hard exercise. In ancient times, before the aspirant was permitted to know a tithe of what has been told you in this curriculum, he had to meet trials and tests that few of us would have courage to face.

No, the work which must be done in order to transform the average sense-bound, illusion-fettered human being into a magician is not easy. It cannot be made easy. What is to be remembered, however, is that when this work has been done, everything that seems difficult to the average person _is_ easy for the magician.

A magician is what the Chinese philosopher, Lao-Tze, called the "possessor of Tao." This is how he described the way to come into possession of Tao, in the chapter of the Tao-Teh-King entitled "Going Home:"

"Having emptied yourself of everything, remain where you are."
"All things spring forth into activity with one accord, and whither do we see them return?"
"After blossoming for a while, everything dies down to its root."
"This going back to one's origin is called peace; it is the giving of oneself over to the inevitable."
"This giving of oneself over to the inevitable is called preservation."
"He who knows this preservation is called enlightened."
"He who knows it not continues in misery."
"He who knows this preservation is great of soul."
"He who is great of soul is prevailing."
"Prevailing, he is a king."
"Being a king, he is celestial."
"Being celestial, he is of Tao."
"Being of Tao, he endures forever; for though his body perish, yet he suffers no hurt."

This is the sacrifice that the altar represents – this giving of oneself over to the inevitable. Throughout these lessons our effort has been to make clear the truth that surrender to the cosmic order, that sacrifice of the illusion of separate personality must come to every human being sooner or later upon the Path of Return. The illusion that we can do anything of ourselves is our only adversary. The failure which results from this illusion is the only sin.

In the earlier part of this lesson we have tried to show you that the cubical altar is the symbol of the coordination of the magician's life with the rhythms of the cosmos. That coordination demands surrender, demands the sacrifice of the childish error that we can "go it alone."

But it is no use to multiply words. Either you will accept this teaching and do all that you can to live it, or you will go about seeking for some other way. Sooner or later, though, the unfoldment of the Life-Power's special work in you will bring you to the point where you will understand and accept this way--the only way to freedom, the only way to preservation.

And then you will understand why the cubical altar of sacrifice is also the work-table of the magician. Then, too, will you see that the same symbol which stands for the surrender of personality is also--by the creative mathematics of the cosmos – the symbol of the preservative Salt, which crystallizes in perfect cubes.

For that which is at once liberation and preservation is the understanding and living of truth. That is perfect coordination and symmetry. That is enlightenment. That is the consciousness which makes a human being "great of soul," that is, what Theosophists call a Mahatma, or a master.

This, in part, is what the altar of ceremonial magic symbolizes. In part, we say, because we have by no means exhausted the significance of this simple geometrical solid.

In the next lesson you will learn more about it, and about the other four regular solids. For, while the occult interpretation of these bodies may seem to be somewhat remote from the subject of magic, it does help to awaken the magical consciousness, which is, primarily, the understanding of the unity and order of the cosmos. Thus we feel that a discussion of the properties and meaning of the Platonic or Pythagorean solids, which were held in high esteem by the schools of theurgy in former times, has its proper place in this course of lessons on the theory of magic.

Platonic Solids

Because the purpose of the Magic of L.V.X. is primarily to develop in the magician a vivid realization of his place in the cosmic order, whatever will tend to deepen or broaden one's mental grasp of the fact that this is truly an orderly cosmos, wherein nothing whatever happens by chance, helps to strengthen the magical consciousness. As you have read in other lessons of this series, ceremonials are of little avail unless they are backed up by knowledge, will and courage. The more, then, you know about the cosmic order, the better will you be able to discern your relation to it.

The purpose of this lesson, therefore, is not merely to make you familiar with the ancient esoteric meaning of the five Platonic solids. We hope, by setting these facts and some of their meanings before you, to intensify your magical consciousness.

The following description of the Platonic solids is taken from Nature's Harmonic Unity by Samuel Colman, N.A. (pp. 14 to 17).

"The Greeks, long before the Christian era, discovered that there could be but five regular solid bodies, or polyhedra, three of these formed by the use of the equilateral triangle, one based upon the square of 90°, and one upon the regular pentagon, which forms we shall now analyze as set forth by Euclid.

"The simplest regular polygon is the equilateral triangle, and since each apex of an equilateral triangle is an angle of 60°, three such triangles can be combined to form a polyhedral angle. It is seen, then, that a regular polyhedron can be formed, bounded by equilateral triangles and having three at each vertex. This has four faces, and is called a tetrahedron. (See fig. A) Since four angles of 60° are less than four right angles, four equilateral triangles can be combined to form a polyhedral angle and it is seen, then, that a regular polyhedron can be formed, bounded by equilateral triangles, and having four at each vertex. There is such a regular polyhedron. It has eight faces and is called a regular octahedron. (Fig. B) Since five angles of 60° are less than four right angles, five equilateral triangles can be combined to form a polyhedral angle, and it is seen then that a regular polyhedron can be formed, bounded by equilateral triangles and having five each vertex. There is such a regular polyhedron. It has twenty faces and is called the regular icosahedron. (Fig. C) No regular polyhedron bounded by equilateral triangles had having more than five at each vertex is possible, for six or more angles of 60° are equal to or exceed four right angles, and cannot form a polyhedral angle.

The regular polyhedron next in order of simplicity to those formed by the equilateral triangle is the polyhedron formed by the square, each of whose angles is a right angle. Three right angles can be combined to form a polyhedral angle. It is seen then that a regular polyhedron can be formed, bounded by squares, three at each vertex. There is such a polyhedron. It has six faces, and is called a cube or regular hexahedron. (Fig. D) No regular polyhedron bounded by squares and having more than three at each vertex is possible, for four or more right angles cannot form a polyhedral angle.

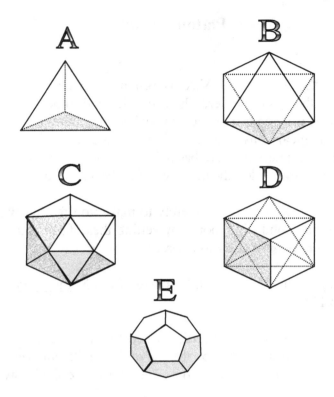

FIGURE 4A — THE POLYHEDRA

"The next regular polyhedron is that formed by the use of the pentagon, each of whose angles contains 108°. Three angles of 108° each can be combined to form a polyhedral angle. It is seen then that a regular polyhedron can be formed, bounded by regular pentagons and having three at each vertex. There is such a regular polyhedron. It has twelve faces and is called the dodecahedron. (Fig. E) No regular polyhedron having more than three angles of 108° at each vertex is possible. These five polyhedra, the tetrahedron, the octahedron, the icosahedron, the hexahedron, and the dodecahedron are the only ones possible.

"It would be well for the serious student to construct models of these five figures in order fully to comprehend their meaning. This can be done easily and with perfect accuracy by drawing on cardboard the following outlines, cutting them out and gluing the edges. It may easily be seen by examination that the square, the pentagon, and the hexagon by its equilateral triangle, are all that appear to the eye in regarding them. This trinity of forms is now disclosed to be harmonic with all five of the polyhedra and they are therefore all that are necessary in an analysis of proportional spaces, excepting the Egyptian triangle with the angles of 38° 30' and 50° 30' and the ideal angles of 42° and 48° which will be considered later."

The patterns referred to in this quotation will be found on the next page. They should be somewhat enlarged for convenience in construction, and the student who succeeds in making good models of the polyhedra will find himself amply repaid for his trouble.

Assuming that the boundary lines of these patterns are all composed of units of the same length (although they are not so represented in the patters given below), the pattern of the tetrahedron will

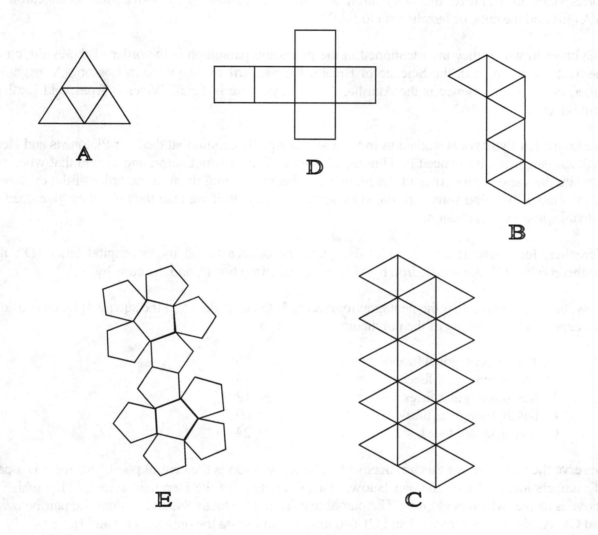

FIGURE 4B – CONSTRUCTION OF POLYHEDRA

have a perimeter of 6 units, that of the cube 14 units, that of the octahedron 10 units, that of the dodecahedron 38 units, and that of the icosahedron 22 units. Each of these numbers is significant to students of the Ageless Wisdom. We need not elaborate upon the significance of 6, 10, 14 or 22. 38 refers by Gematria to אזל, moving one thing through another, spinning; גלה, to uncover, to lay a thing open, to reveal; חל, wall, rampart; לח, new, unused. These meanings are particularly related to the esoteric meaning of the dodecahedron, and we shall explain them presently.

The sum of the numbers 6, 10, 14, 22 and 38 is 90, and its Gematria is given in Lesson 9A, Page 227.

Pythagoras, and Plato after him, together with the Neo-Platonic and Neo-Pythagorean schools (to which we are indebted for so much of our knowledge of the Ageless Wisdom), ascribed special properties to each of the regular polyhedra. In these schools it was taught that the dodecahedron corresponds to ETHER, the octahedron to AIR, the tetrahedron to FIRE, the icosahedron to WATER and the cube or hexahedron to EARTH.

The order in which they are mentioned in the preceding paragraph is the order of the evolution of the Tattvas, as given in the Science of Breath, the Sanskrit work quoted in Lesson 4A, page 54. Ether, or the Quintessence is the Akasha, Air is Vayu, Fire is Tejas, Water is Apas, and Earth is Prithivi. (See Figure 4A)

We know that Pythagoras studied in India, and it is equally certain that the Neo-Platonists and Neo-Pythagoreans were influenced by Hindu philosophy. Thus it is not surprising to find that when we tabulate the various properties of the regular polyhedra, keeping them in the order of the evolution of the Tattvas, we find some striking symmetries which will, if we take the hints they give, lead to valuable practical conclusions.

Hereafter, for convenience, we shall designate the dodecahedron by the capital letter "D", the octahedron by "O", the tetrahedron by "T", the icosahedron by "I", and the cube by "C".

Now, bearing in mind that the pentagon represents 5, the triangle 3 and the square 4, let us consider one aspect of the meaning of the polyhedra.

D.	has 12 pentagonal faces	$= 2 \times 5$	$= 60$
O.	has 8 triangular faces	$= 8 \times 3$	$= 24$
T.	has 4 triangular faces	$= 4 \times 3$	$= 12$
I.	has 20 triangular faces	$= 20 \times 3$	$= 60$
C.	has 6 square faces	$= 6 \times 4$	$= 24$

Observe the symmetry of this arrangement. The tetrahedron is the central point. Above it is a pair of numbers identical with the pair below. This reminds us of the Hermetic axiom, "That which is above is as that which is below." The pair above (D and O) totals 84, and so does the pair below (I and C). Again, the extremes (D and C) also total 84, and so do the opposites (O and I).

The symmetry of the arrangement is striking, but it also points to some very extraordinary conclusions, if we apply the mathematical rule that "things equal to the same thing are equal to each other." For then, since D and I, which represent Akasha and Apas, or the Quintessence and Water, or the Unmanifest and Subconsciousness, are both represented by the number 60, the implication is that Akasha and Apas, Ether and Water, the Unmanifest and Subconsciousness are aspects of the same thing. We may sum this up by saying that the universal, unmanifested reality is identical with the cosmic subconsciousness, and this is a direct echo of Hindu teaching, for we read in Sanskrit works numerous passages like the following:

"She who is pure, etrenal Mulaprakriti (root-matter) is Parabrahman itself and the Devata We (the supreme triad of Hinduism, Brahma, Vishnu and Shiva) worship."

Thus it is that we find the unmanifested Reality compared over and over again to a great ocean, implying that its nature is like Water.

In like manner, because both the octahedron and the cube are represented by the number 24, we may look for an identity between Vayu and Prithivi, Air and Earth, superconsciousness and "matter manifested." This identity is hinted at by the Western symbols for Air and Earth, which are identical in form, but opposite in position. It is also suggested by this passage from the Sepher Yetzirah:

"He created from the formless and made the non-existent exist; and he formed large columns out of intangible air." (Chapter 2, paragraph 6).

At first this may seem difficult to grasp, but it is scientifically true. The property of Vayu, say the Hindus, is motion, and that of Prithivi is cohesion. Cohesion is the result of motion, and just as the root-substance of air is electrons, since the atmosphere is made of molecules of gases composed of atoms, so are electrons the basis of all the solider forms that we call earth.

In like manner, that which we experience through the senses as matter is identical with that which we know in superconsciousness. And here we are very close to the knowledge which becomes fully unfolded in the magical consciousness, the knowledge which overcomes the illusions of appearance, and makes it possible for us to perform works of power firmly established upon our knowledge of reality.

The tetrahedron corresponds to the number 12, which is one-seventh of 84. This suggests that a seven-fold expression of the universal FIRE or Fohat or Astral Light, is represented by all the pairs of elements whose combinations, as represented by the polyhedra, give the total of 84. These combinations are: ETHER and AIR (D and O), ETHER and EARTH (D and C), AIR and WATER (O and I), and WATER and EARTH (I and C), four in all. 4 x 84 = 336, and 336 = 3 x 7 x 16. The sum of these factors of 336 is 3 + 7 + 16 = 26, the number of יהוה.

Since ETHER and WATER are both represented by 60, or 5 times the number of FIRE, we may regard ETHER and WATER as being in some sense a fivefold manifestation of FIRE.

Since AIR and EARTH are represented by 24, or 2 x 12, we may regard them as corresponding to each other, and as being each a duplication, or twofold manifestation of FIRE.

Another table shows the same correspondences, but based on different facts.

> D. (ETHER) has 30 edges
> O. (AIR) has 12 edges
> T. (FIRE) has 6 edges
> I. (WATER) has 30 edges
> C. (EARTH) has 12 edges

Again, the points of the dodecahedron are the same in number as the faces of the icosahedron. Similarly, the points of the octahedron are the same in number as the faces of the cube. Vice versa, the faces of the dodecahedron are equal to the points of the icosahedron, while the faces of the octahedron are equal in number to the points of the cube.

Here is another table, showing the same correspondences, but enabling us to compare the solids by means of the numbers derived from adding together the numbers of the points, lines and faces of each figure:

	Points		Lines		Faces		Total
D.	20	+	30	+	12	=	62
O.	6	+	12	+	8	=	26
T.	4	+	6	+	4	=	14
I.	12	+	30	+	20	=	62
C.	8	+	12	+	6	=	26

TABLE 4A

Here the solids representing ETHER and AIR, AIR and WATER, WATER and EARTH, and EARTH and ETHER give 88 as the sum of the numbers representing each pair. The number 88 is connected with the Pi-proportion and with the Great Pyramid. It is the number representing the circumference of a circle having a radius of 14, because 14 radius = 28 diameter, and 28 x 3 1/7 = 88, which is the circumference number of the circle of Assiah, as explained in Lesson 2 D. 88 is also the number of units around the base of the Great Pyramid, if the height of that structure be reckoned as 14, the number which corresponds to the tetrahedron, or FIRE in the table above.

Note also that in this table 62 and 26 are not only complementary, as being the component numbers of 88, but they are formed by the same digits, so that one is the reflection, as it were, of the other.

By reducing the numbers shown in the preceding table, we arrive at the following:

$$D = 62 = 6 + 2 = 8$$
$$O = 26 = 2 + 6 = 8$$
$$T = 14 = 1 + 4 = 5$$

$$I = 62 = 6 + 2 = 8$$
$$C = 26 = 2 + 6 = 8$$
$$8 + 8 + 5 + 8 + 8 = 37$$

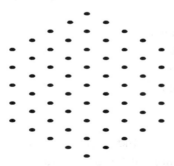

FIGURE 4C – PROJECTION OF CUBE

Thus the number 37 is the sum of the least numbers of the five numbers which represent the geometrical properties of the Pythagorean solids. The digits of 37 are the digits which particularly correspond to the Tree of Life, which has 3 Supernal and 7 Inferior Sephiroth.

Now, if we represent the cube of 4 x 4 x 4, which is built up from 64 small cubes, by a series of points showing the symmetric aspect of that cube in flat projection, the resulting diagram will be what is shown here.

Each point represents one of the 64 constituent cubes in the great cube, and none of these lesser cubes 37 are visible. <u>No more than 37 can be seen at any one time.</u>

The whole 64 stand for Truth, because the Greek word ΑΛΗΘΕΙΑ=64, and thus 37 may be taken to symbolize the revealed or manifested truth.

The reason that this is important is that the Gnosis of the New Testament books indicates, beyond reasonable doubt, that their writers understood the significance of the cube in question. Frederick Bligh Bond, after years of investigation, has made lists of the names, epithets and types of Christ which are multiples of 37. In one of the books written by him in conjunction with T.S. Lea, (their names are given in Lesson 1D) he gives more than a hundred examples. In another book he gives more than 500 Greek words and phrases, used in the New Testament, which correspond by Gematria to 2368, or 37 x 64, which is the number of ΙΗΣΟΥΣ ΧΡΙΣΤΟΣ, Jesus Christ. By the mere operation of the law of averages, something like three percent of all the words or phrases in the New Testament would be multiples of 37, but as Dr. Lea says, "when a large collection exhibits peculiarities for which the doctrine of Chance cannot wholly account, then other causes must be looked for and will probably be discovered."

The root-word from which all these New Testament appellations of Jesus Christ are derived is Hebrew, the proper name H B L, Abel, which is derived from a verb spelt with the same letters, meaning, "to breathe, to wave." Thus the root-meaning is that of the rhythmic motion of the life-breath.

The same noun is used again and again in Ecclesiastes, being translated "vanity" in our English Bibles. The real meaning is "transientness," or "transitoriness." Thus when the Preacher says, "Vanity of vanities, all is vanity," he is saying just what Omar puts thus:

> "The worldly hope men set their hearts upon
> Turns ashes--or it prospers; and anon,
> Like snow upon the desert's dusty face,
> Lighting a little hour or two--is gone."

These are not the accents of despair. They are the wise man's recognition of the fact that all external conditions are fluid, that everything as Heracleitus said, "is becoming, so that a man cannot bathe twice in the same stream." The idea is ominous and sorrowful for those who have believed in the permanence of things, in the importance of the world's standards of success, in the reality of appearances.

They tell us, indeed, that we shall find no permanent happiness in the world of transient forms, in the phantasmagoria of the appearances of the One Reality. We must find THAT which is behind these appearances if we would have a treasure that nothing can destroy. But there is another aspect of this truth. When it is understood that every condition is impermanent, that the external world is plastic and fluidic, that the law of transition is at work in every detail of our environment, the first step has been taken on the path which leads finally to absolute and magical mastery. It is when the imagination is set free from the belief in the permanence of Name and Form that the ground is made ready for the mustard-seed of conviction which develops into the great tree of confident expectation. So long as you believe in the permanence of mountains, you cannot have faith to move them; but when you see that they are mere temporary waves upon the ocean of ETHER, perhaps your belief that they may be moved will take form as the invention of a new high explosive.

But there is an esoteric meaning to this word HBL, behind the dictionary definition. "H" or Heh is the Hebrew definite article "the." בל is a combination of letters which has several meanings. BL is the negative adverb, NOT, equivalent in meaning to LA, which you will remember as the metathesis of AL, strength. It refers to the truth that all things are transitory expressions of the STRENGTH אל which is NOT-anything. בל, again, is the Aramaic word for "heart", and originally it meant, "courage, or strength." בל is also a contraction for BOL, meaning master or Lord. Thus הבל may be read as the (H) No-thing, the Lord, whose strength is the heart or core of all things בל. Again, בל is 32, so that הבל may be read Qabalistically as "The Thirty-two" referring to the complete manifestation of the 32 paths of the Tree of Life.

Now, the fact that the key-number to all the dimensions of the polyhedra is 37, coupled with the fact that this is the key-number of hundreds of names and epithets of Jesus in the New Testament means that liberation from bondage to conditions is the outcome of the realization that all things are transitory, that whatever exists is the temporary self-expression of the power of THAT which is No-Thing. For we must remember always that the very name "Jesus" means "liberation," that it is synonymous in significance with the Hindu word "mukti," and that the whole purport of the teaching of the New Testament is completely misunderstood if we lose sight of the fact that it aims to develop in those who grasp and apply it a truly magical consciousness.

Priestcraft has done its best to conceal the truth. Yet at Christmas-time we read again the story of the visit of the Wise Men, guided by their knowledge of astrology to the birth-place of the Liberator. And not even the effrontery of priestcraft, despite all its false teaching that man is a worm of the dust, has been equal to the suppression of the words which definitely establish the magical quality of the Master's teaching:

"And these signs shall follow them that believe: in my name shall they cast out devils; they shall speak with new tongues; they shall take up serpents, and if they drink any deadly thing, it shall in no wise hurt them; they shall lay hands on the sick, and they shall recover."
The belief, the conviction, which finally leads to such mighty works has its roots in the knowledge that all the conditions of human environment are expressions of an invisible, impalpable Reality, which can only be designated by negatives. The "miracles" of this One Thing which is No-Thing are partially interpreted by materialistic science. But our laboratory researchers cannot get at the heart of the phenomena they observe so patiently and accurately. What is missing? They do not see that all these transformations of electro-magnetic energy which they are so busy cataloguing and reducing to formulae are brought about by the mental activity of the One Power whose outward vesture is that same energy. They do not perceive that the whole cosmos is the IDEATION of the Life-Power.

The last few pages may seem to you to have been a long digression from the subject of the Lesson. What has all this to do with the polyhedra? Quite a good deal. For in the symbolism of the Ageless Wisdom one of these figures is a constantly recurring type of the perfection of the cosmic order. The cube furnished the pattern for the Holy of Holies in the Jewish Tabernacle and Temple, is the New Testament symbol of the New Jerusalem, and was the symbol of Hermes among the Greeks. We are now familiar with the fact that this figure represents יהוה by the sum of its points, lines and faces (as does also the Octahedron). In Hebrew tradition, moreover, it is said that Solomon's Temple was built of cubical blocks, measuring nine units every way, just as does the cube which is the basis of construction for the Vault of Brother C. R. in the Rosicrucian allegory which describes that Vault as "a compendium of the universe." Thus we know that one of the polyhedra, at least, is widely employed to symbolize the perfection of the manifestation of that cosmic order which, in greater detail, is summed up in the properties of all five regular solids.

Now, in a work of Rhabanus Maurus 'de laudibus Sanctae Crucis', there is a plate wherein the Nimbus of Jesus has the letters A. M. Ω., signifying the beginning, Middle and End. These letters, written in their primitive forms give us the outlines of the tetrahedron, the octahedron and the cube, thus:

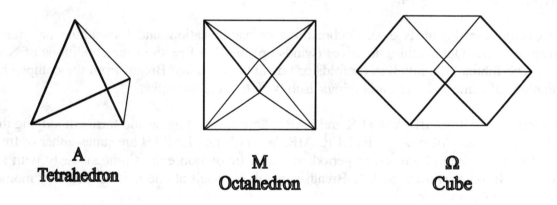

A
Tetrahedron

M
Octahedron

Ω
Cube

FIGURE 4D – AMΩ (primitive form)

Thus, it is evident that behind the esoteric doctrines of Christianity there is hidden an esoteric doctrine, for when we find New Testament titles of the Liberator repeating over and over again the number which synthesizes the properties of the polyhedra, when we find an old Christian writer using symbols that represent FIRE (tetrahedron) as the ALPHA or Beginning, AIR (Spirit) as the mediating principle (Octahedron), and EARTH (cube) as the End, or manifestation, and when, too, we find the opening words of the Fourth Gospel repeating Platonic and Pythagorean philosophy, we must be blind if we do not see that the real Christianity is inseparable from the stream of the Ageless Wisdom which preceded it. It is a truly magical doctrine, aiming at magical results, and accomplishing them (as was said in the first of these Lessons) by the employment of magical words of power.

See now the agreement between the association of the letter ALPHA with the tetrahedron and FIRE, and the older Qabalistic doctrine you have learned from previous lessons. The Sepher Yetzirah says that FIRE corresponds to the Holy Letter, Shin, which is called "holy" because its number, 300, is the value of the words רוח אלהים, <u>Ruach Elohim</u>, the Life-Breath of the Gods. The Sepher Yetzirah assigns this Ruach also to Aleph, and Aleph is identical with ALPHA. Thus in Hebrew as in Christian symbolism the Beginning of manifestation is associated with FIRE, symbolized by the tetrahedron.

From the Table 4A, it is evident that the number 14 is the key-number of the tetrahedron, and to a Qabalist this immediately suggests the name דוד, David, or LOVE, and thus links up the ideas of Beginning and Creative FIRE with that of the attraction between complements which pervades all existence. But this is an aspect we may pass for the time. We shall pass, too, all the interesting deductions which might be drawn from the fact that 14 is the diameter number of the Creative World, as explained in Lesson 2 D. What we wish now to emphasize is that 14 is a numerical representation of the movement of the cosmic Life-Breath.

Traditionally the Elohim אלהים are the seven spirits of God. Thus Ruach Elohim may be understood as "Life-Breath of the Seven." (Incidentally, this fact as well as tradition, for the cosmic breath has seven aspects). Therefore, because breathing consists of two movements, inspiration and exhalation (with a pause between them, which is not a movement, but a cessation of motion), the idea of breathing is numerically represented by 2. Hence the motion of the sevenfold Cosmic Breath may be represented as 2 x 7 = 14.

The Cosmic Fire-breath is dual, Outbreathing or manifestation, and Inbreathing or return to the unmanifest. The Outbreathing involves (winds up) the Fire-Breath in the conditions of Name and Form. The Inbreathing involves (unfolds or unwinds) that same Breath from the complexities and limitations of name and form, and brings itself back to the Unmanifest.

All states of ETHER, AIR, WATER and EARTH are states of name and form embodying the FIRE of the Life-Breath. All states of ETHER, AIR, WATER and EARTH are states either of Involution or of Evolution, and at any given period, states of Involution exist simultaneously with states of Evolution. In other words, the Life-Breath is involving itself at one point at the very moment it is evolving itself at another.

The symbol of this is the turning wheel or ROTA, and in previous lessons you have learnt that R.O.T.A. in Hebrew letters adds up to 671, (another 14), which may be represented in our alphabet by A.O.M. (reckoning final M as 600). Of this A.O.M. the Hindu Pranava AUM is a variant, and so is the A.M.O. (mega), that has been studied in this lesson.

It will not escape you, either, that A.M.O. is the spelling of LOVE in Latin[2], so that the word which makes 671=14 in Hebrew utilizes the letters that spell LOVE in the later tongue of science, but has a numeral value which is the number of LOVE (DVD) in Hebrew, and the number also of the tetrahedron.

The name Elohim also points at the same thing. Its total numeration is 86 = 8 + 6 = 14. This 14 also reduces to 5, the number of the polyhedra, and of the elements and Tattvas. (Note, too, that 14 expresses numerally the idea of the manifestation of ORDER (4) through unity (1)). And each letter

---

[2] Ed. note: AMO = "I love", "Love" = AMOR (noun) or AME (imperative).

of ALHIM corresponds to one of the elements, thus:

> A: letter of Ruach, really ETHER (D)
> L: letter of Libra, therefore AIR (O)
> H: letter of Aries, therefore FIRE (T)
> I: letter of Virgo, therefore EARTH (C)
> M: letter of the element of WATER (I)

The order of the elements in this word is the order of the evolution of the Tattvas, except that the last two are reversed. FIRE is central, ETHER and AIR are above, and WATER and EARTH are below. The purport is evident.

Nor should we overlook the significance of the number 86, which is the value of Elohim. It represents the expression of RECIPROCATION, interchange, and the like (6) through the RHYTHM, periodicity, and alternation represented by 8. Thus, from another angle we arrive at the very same idea that the Life-Breath is a rhythmic pulsation of Evolution and Involution.

There is another detail about the polyhedra which we must take into consideration. Three have faces formed from equilateral triangles, one has faces formed from the square, and one has pentagonal faces. The triangle is the number 3, the square the number 4 and the pentagon the number 5, so that in the construction of the polyhedra we find once more the familiar numbers of the old Egyptian triangle of Osiris (3), Isis (4) and Horus (5). The sum of the squares on the three sides of this triangle is 50 ($3^2 + 4^2 + 5^2$) and 50 is the number of the faces of the polyhedra and also the number of their points or verticles. Thus we find the basic numbers of the triangle in the construction of these Platonic solids. Furthermore, the angle formed by the lines of Osiris and Isis is the angle of 90°, and this angle's numeral value is represented by the total number of edges in the polyhedra, which is also 90.

The polyhedra with triangular faces represent AIR, FIRE and WATER, and they correspond to Osiris, or 3. That which represents EARTH corresponds to ISIS, or 4. That which typifies ETHER corresponds to Horus, or 5. Osiris is a sun-god (Fire), a Nile-god (Water), and, as careful examination of Egyptian myth will show, an atmosphere god also (Air). Isis typifies Mother Earth. Horus, son of Osiris and Isis, represents the Ruach, or ETHER, which is the Quintessence, or fifth essence, of the alchemists.

We hardly expect you to see the force of some of these details at first reading. The reason that this lesson on the polyhedra has been introduced at this point is to show that there is a thread of connection between the mystery symbols of Egypt, India, the Neo-Platonists and Christianity. In these days when the land is filled with the disputes of jarring sects, the fact seems to be forgotten that Christianity is essentially a magical religion, that its aims are precisely the same as those of the older faiths which preceded it.

One of our aims is to revive this fundamental aspect of Christianity. And although all this xplanation of numbers and geometry may seem to be very complex (and to many readers, perhaps, more or less far-fetched) we know from experience that the contemplation of these mathematical truths will lead the mind at last to a deeper perception of the hidden symmetries of the cosmic plan. The real meaning of what lies behind all this strange symbolism is simple enough. Everything that exists is an appearance of a single reality. All the appearances are transitory. None has permanence. For the knower of Self, therefore, no obstacle is insuperable, no condition unalterable, no limitation so fixed that it cannot be overcome.

But the mere assertion of this truth is not enough. The Emerald Table advises us to separate the subtle from the gross, the fixed from the volatile with great ingenuity. That is, we must devise as many means as we can to help us in the work of distinguishing the Permanent or Real from the Impermanent or Apparent.

The study of the mathematical properties and correspondences of the polyhedra is one such application of ingenuity. Many others are required in order to overcome the hypnotism of those volatile, ephemeral conditions of Name and Form which seem to us so fixed and unyielding. It is not that these manifold symbols have any magical power of their own. That is not why you are asked to become familiar with their esoteric meaning. The value of this kind of study is that it exercises a power of the mind which is not properly developed by our modern methods of schooling. From the perception of the symbolic correspondences between the letters of the alphabet of nature the mind is led to the realization of the unity which is veiled behind the multiplicity of appearances.

This is the important thing to grasp, and this is the really valuable result of the study of comparative symbology. At first one seems to be lost in a maze of strange signs and emblems, but finally comes the realization which Eckhartshausen expresses in The Cloud Upon the Sanctuary, when he writes:

"As infinity in numbers loses itself in the unit which is their basis, and as the innumerable rays of a circle are united in a single centre, so it is also with the Mysteries; their hieroglyphics and infinitude of emblems have the object of exemplifying but one single truth. He who knows this has found the key to understand everything, and all at once... He who has discovered this way possesses everything therein; all wisdom in one book alone, all strength in one force, every beauty in a single object, all riches in one treasure only, every happiness in one perfect felicity."

Magical Instruments and Vestments

In ceremonial magic four principle implements are employed: the Wand, the Cup, the Sword and the Pentacle. These implements are represented by the four suits of the Tarot, and what you have already learnt concerning the symbolism of those suits should prepare you to understand the further developments set forth in this lesson.

Eliphas Levi gives the following description of the magic wand, a description full of blinds, but one which contains many clues to the real significance of this implement:

"The magic rod, which must not be confused with the simple divining rod, nor with the fork of the necromancers, nor with the trident of Paracelsus, the true and absolute magic rod, must be a single and perfectly straight beam of the almond or hazel tree, but by a single blow with the magic pruning-knife, or golden sickle, before the sun rises, and at the moment when the tree is about to blossom. It must be longitudinally perforated without splitting or breaking it, and a needle of magnetized iron, occupying its whole length, must be introduced; then a polyhedral prism triangularly out (that is, a tetrahedron), must be fitted to one of its ends, and to the other a similar figure of black resin. In the middle of the rod must be placed two rings, one of red copper, the other of zinc; the rod must be gilt on the side of the resin, and silvered on the side of the prism up to the central rings, and it must be wrapped in silk to the extremities exclusively. On the copper ring must be engraved these characters ירושלים הקדשה = (596 + 414 = 1010), and on the zinc one המלך שלמה (=95 + 375 = 470). The consecration of the rod should last seven days, beginning at the new moon, and should be made by an initiate possessing the great Arcanum, and himself having a consecrated rod. This is the transmission of the magical priesthood, which has never ceased since the misty origin of the transcendent science. The rod and other instruments, but the rod above all, must be carefully hidden, and under no pretext should the magus permit it to be seen or touched by the profane; otherwise it will lose all its virtue. The manner of transmitting the rod is one of the secrets of science which it is never permitted to reveal. The length of the magic rod should not exceed that of the operator's arm; the magician should never use it except when alone, and should not even handle it unnecessarily. Many ancient magi made it only the length of the forearm, and concealed it beneath their long mantles, showing the simple divining rod only in public, or some allegorical scepter made of ivory or ebony, according to the nature of their operations. The magic rod is the Verendum of the magis, he should not so much as refer to it in any clear and precise was; no one should boast of having it, and the secret of its consecration should be transmitted on condition of absolute confidence and discretion alone." The Mysteries of Magic, p. 206 (Parentheses are ours.)

Even a cursory reading of this description ought to be sufficient to show that it is not intended to be taken literally. But the clues to the real meaning are abundant.

In the first place, the material of the wand is to be the wood either of the almond or hazel, and both these trees are symbolic of the power of Kether. The almond about to blossom refers to Kether itself. The hazel is especially attributed to the Moon, and so to the path of the letter Gimel, which proceeds from Kether. The rod must be a single, straight beam. It must be cut with a single blow. Note the emphasis on the idea of singleness or concentration.

In Hebrew the almond is שקד (=404), and the name refers to the earliness of its flowers and fruit. The derivation is from a verb spelt with the same letters, which means 1) to hasten away; 2) to be zealous, to be eager for or intent upon something; to attend carefully. These ideas, as you can see, are directly connected with Kether, because Kether is the first, or earliest of the Sephiroth, and because it therefore represents the first awakening of the Life-Power into activity at the dawn of the Cosmic Day.

By Gematria, שקד corresponds to קדש, sacred, (which is a transposition of the letters) and to דת, a law, edict or commandment. These words represent the outgoing affirmative quality of the primal Will of Kether. The last is particularly interesting because it combines the letters of Venus (D) and Saturn (Tv) and so indicates that the Law is an expression of the creative imagination (D) in activities leading to concrete, specialized results.

The alternative wood, hazel, is named לוז (=43), and this was the name of the place where Jacob is said to have had the dream of angels ascending and descending a ladder. לוז is also a verb whose primitive meaning is "to turn away, to deviate." Later connotations include the idea of forwardness and perversity; and these have a bearing upon later meaning of the path of the letter Gimel. For that path is the path of the Moon, and it is the symbol of the departure of the energy from Kether on its way down to Tiphareth. This departure, descent, or involution is, as we have tried to make clear throughout these lessons, the cause of all limitations and "evils" on which account the feminine principle represented by the moon has always been designated in the books of the wise as the cause of the "Fall".

Corresponding to לוז by Gematria are גדול, which means "great" in a wide variety of applications-- great in mass or size (weighty, important); great in vehemence (violent); in dignity (authority); in eminence (distinguished). To a Qabalist, therefore, LVZ would suggest intense power and value, so that it is symbolically representative of the potency ascribed to the magic rod. Another word which corresponds to לוז by Gematria is חלה, Challah, which is interpreted by Qabalists as representing the Shekinah, or divine agency through which God rules the world. This Shekinah (which Qabalistic Rabbis call the cohabiting glory) is in every respect the same as what the Hindus call Shakti, the feminine power which is the Mulaprakriti and working principle in all things. חלה, as corresponding to this power and to לוז, represents the intermediary power between the Primal Will and its manifestations. That power, on the Tree of Life, is represented by the UNITING INTELLIGENCE of the 13th path, and to this path both the almond שקד and the hazel לוז are attributed. The magic rod, therefore, is to be made of a single beam of this UNITING INTELLIGENCE, that is to say, is to the fashioned from a single ray, or one particular specialized expression of the power which descends from Kether through the 13th path.

Notice, too, that all these words referring to hazel wood are represented by the number 43. They therefore direct our thought to something which combines growth and augmentation (3) with order and regulation (4). And the words which correspond to שקד, or 404 are designated by a number which shows the essential order (4) of the Limitless Light (0) expressing itself in the regulation of all things (4). These ideas, of course, are directly related to the notion of magic power expressed by the rod.

The prototype of the magical rod is described in the Bible as being of almond wood (Numbers 17). This was the rod of Aaron, the first High Priest of Israel, whose name means "enlightened or lofty".

The needle of magnetized iron represents the Mars-force, or Rajasic energy of desire which must animate the volition of the magus.

The two prisms refer to the fire-power symbolized by the tetrahedron. One is of crystal, representing the transmission of light. The other, of black resin, represents the absorption of light.

The rings in the middle of the rod are of copper and zinc. The red copper ring refers to Venus, and the zinc refers to Jupiter. The gilt at one end of the rod is a symbol of the sun. The silver at the other end is a symbol of the moon.

The Hebrew letters on the copper ring may be translated "Jerusalem the Holy". Note that their numeral value is a double 10. The letters on the ring of zinc may be translated "(The) King Solomon", or "(The) King of Peace". This name has the value of 470, which corresponds by Gematria to DVR DVRIM, a cycle of cycles, or eternity, so that we have here the essence of the idea which Levi expresses elsewhere when he says that a magician should work as if he had all eternity in which to complete his operation. The total value of these Hebrew letters is 1480, and this is the numeration of שבע שבתות, which is literally "Seven Sabbaths". Seven periods of seven days are forty-nine days, and this number 49, which is the square of seven, and so related to the powers of Venus, is one with which we meet constantly in works devoted to practical occultism. Note that its reduct is 13, and its least number 4. The same results come from the reduction of 1480, so that the Qabalistic treatment of the letters on the wand bring us at last to the consideration of Unity and Love (both represented by 13) and finally to the idea of Order, symbolized by 4.

Hence, no sooner has Levi mentioned these letters, than he tells us the consecration of the wand should take seven days. He follows this by a reference to the moon as being important in connection with the consecration, and we have seen that the hazel and almond both refer to the path of the Moon. This, too, is the 13th path, and the reduction of the total value of the Hebrew letters on the wand gives the number 13.

Furthermore, the very word "rod" in Hebrew is מט =49. Consider, too, what its letters mean. There is M, corresponding to the Hanged Man in the Tarot, and Th, the symbol of Fohat and of its direction, as represented by Strength in the same book of symbolic wisdom.

It is said that "the length of the rod should not exceed that of the operator's arm," to indicate that the extent of the aspiration, or one-pointed purpose which it symbolizes should not be out of his reach. It is called the Verendum, a Latin word synonymous with lingam or phallus, but having special reference to secrecy or privacy, because the immediate source of the power of any magician is actually the nerve-force ordinarily expressed through the organs of reproduction.

We have been at some pains to indicate the clues to the real meaning of Levi's description of the magic wand, because it is an excellent example of the way in which a writer well versed in symbolism can convey occult instruction for the initiated in terms which make apparent sense to the uninitiated.

What he is talking about is the magician's central, dominant purpose--the one particular tendency of the Life Power which he has set himself to realize. And he gives priceless practical instruction when he says that it must be kept carefully hidden, so that the profane may never touch or see it.

For the true rod of miracles in the ONE AIM which you have set yourself to realize in life. Keep it concealed. Do not talk about it. Do not handle it unnecessarily, even when alone, says Levi. This means that the ONE AIM must be kept sacred, that it must not be the subject of too much thought, above all, never of light or doubtful thought. The times when you dwell upon it should be times set apart for the very best that is in you.

This emphasis on secrecy is not to be lightly passed by. None may become a magician who cannot keep his own counsel. Your true, innermost purpose must come to you as an intimation from the highest Self, from that indivisible principle of unity, seated in Kether, which is names IChIDH, Jechidah. That Self is the "initiate possessing the Great Arcanum," and that Self already possesses a consecrated rod.

From that self alone may you learn the one high purpose for which you have entered into incarnation, and it is what happens when you receive this inner teaching that Levi means when he says, "The manner of transmitting the rod is one of the secrets of science which it is never permitted to reveal."

Now, in ordinary ceremonial, no such elaborate preparations are required. One magician of our acquaintance uses a common black wand with ivory tips, such as may be bought at the shops which deal in supplies for stage conjurors. This form of wand is excellent from the point-of-view of symbolism. The ivory tips are symbols of the elephant-god of India, Ganesha, the god of wisdom. The black body of the wand represents the hidden force of the magical will, and the secrecy which the magician must maintain concerning his one aim. The contrast of colors, black and white, serves the same symbolic purpose as the more elaborate symbolism of the wand described by Levi. For white is the synthesis of all colors, and black is the absorption of every hue. Consequently every aspect of color-vibration is included in this combination of black and white, which, moreover represents the combination of Will (Kether) and Understanding (Binah) since Kether is white and Binah is black. For each magician, the wand must represent all these ideas, plus the special aim or purpose which he has come to realize as a result of listening to the Voice of his innermost Self.

Every time the wand is used in ceremonial, it must be employed to make some gesture or other indication of the power descending through the path of Gimel from Kether. Hence it must invariably remind the magus of the eternal self-direction of the Life-Power toward the production of beautiful results, inasmuch as the path of Gimel ends in Tiphareth. Hence, in making rituals, one must be careful that the wand is used in the right places, and to represent the correct ideas, for otherwise the ceremonial will be more or less confused, and the auto-suggestive value will be lessened.

The prototype of the magic cup is the silver cup used by Joseph for divination. It is primarily a symbol of receptivity, in contrast to the wand, which, as representing the lingam, corresponds to the letter YOD, the archetypal world, and to the powers of Kether and Chokmah. The cup represents the second letter of IHVH, and this letter is assigned to Binah.

It should be made of crystal (which costs too much for ordinary students) or of glass. The preferable material is black glass, but when this cannot be procured, an ordinary glass goblet may be painted black, inside and out, and then varnished with some water-resisting substance. We recommend having this done by somebody who understands all about paints and their application to glass.

The reason the cup should be black is that it is intended to symbolize Binah, the sphere of Saturn. This is one reason, rather. Another is that black is the best color for a magic mirror or divining crystal, and the cup is sometimes used for this purpose.

A goblet of the shape shown here, which is not very unusual, will serve perfectly, after it has been painted black, and the whole cost will be well within the means of the average student.

It is used to contain the water of purification used in ceremonial work, and, as said before, for the kind of divination commonly known as crystal-gazing.

Around its base, in Hebrew letters, should be written the words בינה, אלהים and אימא.

**Figure 5A –
GOBLET**

Because the cup corresponds to Binah, it is the particular symbol of intuition, and its use in ceremonials has always to take this into account.

It contains the water of purification, and this water is the symbol of the Astral Fluid, or universal substance. Thus, in a sense, the cup represents the Great Sea of undifferentiated substance whence all forms are generated. And as a cup gives a temporary form to the water which is poured into it (so that if the water be frozen it takes the shape of the cup) this implement of the magician typifies the formative power of Understanding, with which we make our personal contact through intuition.

The cup is a symbol of receptivity, and as such represents the descending current from Kether which traverses the 12th path of the letter Beth. Into the cup of Binah, moreover, are poured the currents of the Life-Force from Chokmah, through the path of Daleth, the 14th path. Hence the water in the cup represents the mingling of the Primal Will with the Life-Force, but that mingling, we must remember, is also a mixture of the qualities of Mercury and Venus. For the 12th path which leads from Kether to Binah is tinged with the quality of Mercury, and is symbolized in the Tarot by the Magician. Thus it represents the volition and attention of the self-consciousness. And the life-force חיה, Chaiah which comes to Binah through the path of Daleth, is tinged with the Venusian quality represented by the Empress, who is subconsciousness as the generatrix of mental images.

Our magical cup then holds the impulses of the Primal Will, expressed as self-conscious attention to the facts of self-experience, and as intelligent classification of those facts, mingled with the life-force proceeding from Universal Wisdom, and expressed as mental imagery proceeding from the principles of that Wisdom.

This combination is what is symbolized by the water in the cup, and all the lustrations and other applications of that water refer to the paths proceeding from Binah. The first of these is the 17th path of Zain, and the other is the 18th path of Cheth. The 17th path is completed in Tiphareth. The 18th is completed in Geburah. The 17th, because it corresponds to Gemini, ruled by Mercury, carries and elaborates an influence which has its origin in the 12th path. The 18th, because it corresponds to the sign Cancer, ruled by the Moon and the exaltation of Jupiter, is a path in which the powers of the subconsciousness, represented by the path of Daleth, predominate. In ceremonial uses of the water in the cup, to produce the most satisfactory results, every emblematic employment of the fluid must express ideas connected with one of other or these two paths.

The magical sword is thus described by Levi:

"The sword is less occult, and must be made in the following manner: - It must be of pure steel with a copper handle made in the form of a cross with three pommels, as it is represented in the Enchiridion of Leo III, or else with two crescents for guard. On the middle knot of the guard, which should be covered with a gold plate, the sign of the Macrocosm must be engraved on one side, and that of the Microcosm on the other. On the Pommel must be inscribed the Hebrew monogram of Michael, as it is seen in Agrippa; the characters באילים יהוה סי במכה (93+26+50+67 = 236) must be engraved on one side, and on the other the monogram of Constantine's labarum with the following words, <u>Vince in hoc, Deo duce, comite ferro</u>. The consecration of the sword must take place on Sunday, in the hours of sunlight, under the invocation of Michael. The sword must be thrust into a fire of laurel and cypress wood; it must then be dried and polished with ashes of the sacred fire, moistened with the blood of the mole or serpent, these words being said: - <u>Sis mihi gladius Michaelis, in virtute Elohim Sabaoth fugiant a te spiritus tenebrarum et reptilia terrae</u>; it must then be perfumed with the perfumes of the Sun, and wrapped up in silk with branches of vervain[3], which must be burned on the seventh day."

The key to the understanding of this symbolic description is to be found in the fact that the sword is to be consecrated on Sunday, in the hours of sunlight, under the invocation of Michael. For Sunday, sunlight, and the Angel Michael all refer to the sixth Sephira, Tiphareth, to which Qabalists particularly assign the V or IHVH, and of this letter V, in this connection, the sword is the symbol.

Its steel blade represents Mars and the Sephirah Geburah. Its copper handle represents the Sephira which is the complement of Mars, namely, Netzach, sphere of Venus. The middle knot of the guard, with its gold plate, is the sixth Sephira, because gold is the metal corresponding to the sun. The sign of the Macrocosm is the six-pointed star or Hexagram, and the sign of the Microcosm is the five-pointed star, or Pentagram. They are combined in the sword, because this implement represents the personal (microcosmic) expression of universal (macrocosmic) powers. The Hebrew characters (which are printed with many typographical errors, here corrected, in Levi's book) may be freely rendered "In the powers of IHVH how shall there be defeat?" The Latin motto means, "I conquer in this, with God my guide, my sword my companion."

If you will study the diagram of the Tree of Life, you will see that from Kether to Tiphareth inclusive there are six Sephiroth. These are represented by the Hexagram, or seal of the Macrocosm. From Tiphareth to Malkuth inclusive there are five Sephiroth. These are represented by the pentagram, or seal of the Microcosm.

The successive numbers of the Hebrew words are also significant:

באילים = 93 = בני אל, Beni El, the sons of God; לבונה, frankincense, symbol of aspiration; מגן, a shield, used in Hebrew as emblem of God the Protector, and especially connected with the Hexagram, called מגן דוד, Mogun David or Shield of David; נחלה, possession, property, destiny,

---

[3] Ed note: also called Verbena.

fate; and TzBA, a host, and army (of which the plural, צבאות, Tzabaoth, is used in the divine names assigned to Netzach and Hod).

יהוה = 26, and the other words given under that number are to be found in the Qabalistic dictionary. It emphasizes the powers of the Self-Existent One.

מי = 50, and this refers to the Gates of Understanding, to the squares of the Pythagorean Triangle, and to the various words having the same number given in the Qabalistic dictionary.

במכה = 67 = a number also given in the dictionary, which is particularly referred to בינה, Understanding and זין, sword, the name of the seventh letter.

236, the sum of all these names, is the number of the Rabbinical word קומץ, which Knorr von Rosenroth translates as <u>Pagillus</u> in his <u>Kabbala Denudata</u>. This word signifies the hand as a weapon, (as may be seen from the English word <u>pugilist</u>, derived from it). Rosenroth says it is YOD (the Hand), or Chokmah (because I of IHVH is assigned thereto), which may be resolved into five fingers, i.e., Binah, since to Binah is referred H (=5) and the fifty Gates. It therefore denotes the powers collected and hidden in the supernals prior to manifestation, whose extension (the opening of the fist) is effected in Binah.

This curious and characteristic bit of Qabalistic symbology is a clue to the Hebrew motto on the sword. The powers of the sword are primarily the powers of Chokmah, of the Father. And, as we have learned that Chokmah is the sphere of the zodiac, here is a hint that all the powers which are symbolized by the magical sword are really the vibrations of the cosmic light manifested through the zodiac. Of like import is the sign of the Hexagram on the pommel. What is meant is that all the activities of personality are really specializations of cosmic forces.

The Latin motto implies the same idea. Vince in hoc signes or "I conquer in this sign" refers to the cruciform shape of the sword, which designates the letter Tau, the vibration of Saturn, and the crystallizing, specializing power of human activity. This, indeed, is the secret of our magical victories. We win them because in our theurgy, or god-working, we consciously wield and direct, not our own puny personal forces, but the infinite powers of the One Life.

We do so as conscious instruments of the Life-Power, and this is what is meant by <u>Deo duce</u>, "with God for my guide." Finally, the magical sword is our companion, our agency, our aid, and this is signified by "Comite ferro."

Now, the V in יהוה refers to the Sephiroth from Chesed to Yesod inclusive, and thus symbolizes the powers of the personal consciousness. Chesed is the sphere of MEMORY, Geburah is the fiery Mars-force which we feel as WILL; Tiphareth is IMAGINATION; Netzach is DESIRE; Hod is INTELLECT; Yesod is the AUTOMATIC CONSCIOUSNESS, or the cell-consciousness of the animal organism. These powers, and the connecting activities, represented by the paths joining these Sephiroth, are what is represented by the magical sword. Careful study of the diagrams in Lesson 10 of Section A will help you to understand it better.

Nor should we forget that the magical sword, as corresponding to V of יהוה does, in a measure, represent the particular powers associated with Vau as a letter. To Vau the Sepher Yetzirah assigns the power of HEARING, so that it is the letter which particularly represents the subtle principle of

Sound, or Akasha. To wield the magical sword is to make use of the potencies of sound-vibration – and this is the basic power in all production of forms.

Finally, we come to the Pantacle, represented in the Tarot by the suit of Coins, and so corresponding to the final Heh of IHVH, to the world named Assiah, to the element of Earth, and to Malkuth among the Sephiroth.

Tradition says it is a disk, made of beeswax, and engraved with the sigils and names relating to the particular magical operation to be performed. Thus, if the work be a work of light and wealth, under the patronage of the Sun, the pantacle will have the sigil of Michael, angel of the sun, will bear the magic square of 6 x 6, and the magical names belonging to the Tiphareth. It will be encased in a bag of orange silk, and the names upon it will be filled in with orange paint or with gold. For works of divination and mysteries, under the patronage of the Moon, the names and sigils will be those belonging to Yesod, sphere of the Moon, the magic square will be one of 9 x 9, and the writing will be in silver or blue. So for all the other works. Each is under the presidency of one of the planets, and the pantacle used must bear the magic square, sigils, and names corresponding to the Sephira which is the sphere of that planet, written in the corresponding color; and when not in use will be wrapped in a bag of the same color.

On the reverse side of the pantacle, written in the color which is complementary to that in which the sigils, names, etc. are written, should be a brief statement of the specific result which the operation is intended to accomplish. Thus, if the work be an undertaking which is under the presidency of the Sun, whose names and sigils are written in orange, the statement of the work to be done will be written in blue, the color complementary to orange. These names and sigils are first engraved on the surface of the wax with a stylus, and then filled in with the proper colors.

The material, beeswax, is particularly susceptible to impression by certain of the finer vibrations of the astral light. Its plasticity represents the amenability of the external world to control by mental imagery. As a product of the work of bees, it is of course a symbol of the results of industry, but there is a deeper meaning than this obvious one, which will be easier to grasp if we know the mythological significance of the bee.

Concerning this, the Neo-Platonist, Porphyry, writes:

"The Ancients, moreover, used to call the priestesses of Mother Earth Bees, in that they were initiates of the Terrence Goddess, and the Maid herself Bee-like. They also called the Moon the Bee, as Lady of Generation; and especially because (with the Magians) the Moon in exaltation is the Bull, and Bees are Ox-born--that is, souls coming into birth are Ox-born – and the 'God who steals the Bull' (Mithra) occultly signifies generation."

The Moon, whose sphere is in Yesod, the Foundation or basis, is the subconscious plane of mind, and beeswax, as the product of the Bee or Moon, thus represents the sphere of the elements, Malkuth, which proceeds from the ninth Sephira. In other words, the use of beeswax for the pantacle is a symbolic reminder of the fact that the appearances of the external world are really differentiations or projections of subconsciousness in terms of time, space, name and form. The things which make up our environment are emanations of the subconsciousness. Their very substance is the subconsciousness. And he who is master of his mental imagery is able to make his environment what he will by reason of his power to express patterns upon this universal subconscious plane of being through the channel thereto provided by his personal subconscious mind.

In addition to the four implements, ceremonial work requires incense, fire, and for some rituals, consecrated oil. The incense is of various sorts. Each kind has its particular correspondence to one of the planets.

For works of the Sun, the principle ingredients are clibanum (frankincense) and cinnamon. For works of the Moon, camphor and aloes. For works of Mars, pepper, dragon's blood, and like hot, pungent odors. For works of Mercury, mastic, white sandal, mace and storax. For works of Jupiter, cedar and saffron. For works of Venus, rose, red sandal, and the leaves of myrtle. For works of Saturn myrrh (and in evil magic) assafetida and sulphur.

The base of the oil is pure olive oil (representing the order and measurement of the sphere of Jupiter). With it are combined liquid storax, (for Mercury), camphor (for the Moon) and benzoin (for Venus). Since this course of lessons is concerned principally with the theory of ceremonial, the exact proportions of the elements used in the incense and oil are not here given.

The ashes of the incense are mixed with salt, and are mingled with the water of purification. Rituals of magic include formulae for the consecration of the ash and salt, and for the consecration of the water into which they are cast. The ash represents the material element in aspiration, which is symbolized by the incense. The salt is a symbol of preservation. These are mingled and cast into the water to represent the nucleus of the Tmasic quality around which are crystallized the material results of the magical work.

The magical fire may be a small red lamp, such as is used on altars in the Roman church, containing a large wax candle. It is used for lighting the charcoal on which the incense is cast. From it, also, are lit all the fires or lights which may be required in certain ceremonials; and it serves, too, for the ceremonial purification of the blade of the magic sword, before it is used in making the signs of the Pentagram or Hexagram. This fire represents the cosmic fire, as the ash and salt represent earth, the incense (in process of combustion) air, and the oil one aspect of the watery element.

We have left the description of the magical vestments to the last, not because it is unimportant, but because in this elementary study of the subject, it would be futile to enter into detailed descriptions.

Some writers are of the opinion that the vestments should include an outer robe and an inner robe, a girdle in the form of a serpent, an apron similar to those worn by Free Masons, and a crown. Others substitute a hood or cap for the crown. Others say that the two robes and a silken girdle are sufficient.

The inner robe should be of woolen stuff, and its color black. Thus by color it represents the primal Night which to uninitiated eyes appears to be night but which every seer who has experienced superconsciousness declares to be a radiance surpassing any light we see on earth. It is darkness to our eyes and intellects, but it is also the Primordial Glory, wherein all lesser lights are swallowed up. Thus the black inner robe is often called "The Robe of Glory". It symbolizes AIN SVP AVR, the Limitless Light.

The outer robe may be of a color appropriate to the specific work--orange for works of the Sun, Blue for operations under the dominance of the Moon, Scarlet for works of Mars, Yellow for those of Mercury, Violet for those under the influence of Jupiter, Green for those of Venus, and deep Indigo for the works of Saturn. When these colored outer robes are used, the silken girdle should be of the complementary color. (Color complements are those which are opposite each other in the color-chart.)

But we may simplify matters by using only a white robe, inasmuch as white is the balance or equilibrium of all colors. With this will be worn a girdle of yellow silk, symbolizing the restrictive power of the intellectual selfconsciousness, under the rulership of Mercury.

The black inner robe may be cut like the outer one, or hereafter described, or it may be a cassock such as is worn by priests. Its cut is unimportant, because it is the symbol of the formless Light.

The outer robe, which is called the Robe of Concealment because it is either of a specific color, or else of white linen or silk representing all colors, (we say because on account of the derivation of the word "color," from the Latin celare, to conceal), is cut so as to represent one form of the Tau-cross, as seen on the following page:

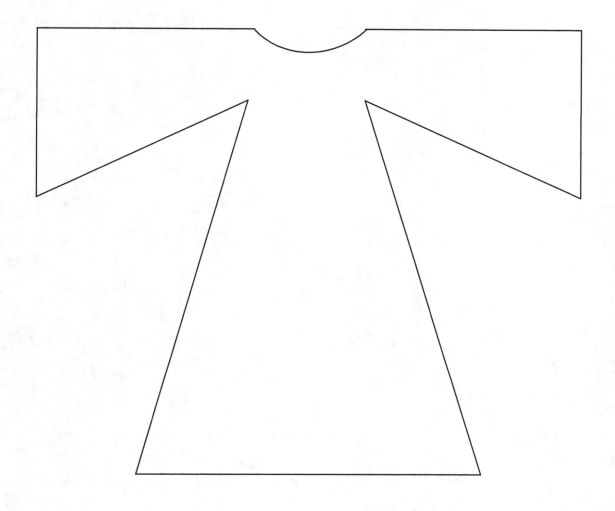

Figure 5B - GARNMENT

The shape of this garment refers to the letter Tau, and to the 32rd path on the Tree of Life. The name of that path, Administrative or Assisting Intelligence, describes the magical consciousness, because a magician is one who by his knowledge of the hidden laws of the Life-Power's self-expression, takes a conscious active part in the administration of those laws. Tau also refers to Saturn, and so represents the force of crystallization which is at work in all practical applications of occult law.

Embroidered upon the breast of the outer robe, or hung by a white cord from his neck, the magician also wears a lamen, or symbolical summary of his understanding of the cosmos. Some use a simple crucifix--which is a perfect symbol if only it be understood, but worse than useless if it be worn without a real knowledge of its meaning. Others wear some variation of the Rose and Cross. Yet others find it best to devise their own lamen, and many enclose it in a <u>vesica piscis</u>. Such a lamen is pictured in a little book on magic which is meat for those who can digest it, entitled, <u>Book Four, Part 2</u>. We prefer the lamens which are the result of the magician's own ingenuity. The simpler they are, as a rule, the better.

The Four Maxims

As the implements of magic are four, as the letters of the Great Name are four, as the Qabalah speaks of four worlds and of four principles in the constitution of man, so does magic, which is the conscious operation of the cosmic order through a human personality, sum up its theory in four words. These have come down to us from the past in the formula:

TO KNOW, TO WILL, TO DARE, TO BE SILENT.

Knowledge, will, courage, silence – this is the four square foundation of magical practice. And since the art of magic is founded upon a tradition which, for us of the Western world, comes in its clearest and simplest form by way of the channel of the Secret Wisdom of Israel, we purpose in this lesson to give some account of the esoteric meanings of the four Hebrew words which embody these ideas. Knowledge in Hebrew is דעת, Will is רצון, Courage is אמץ, and Silence is הסה.

דעת signifies insight. Its first letter is D, the Door, suggesting entrance. The second letter is O, the Eye, or instrument of vision. The last is Tau, the mark or sign, signifying definiteness. True magical knowledge includes all these elements. It opens a door from the outer world of effects and appearances, leading inward to the realm of causes. It develops vision of the inwardness of things. It is, finally, definite and particular, not vague and general.

The first letter of the word דעת is the letter assigned to the 14th path on the Tree of Life, connecting Chomah with Binah. Therefore traditionally it is said that Da'ath is the union of Chokmah and Binah. This path, named Luminous Intelligence, is represented in the Tarot by the Empress, and since we have learned that she is a symbol for the response of the subconsciousness to self-conscious stimuli, in the generation of ideas, we find that the beginning of magical knowledge, as represented by the letter D, is really creative imagination.

It follows, therefore, that he who would attain to this knowledge which combines Wisdom and Understanding, must not only have a mental grasp of principles, but must also develop as much skill as he can in developing his understanding of the application of these principles.

In other words, magical knowledge requires us to exercise the deductive processes of the subconsciousness. And those deductive processes cannot be exercised unless we given them something to work upon. This, indeed, is the reason for all the work that you have received up to this point in your studies. This is why you have been asked to learn numbers and their meanings, the Hebrew alphabet and its correspondences, alchemical and astrological symbols, and their correlations. For these symbols are all that we can communicate to you. These symbols, the Tarot pictures, and some commentary upon them, couched in language which is itself symbolic and inadequate.

The real magical knowledge, however, cannot be communicated. It must be evolved. You may read thousands of books, attend innumerable lectures, but the only way in which you can come into conscious possession of the true magical DOTv <u>is by evolving it from within</u>.

The first step in that evolution is to learn the symbols. They are the seeds which you plant in your mental garden. They are not planted if they remain between the covers of the notebooks in which you preserve these lessons. Not until they are incorporated in the substance of your brain-cells can the life within them begin to manifest itself. For not until they become interior objects, so to say, can the eye of the mind begin to perceive the relationships between them.

It may well be that in earlier lessons we have not sufficiently emphasized the importance of thorough familiarity with the Hebrew letters, the 32 Paths of Wisdom, and the peculiar arithmetical processes of the Qabalah. If we have been at fault in this particular, let this be the opportunity to correct the short-coming. It is absolutely necessary to be letter-perfect in these matters, and to keep oneself letter-perfect by daily exercise. It is necessary primarily because this material has life in itself, so that if it be really deposited in the subconscious it will begin to grow. It is necessary secondarily because this particular system of symbols is, and has been for many centuries, the means of communication between adepts of the Inner School.

What will sooner or later happen to you if you become thoroughly familiar with these symbols is precisely what would happen to you if you learned the Morse alphabet, or the signals used in sending Marconigrams. Some day you might be passing a telegraph office, and instead of hearing meaningless noises from the sounder, you would hear a definite message. Or, if you know the Marconi signals, you might some day find, to your delight, that the crash of the wireless in your receiving set had become significant. But with a notable difference. From the telegraph sounder or from the wireless you would receive nothing but scraps of information concerning mundane affairs of little or no importance to you. When full possession of the code language of the Inner School has put you on rapport with the mental broadcasting of its adepts, you will be able to "listen in" on a priceless store of wisdom. We make no secret of the fact that some of the best things in these lessons have come in just this way.

Once experienced, this "listening-in" will never be confused with one's own subconscious elaboration of the symbols. Often it has a distinctive tone of its own, so that after many experiences of this kind one is able to recognize the characteristic quality of the "sender."

But we would not have you underestimate the importance of the subconscious elaborations just mentioned. To make these possible, indeed, is the main reason for learning the symbol-language thoroughly. It is interesting to listen in, and the experience forever settles one's doubts as to the real existence of the Inner School. But one's own needs are best met by the deductive process which begins as soon as the numbers, letters, Sephiroth and Tarot Keys are firmly fixed in mind.

In a later lesson, on the Great Arcanum, we shall recur again to the fact that the highest teaching is incommunicable, and shall consider some of the reasons why this is so. At present it is sufficient to say that דעת is an interior illumination.

The subject of that illumination, that with which it is concerned, is the Great Magical Agent. Eliphas Levi tells us that this agent is "the devil of esoteric dogmatism," and thus we know that it is represented by the letter Ayin, corresponding to the 15th Key of the Tarot. We may say explicitly that the symbolism of this Tarot Key, rightly understood, leads directly to magical knowledge of practical value. That knowledge, moreover, is definite, not vague, practical rather than abstract. Certain aspects of it, perhaps, might possibly be put into words. Jacob Boehme and the alchemists, indeed, have tried to do so. And here and there in these lessons we have made one or two like attempts. But we are of the opinion that our efforts have been no more successful than those of Boehme or the alchemists, so far as they affect people who have not already developed within themselves an inkling, at least, of the truth. For there seems to be something in the very nature of the spoken word which makes it an inadequate medium for the transmission of this class of ideas, no matter how clearly the words one uses appear to the writer or speaker to convey his meaning. But we can at least put you upon the right track. The magical knowledge is knowledge of that which is symbolized by the Devil, and when it blossoms in the garden of the mind it is truly an experience that is properly named "The Renewing Intelligence," for as a result of it one comes to see – to see with his inner eye, and to perceive, too, with his outer sense of sight – that the world in which we live is quite other than what we formerly supposed. And this vision is an inner and outer perception of the Beauty which dwells in all things whatsoever, which leads to confident, yet cool and intellectual, expectation of the ultimate perfection of the Great Work in which we all have a part.

The last letter of דעת, and the last letter of the Hebrew alphabet, refer to this new vision. So does the 21st Key of the Tarot. Remember what we have just said. Although it is apparently incommunicable, it is not in the least vague. When you experience it you will know it as the most certain knowledge that you have. Nothing can shake this certainty. Nothing can take away from you the recollection of the experience. The experience itself, because of its intensity, is commonly of short duration. From a few minutes to an hour is the average length of this clear vision of reality. But the memory never fades. And when one has thus truly seen, one knows beyond per-adventure that he has a place in the schema of things, a work to do, a part of the Great Plan to materialize. He knows too that this special part of the work is indispensable. He has entered the kingdom, and has, in effect, become the King Himself, inasmuch as he knows that every part of his personal life has, as its raison d'être, the working out of a particular aspect of the Creative Will.

Such, in brief, is the nature of the magical knowledge, but we fear that we have fallen far short in our attempts to declare it. But enough has been said, we think, to make you understand that it is not ear-knowledge, not book-knowledge, not formula-knowledge, and that above all, it is knowledge received from within. Our understanding of psychology enables us to determine that it is not miraculous (except as all natural processes are miraculous). That is, we can say definitely that this experience comes as the result of subconscious elaboration of the symbols of the Ageless Wisdom which have been transmitted to us from the past. But none but those who have entered the Door, and seen with the inner Eye, can have any adequate idea of the glory and wonder of this experience.

Will comes next, because it is only when we truly know that we can really will. Yet the word רצון affords many clues. Some of these have been considered in other lessons, but if there be some repetition here, it will serve to fix the ideas more definitely in your minds.

In the first place, the magical will is recognized by the initiated as the out-pressing into manifestation of that Limitless Light which centers itself in our world-system in the Sun. Will, for magicians, is no abstraction. It is primarily a force, and a physical force, at that. Literally, and without reservation, it is the power that radiates to us from the sun. We regard it, therefore, not in any sense as being any person's possession, but as a common principle in which all of us have a share. And, because it is primarily this One Energy which always is pressing itself into manifestation, and always in harmony with itself, we reject as unthinkable and unreasonable the notion that it can anywhere be turned against itself, or made (even temporarily) to defeat itself. This is the basis of the metaphysical determinism which has been referred to so often in these pages.

Secondly, we regard the magical will as being something perceptible throughout Nature. Thus it is correctly described, in one aspect, as Natural Intelligence. And, furthermore, we accept the testimony of the wise in every age who declare, over and over again, that he who learns by practice the art of true meditation becomes a powerful center of that Natural Intelligence. We accept as worthy of credence the following statements of the great Hindu psychologist, Patanjali:

"By making Samyama (defined as the combination of concentration, meditation and Samadhi with reference to some particular thing) on the three sorts of changes comes the knowledge of past and future. By making Samyama on word, meaning and knowledge, which are ordinarily confused, comes the knowledge of all animal sounds. By perceiving the impressions, knowledge of past life. By making Samyama on the signs in another's body knowledge of that mind comes; but knowledge of its contents, that not being the objects of the Samyama. By making Samyama on the form of the body the power of perceiving forms being obstructed, the power of manifestation in the eye being separated, the Yogi's body comes unseen... By making Samyama on the elements, beginning with the gross, and ending with the superfine, comes mastery of the elements."

And these are only a few of the powers enumerated by Patanjali. They are the natural powers of the man who by meditation identifies himself with the very essence of the various modifications of the one Life-Power. Such a man is in absolute harmony with the One Will, and through him its omnipotence will be manifest. Will he, then, be a miracle-worker? Not necessarily. Indeed, it is more than likely that wonder-working is the very rare exception among those who have gained the powers mentioned above. For after all, there is very little reason for miracles, as a rule, so that even if an adept had these powers, he would never exercise them except in case of absolute necessity. We may be sure that he would not (unless his was a particular vocation to world-enlightenment, such as that of Jesus) do anything out of the ordinary as evidence of his superior attainments. And because of this, too, we may be sure that no real magician will ever exercise his power to satisfy either doubt or curiosity.

The third letter of רצון is a consequence of the two that precede it. He who knows the One Will is a Yogi. He goes through life guided by an Inner Voice, and many who have attained this unfoldment have borne testimony to this. Thus Jesus, "As I hear I judge, and my judgment is just." Appearances never deceive such a man, even though the illusion that they present will affect him just as certainly as they will anybody else who is incarnate in terrestrial conditions. But he who has identified himself with the One Will never judges by appearance. He always <u>listens</u>. In him the magical will is the reverberation of the Soundless Sound of the Voice of the Silence. To him that Will presents itself as the revealer (Hierophant) of all mysteries and secrets.

Finally, the magical will is a power of development, and a dissolving power, also. It is a power which taken form in mental imagery. It is a power which can, as Levi says, reduce the whole world to a chaos. It is a power which impels him through whom it works to be ever on the side of progress. Magicians, therefore, are always among the radicals, not on the side of the conservatives who rely upon the power of precedent. Magicians have been the hidden force at work behind every step in human progress toward the better realization of the ideal of freedom. It is the magical will which has practically overthrown monarchy, which has done so much to change the status of women and children, which is necessarily a perpetual menace to the cant, hypocrisy and formalism of organized exoteric religions. Thus priests have ever been foremost among the persecutors of magicians, and kings have seldom been their friends.

The third aspect of the magical consciousness, Courage, valor, or strength, is the consequence of magical knowledge and magical will. Its three letters are in a sense a summary of all that has been said on the preceding pages concerning magical realization of the inner meaning of דעת and רצון. The first letter of אמץ is Aleph, and represents the path of Fiery or Scintillating Intelligence, which joins Kether, the Hidden Intelligence of the Primal Will, to Chokmah, the Illuminating Intelligence of Wisdom. To Aleph the word Ruach is especially assigned, as if to emphasize the thought that this path is the one whence we may learn the real nature of spirit, or the Cosmic Life-Breath.

Reference should here be made to the Qabalistic analyses of the word רוח in earlier lessons. In the Name of the 11th Path its fiery, sparkling quality is particularly emphasized. And the letter with which this energetic, coruscating, blazing aspect of the Great Breath is associated is appropriately the first letter of the word representing the magical courage. A magician must be spirited. He must have contempt for danger. A degree of audacity must be part of his psychic make-up. He must have fortitude in the face of uncertainty and peril.

This does not mean that he is to be fool-hardy, but it does mean that the world will often judge him as being just that. The magician must meet problems that make the uninitiated flinch, must face perils that strike terror to timorous souls whose imaginations are fertile in conjuring up pictures of disaster. His attitude toward life will be inexplicable to those who do not have his knowledge, and if he does not carefully observe the last of the four occult maxims, he is sure to be called a fool.

This, indeed, is one implication of the Tarot Key which represents the letter Aleph. But the magician's folly is such only when judged by the false standards of the unenlightened. He is not really foolhardy. His daring is based upon his vivid realization of his place in the scheme of things. If he seem unduly venturesome to lesser minds, it is only because they do not know how adequate are the grounds for the security that he feels.

To all puling, sickly prudence of the worldly sort he is necessarily a stranger. And they who watch his progress through the world are likely to suppose that he is almost a monster of determination and refusal to be bound down to the mean standard of averages which is accepted by the masses of his fellow-men. To the outsider, the magician always seems a great egoist, if not an insufferable egotist. Yet this, of all mistaken opinions, is farthest from the truth.

For the daring of the magician, as shown by the second letter of AMTz, is the result of a reasoned surrender to Life itself. It is by no means an egotistic confidence in one's personal adequacy. On the contrary, it is the result of a calm reliance upon the ability of Life Itself to adjust all conditions so as to produce good results. For the magician, remember, is one who knows, one in whom the ripening of consciousness has brought out a realization of his exact place in the scheme of things. He does not depend upon appearances. The mental imagery that take form in his thought and word and action is not motivated from without, but from within. Like Moses, he has seen the "pattern in the mount," and his courage to go ahead through every peril, and in spite of every opposition, is born of his certainty that this pattern is true.

He does not depend upon his own will and vision, but makes himself receptive to the One Will and the One Vision of the Inner Seer. Thus his consciousness is not only enterprising and adventurous, but it is also fixed or stable, as the name of the path to which Mem is attributed shows. He has the resistless courage of One Aim, which he <u>knows</u> must be realized, because it is the tendency of a resistless will.

Thus his impetuosity is balanced by calmness. However spirited he may be, he is always poised. He does not "go off half-cocked." And thus the faces of great magicians are notable for their placid calm, and their words and actions, ever full of force, are free from the least trace of haste or bluster.

The last letter of אמץ is the second of רצון, because the magical courage is the fruit of conscious possession of such powers as we have enumerated in the quotation from Patanjali. Intellectually we may even now grasp the idea that such are the powers which <u>ought</u> to be expressed in the life of a man who measures up to the fullness of his inheritance as a son of God. It is, perhaps, less easy to grasp the idea that all these powers are at this very moment latent within us, like seeds that have scarce begun to grow, if, indeed, they have begun at all.

Yet this is what the Ageless Wisdom has always taught. These powers are not acquired. We cannot have them imparted to us by any mysterious process whatsoever. Thus more than one alchemist has written "To make gold, you must have it." Nor is this to be interpreted (as some unfriendly critics would have us believe) as being a veiled admission that all the mysteries of Hermetic Science are nothing more than veils for conscious chicanery. You <u>must</u> have gold to make it. You must have the powers if ever you are to develop them. And you who read these pages must begin by training your intellect to grasp the truth that all these powers are YOUR powers NOW. From this initial perception every magician has begun the process of his unfoldment. You, too, must follow the same path. And when the work is perfected, then you will understand that the magician's courage is the natural expression of his clear perception of the actual facts about the world in which he lives and works. He knows that through him are working the powers that make a nebula appear in empty space, that form that nebula into a solar system, and people it with living things. He knows that in him and through him work the powers that form the veins of precious metal in the bowels of the earth, the powers that determine the number of electrons in every atom, the powers that shape crystals and fashion all the marvelous perfection of line and color that meet our eyes on every hand. Furthermore, he knows himself as one with the Source and Controller of all these processes. And this knowledge he has gained by ceaseless meditation, whose fruit is absolute identification of his whole personal activity with the working of the Life-Power in the cosmos. By meditation he unites himself with nature (Tz), by imagination he builds specific images of the consequences of that union (D) and by his works he confirms and realizes what he sees (I).

Magical courage, then, is the natural outcome of the magician's unusual responsiveness to the influx of the Spirit of Life, of his perfect surrender to the direction and guidance which that spirit exerts upon all of its centers of expression, and of his conscious identification with the sum-total of cosmic processes. The possessor of such a consciousness is daring because he is absolutely certain that he will succeed, courageous because none of the phantoms of appearances has any power over him. His will is the Cosmic Will. His powers are the Cosmic Powers. His knowledge is Wisdom itself. And by this realization fear is banished from his mind.

The last of the four aspects of the magical consciousness is silence. You remember the story of Elijah, and how he identified the Lord as a "still, small voice." The Hebrew word for "still" is elsewhere in the Authorized Version translated "silence." Thus we know that what Elijah heard was what Theosophists term "the Voice of the Silence." This is that "god-nourished silence" whereof the Chaldean Oracles also tell us. It is the Soundless Voice of the Inner Life.

The Lord was in this Voice. The ruling power in the cosmos is not noisy. Its Creative Word is the silent Word of thought. And we, if we would be theurgists, or "god-workers," must remember this and apply it to our practice of the art of life.

When people first escape from the swaddling-bands of orthodoxy, their enthusiasm over the new thoughts which stimulate their imaginations makes them eager to proselyte. Like St. Paul, they preach the good news "in season and out of season."

Yet Jesus, although he bade his disciples preach the Gospel to every creature, bade them also be "wise as serpents," and serpents are among the most silent of silent beasts. And in early Christian times the meaning of this injunction was understood and observed. Christianity began as a secret society, and following the example of the Master, reserved many things for secret instruction of pupils tested and tried with "milk for babes."

This rule still holds good, and those who fail to observe it pay the inevitable penalty of loss of power. For of all wasters of energy, an unmanageable tongue is one of the worst. He who expends all his force in talking cannot have much left for doing.

Possibly this may be one of the reasons why teachers of the Law in Eastern lands are recognized as meriting particular care from their pupils. They use their force for the purpose of instruction, and thus have less to expend upon the acquisition of worldly goods. Yet we are by no means sure that the Eastern methods will work in Western Civilization, and perhaps the necessity which the European or American expounder of cosmic law is under – the necessity of making his teaching pay for itself – may work out to good results in the long run.

But this is a digression. The Hebrew word for silence, HSH, claims our attention now. Its first letter is Heh, and so is its last. Our teachers in the Qabalah tell us that the first Heh is the Heh of the Mother, AIMA, or Binah, which the last if the Heh of the Bride, Malkuth. The first Heh, therefore, corresponds to the creative world and to the faculty of intuition.

Thus is reminds us that to receive the interior tuition which reveals to us the mysteries of cosmic law, we must learn to keep silent. The Inner Voice is not heard by those who indulge in needless talk. Furthermore, the letter Heh is the letter of Sight, and for the clearest, most intense vision, silence is essential.

The second Heh may serve to remind us of Lao-Tzu's dictum: "The state should be governed as we cook small fish, without such business." When we come to apply whatever magical knowledge we may possess to the actual work of taking our part in the administration of the Kingdom, we shall accomplish more work and do it better if we don't have too much to say about our plans and projects. The middle letter of HSH, Samekh, hints that in silence there is a supporting or sustaining power. That this is true every practical occultist learns sooner or later. The practice of silence as to what you aim at, as to what you are doing, has two very important practical results. First of all, it prevents other people from learning of your plans, and perhaps setting themselves in opposition to you. Thus silence is over and over again a time-saver and an energy-saver. Secondly, the practice of silence serves to intensify desire-force. Your one aim (the arrow of the Archer, represented by the letter Samekh) is something that you must keep religiously to yourself. Not even your closest friends should know of it. This one aim is typified in Revelation by the white stone, upon which is written a name which to man knoweth, <u>save him that receiveth it</u>. The one thing you have to do in order to fulfill your destiny will be, or perchance has been, revealed to your from within. See that you tell no man. For in silence and secrecy the strength and potency of that aim will be intensified until it dominates your whole life.

But if you tell your secret to other people, virtue goes out of you, and you are almost certain to incite somebody to acts of open or veiled opposition.

Pythagoras, it is said, required several years of silence from his pupils. And because of that training, some of his pupils became mighty men among the magicians of that day.

To enforce such a rule now would be difficult indeed, so confirmed are we in the habit of telling all we know, and a great deal more than we know. But we urge you, as you hope for the unfoldment of the magical consciousness, to practice silence. Keep your counsel. Do what you have to do without one needless word. Spare your wife or husband the ordeal of listening to all your little plans. Be self-contained and quiet.

Practice, we say, because of all the occult maxims, this one is the hardest to observe, the one that will take the greatest amount of ingenuity in the way of devising strictly technical exercises (like a musician's scales) before the degree of magical perfection is attained.

Remember, this maxim, BE SILENT, is placed last among the four, in the most emphatic position, that is. Think out what this means, and then begin to live, in so far as you are able, a life of wise silence. Nothing will do more to hasten your progress toward final liberation, toward ability to demonstrate your god-likeness.

The Great Arcanum

This is what Eliphas Levi says concerning the Great Arcanum:

"There exists a principle and a rigorous formula which is the Great Arcanum. Let the wise man seek it not, for he has already found it; let the vulgar seek for ever, they will never attain it. This universal arcanum, the crowning and eternal secret of supreme initiation, is represented in the Tarot by a young and naked girl who only touches the earth with one foot, who holds a magnetic rod in each hand, and appears to be running inside a crown which is supported by an angel, an eagle, a bull, and a lion. This figure is fundamentally analogous to the cherub of Ezekiel, and to the Indian symbol of Addhanari, corresponding to the Adonai of the prophet just mentioned. The comprehension of this figure is the key of all the occult sciences. The Great Magical Secret is represented by the lamp and poniard of Psyche, the apple of Eve, the fire stolen from heaven by Prometheus, and the burning scepter of Lucifer, but also by the Cross of the Redeemer. It is the ring of Gyges, the Golden Fleece, the allegorical picture of Cebos, which is its most audacious demonstration. It is also represented by the lingam, for the Great Arcanum is connected with the mystery of universal generation, and by the serpent pierced with an arrow, with formed the seal of Cagliostro.

"The secret is the kinghood of the sage, the crown of the initiate, whom it renders the master of gold and of light, which are fundamentally the same thing. By its means he solves the problem of the quadrature of the circle, directs the perpetual motion, and possesses the philosopher's stone. This great and indicible arcanum was never referred to even among adepts; it is essentially unexplainable in its nature, and is destruction both to those who divine it and those who reveal it.

"The Great Magical Secret is the secret of the direction of the Great Magical Agent; it depends upon an incommunicable axiom, and on an instrument which is the supreme and unique Athanor of the Hermetists of the highest grade. When the adepts in alchemy speak of a great and unique Athanor of which all can make use, which is within the grasp of all, which all men possess without knowing it, they allude to the philosophical and moral alchemy. A strong and resolute will can arrive in a short time at absolute independence, and we all possess the Athanor, the chemical instrument, by which that which is ethereal is separated from that which is gross, and the fixed is divided from the volatile. This instrument, complete as the world, and precise as mathematics themselves, is designated by the sages under the emblem of the Pentagram, the body of man and the absolute sign of human intelligence. The incommunicable axiom is kabbalistically enclosed in the four letters of the Tetragram, arranged in the following manner: in the letters of the words AZOTh and INRI kabbalistically written, and in the monogram of Christ as it is embroidered on the labarum, which Postel the Kabbalist interprets by the word Rota, from which the adepts have formed their Tarot.

"To understand the alternative or simultaneous proportion of the forces which produce equilibrium is to possess the first principle of the Great Magic Arcanum, which constitutes true human divinity. It is the science of fire; everywhere we find the enchanter who pierces the lion and leads the serpents – the lion is the celestial fire, and the serpents are the magnetic and electrical currents of earth. It is to this great secret of the Magi that we must refer all the marvels of Hermetic Magic,

157

which still declares in its traditions that the Arcanum of the magnum opus consist in the government of fire.

Figure 8A

Thus far Eliphas Levi, and at first reading it may seem to you that he has left nothing to say. Has he not declared that the Great Arcanum is incommunicable – that it is destruction for him who divines or reveals it? How then may we dare to venture in explaining it?

Well, you have had occasion before this to learn that our French magus, writing for a world that he rightly judged as having few who would in his day understand him, veiled his actual meaning in subtleties of language, after the fashion of adepts in every age. We do not pretend to be able to tell you the Great Arcanum, but we can do something in the way of lifting Levi's veil of words, and perhaps a little something, too, to bring you a step or two nearer to the discovery of the Great Secret.

First of all, the Great Arcanum is twofold. It is a principle, and it is also a formula. A principle is a source, or something from which other things proceed. In physics it is a fundamental energy or substance. In meta-physics it is a fundamental truth or postulate. The Great Arcanum is a principle in both senses. It is an actual or real energy. It is also a fundamental, archetypal idea.

This idea, wherein real energy or working power resides, exists, or comes into manifestation, as a formula. A formula is a fixed, prescribed, arranged method by which something is said or done. And when Levi says the Great Arcanum is a "rigorous formula" he is referring to the exactitude and severity of the order of manifestation by means of which the power of the Originating Idea or Principle comes into manifestation, or exists.

The wise man has no need of seeking it, for the wise man, as Levi uses the term, is one who has found this principle and formula. The vulgar, that is, the general run of human begins in any age, cannot find it, because their seeking is invariable in the wrong place. Moreover, even if they should happen to look in the right direction, it remains true that they would not <u>attain</u> it. For it is absolutely true that no man ever attains this secret, <u>because he already possesses it</u>. What happens is that its meaning dawns upon him. Aladdin, says the Eastern tale, had the magic lamp for some days before he learned its secret. And that story of the Wonderful Lamp is only another variation of the allegory of the Great Arcanum, to be added to those enumerated by Levi in our quotation.

When he describes the 21st Key of the Tarot as a glyph of the Great Arcanum, Levi is perfectly correct, but he might have chosen any of the major trumps for the same purpose, because each of them has this "crowning and eternal secret of supreme initiation" for its central theme. A little farther on in this lesson we shall consider another of the major trumps from this point-of-view. But let us continue with our interpretation of Levi.

"This secret is the kinghood of the sage," our Qabalist tells us, "the crown of the initiate." Look at your diagram of the Tree of Life. The "King" is MLK, Melek, the Divine Name of Malkuth. The "crown" is Kether. And the Great Arcanum has to do with the identity of the two Sephiroth, indicated by the doctrine that "Malkuth is in Kether, and Kether is in Malkuth." But the kinghood of the sage who possesses the great Arcanum is more than this metaphysical realization of the identity between the opposite extremes of the Tree of Life. It is a practical secret, which makes the true sage really dominant in his world, which makes its conditions subject to the Will expressed in all his thoughts and words and acts. Here we deal with no figure of speech at all. Whoever has made sufficient progress in the study of occult science to be able to understand this lesson knows that the affairs of this world are truly directed by an "invisible government." Those who sit in the high places of external authority are only so many puppets, working out (in ways which often puzzle, and often, too, distress us) the details of the Cosmic Plan. The invisible hierarchy of adepts and masters are the real governors of this plane and its affairs, and their rule is through the application of the principle and formula with which we are not concerned.

Literally, too, the sages are masters of gold and light. (Notice, too, how Levi anticipated modern scientific ideas about matter.) They have at their command practically limitless resources, and nothing could be farther from the truth than the idea that the poorer a man is the better occultist he is. The wise, to be sure are not burdened with a weight of personal possessions, but no person at all familiar with the innumerable him, as to the workings of the occult hierarchy, which are to be found here and there in the literature which they have inspired or sponsored, can doubt that they always have enough actual material wealth to carry out any undertaking with which they are concerned.

Yet, because Levi's writing conforms to the occult rule of "a meaning within a meaning" it may also be understood to refer to the mastery of the powers which Qabalah associates with Tiphareth, the sphere of the sun or alchemical gold. Thus we may know that knowledge of the Great Magical Secret makes the sages masters of the Intelligence of the Mediating Influence. That particular kind of intelligence is identified in Qabalistic psychology as Imagination, and Tiphareth, as the seat of Imagination, is called BN, Ben, the Son. For imagination is actually the personal expression of the original creative power of the One Life, and in nothing is the truth that man is the son of God so perfectly demonstrated as in the fact that the dominant images in each human mind set the pattern for the world in which each man lives.

Levi goes on to tell us that the Great Magical Secret enables its possessor to solve the problem of the quadrature of the circle. He does not refer to the mathematical problem. What he means is the very same thing that is meant by the words of the Lord's Prayer, "as in heaven, so on earth." For the symbol of heaven, or the world of archetypal ideas, is the circle, and the square is the symbol of the physical world wherein those ideas are actualized. This metaphysical "squaring of the circle" is also what is symbolized by the square and compass of the Masonic fraternity. It is the bringing into actual, concrete expression to the physical plane of the hidden potencies of the archetypal world.

The accomplishment of this result is the Great Work, and it is rightly described as the direction of the perpetual motion. Read Levi's words carefully and you will see that he says nothing whatever to justify the belief that one can make a perpetual motion machine. He only declares that the sage "directs the perpetual motion," the eternal self-activity of the Limitless Life.

Finally, he tells us that the sage who knows the Great Secret "possesses the philosopher's stone." We have referred to this "stone" in other lessons. You will remember that it is named ABN, Ehben, in Hebrew. Jesus, who spoke Aramaic, said, "What is this then that is written, the stone which the builders rejected, the same is become the head of the corner?" Thus he quoted from Psalm 118: 22, and went on to identify this stone with the stone of Nebuchadnezzar's dream, mentioned in Daniel 2:35.

The "builders" rejected the stone because they were the line of theologians who developed the monotheism of Israel, with its conception of a far-away God. But the very word אבן is itself a glyph for the Great Arcanum. This it is because it combines in one word the names אב, Father, and בן, Son. And the most open and audacious declaration of the Great Arcanum ever given, in spite of what Levi says about the allegorical picture of Cebes, is to be found in three sentences of Jesus: "I and the Father are one. He who hath seen me hath seen the Father. The things that I do shall ye do also, and greater things shall ye do, because I go unto the Father."

Yet even these words cannot reveal the Great Secret to any man. Rather must their meaning be forever veiled from those who have not come into possession of that Arcanum. For this is truly an indicible arcanum. "Indicible" and "incommunicable" must be understood in their most literal sense in this connection. The secret is one that cannot be told. Its nature is such that it cannot possibly be imparted. It is not that people know and will or dare not tell. It is that those who know find no means for transmitting their knowledge. And Levi is particularly explicit upon this point.

He says, furthermore, that the Great Arcanum is destruction both to those who divine it and those who reveal it. Here is an echo of Jesus' teaching about the Stone. Jesus declared, "Whoseever shall fall upon that stone shall be broken; but on whomsoever it shall fall, it will grind him to powder." We would have you ponder long and earnestly upon these words. Yet ponder them without fear. True it is that the Great Secret is "destruction." And in this aspect it is symbolized by the 16th major trump of the Tarot. But not only is it the destruction of all false notions of personality. In itself, essentially, it is a secret of destruction, of the dissolution of forms, of the disintegration of matter. And on this account the Hindu teaching which so wonderfully parallels the Western occultism gives us to understand that the final liberation of the Yogi is brought about by the destruction or transforming aspect of the Life-Power personified as Shiva.

We do not believe that Levi's remarks about the Athanor will give readers of these pages very much trouble. His meaning is plain. The Athanor, or chemical instrument, is the human body. This is the tool wherewith we are able to demonstrate our knowledge of the Great Arcanum. Hence the Ageless Wisdom, teaching reincarnation, declares that its purpose is liberation. We come into bodies again and again until at last we learn the secret which makes their rebirth needless. How foolish, then, to neglect or misuse our bodies! How impossible to find liberation until we learn that the body is indispensable thereto it is ridiculous to suppose that the goal is to become bodyless, especially when we remember the plain teaching which pervades the New Testament! Liberation from the necessity for rebirth is attained when one is so perfectly adapted to cosmic law that one has learned how to make an indestructible body. The last enemy to be overcome is death we are told, and if this means anything, it means that the completion of the Great Work brings a man into the control of natural forces that he is the master of the occult forces of disintegration which now bring his earthly body to the grave.

The diagram which we reproduce from Levi needs explanation for students of these pages. It is plainly derived from the Tree of Life. The white triangle top, enclosing the letters YOD and HEH, refers to the supernal Triad. The Hexagram in the middle indicates six Sephiroth which are referred to the VAU of IHVH and the circle at the bottom, enclosing a square, is Malkuth, מלכות, its meaning is the same meaning which is repeated over again in the Tree of Life. That is: every apparent separate aspect of the One Life includes all the rest.

Consciousness of this, as distinguished from the outline conveyed by the words, is the Great Arcanum. Consciousness cannot be communicated. It seems, indeed to be preposterous to the great majority of human beings, and even you, who have spent much time ripening yourself, may find more of sound than of sense in the words.

We have said that every major trump symbolizes an aspect of this consciousness, so that Levi is correct in describing the 21st Key as a synthesis of the Great Arcanum. But there is another trump which to us has had particular significance from this point-of-view because it is connected with the path on the Tree of Life named "Intelligence of the Secret of All Spiritual Activities."

The Hebrew name for this path, סוד הפעולות has been dealt with in other lessons, but there are other aspects of its meaning with which we shall now deal. It will be well for you to reread, before going on with this lesson what has been written concerning הפעולות in Section C, beginning at page 137.

In that lesson we have said that the Secret of All Spiritual Activities is the secret of the Word made flesh. The eighth Tarot Key shows the nature of the law whereby this comes to pass. The Word or Thought, formulated by the intellect, or self-consciousness, passes into the subconscious plans of mental activity, and this results in a modification of the subconsciousness, represented in the 8th Key by the sign of the Holy Spirit (∞) over the head of the woman.

One of the essential meanings of that sign is that the various pairs of opposites in the illusive world of actuality which affects our senses are all produced by a single cause. In other words, this sign stands for the idea that the manifested universe is the expression of One Power, which produces opposite forms of expression. It is the contradiction of the various dualistic interpretations which see the world as something developed from, or the playground of, two contending forces.

The intellectual perception of the unity of causation is the beginning of the gradual change in consciousness which leads from bondage to freedom. So long as we are enmeshed in the net of dualism (however subtly stated) we are in bondage to the pairs of opposites. But when we perceive clearly that whatever happens is the outworking of the potentialities of a single cause, we have taken the first step on the Way to Freedom.

The noun דבר, Word, which corresponds by Gematria to הפעולות, begins with the letter Daleth, symbol of Venus, and so referable to the emotional nature, since the sphere of Venus is Netzach, the sphere of Desire. This is important, as showing that the beginning of every Word or Thought is a feeling.

"As below, so above." The Creative Logos, the Word or Thought which calls the cosmos into existence must begin as feeling also. Pure Spirit, which the Qabalists call No-Thing, or AIN, transcends all the states which we call mental, yet every sage tells us that Pure Spirit is Pure Consciousness. But Pure Consciousness as it is prior to self-manifestation cannot be consciousness of anything, or consciousness of any relation. Feeling, or self-awareness, therefore, is the only mode of consciousness which is conceivable at this point. And as Judge Trovard has said, in The Creative Process in the Individual, this initial feeling must be that of being alive.

This, indeed, is Qabalistically shown in the letters of the word אין, inasmuch as the first, A, is the symbol of Ruach, or Life-Breath, the second, I, a symbol of potential humanity (because I="hand"), and the third, N, by its name, Nun, (taken as a verb), a symbol of the potency of growth. That which is אין, No-Thing, is nevertheless that which has for its primary self-awareness or feeling, the feeling which is subsequently developed as actual Life (A), as actual humanity (I), and as actual development (N).

It is this primary feeling of the No-Thing which is represented by the first letter of דבר. That feeling is rationalized into the self-conscious awareness indicated by the letter B. For no sooner does Spirit feel itself alive than it must also experience a further modification of consciousness, described by Troward in the book above-mentioned as follows:

"Then to feel alive it must be conscious, and to be conscious it must have something to be conscious of; therefore the contemplation of itself as standing related to something which is not its own originating self in propria persona is a necessity of the case; and consequently the Self-contemplation of Spirit can only proceed by its viewing itself as related to something standing out from itself, just as we must stand at a proper distance to see a picture – in fact the very word 'existence' means 'standing out'. Thus things are called into existence or 'outstandingness' by a power which itself does not stand out, and whose presence is therefore indicated by the word 'subsistence.'"

Yet this outstanding is illusive, because there is really no "outside" into which the omnipresent Spirit may project itself. Hence a Gnostic writer is careful to say that the "Noughtness emanates, but does not really emanate" the cosmos. Qabalists, too, are careful to say that the ten Sephiroth, or "emanations" begin by the concentration of the Limitless Light in and upon itself. Time and Space are therefore labels for relations existing between the points of the Life-Power's self-expression within the boundless Presence of its own subsistence. The relative is not a projection from the Absolute. Neither is it to be understood as a development of the Absolute. More accurately is it described as an apparent self-limitation of the Life-Power which happens within the boundless area" is an alogical (as distinguished from "illogical") expression. The limitations of language are such that words will not serve to formulate a logical statement of this first stage of the creative process. But because THAT which eternally does so manifest itself to itself is the central reality of your experience, you may, by maintaining a mental attitude of receptivity, receive from that Source of Pure Knowing a confirmation of this teaching which will carry your consciousness beyond the limitations of words.

The last letter of דבר, as you know, is the letter of the Sun, and here it typifies the third stage of the creative process, in which the Life-Power completes its expression of its feeling of Life in the establishment of a systemic center of activity. That center may be the nucleus of the miniature solar system of electrons composing an atom. It may be the central sun of a universe of solar systems. But whether the scale be large or small, the quality of consciousness manifested is always the same. It is the consciousness of relative centrality, the consciousness of being a center of positive, self-directed energy.

The three stages of creative activity represented by the letters of DBR, the Word, are therefore as follows:

D: The simple feeling of being alive.
B: The consciousness of that life as finding expression in specific, existing or "outstanding" activities.
R: The consciousness that whether the range of those activities be relatively great or small, the Life is the directive center of the whole system.

The reproduction of the Life-Power's own consciousness of this creative process in a personal center is what makes a man an adept, a master and a magus. The words we have used to indicate that consciousness are more than inadequate, but we believe that they are words which will point the way for you.

Thus, although the Great Arcanum is incommunicable, we may do something to indicate the way to be followed in order to come into possession of it. We may also make known the fact that the psychical and physical transformations which make a human being able to receive this knowledge from within are those which happen according to the law symbolized by the 8th Tarot Key. By the study of its symbolism, by the contemplation of the position of its path upon the Tree of Life, by the earnest demand that its deeper meaning be made known to you, you will establish the state of receptivity which makes possible the influx of the higher wisdom from superconsciousness.

In addition to this practice, you will probable find it to your advantage to read, ponder, and develop in your times of meditation the following extracts from the Chaldean Oracles.

Attributed by the ancients to the magi, these Oracles are sometimes called the Oracles of Zoroaster, but theirs is the spirit of Egyptian Neo-Platonism, rather than that of Persian dualism. This is made clear in the first of these fragments. No complete version of the Oracles has come down to us. These fragments are mostly quotations given by various Greek writers of Neo-Platonism. They are taken from Volume 6 of the Collectanea Hermetica. The translation is by "Sapere Aude," which is, I believe, the Rosicrucian motto of Dr. W. Wynn Westcott.

SECTION FROM THE CHALDEAN ORACLES

1. But God is he having the head of the Hawk. The same is the first, incorruptible, eternal, unbegotten, indivisible: the dispenser of all good; indestructible; the best of the good, the Wisest of the Wise; He is the Father of Equity and Justice, self-taught, physical, perfect, and wise – He who inspires the sacred philosophy.

"The hawk," says Horappalo, "stands for the Supreme Mind, and for the intelligent soul. The hawk is called in the Egyptian language biaeth, from bai soul, and eth heart, which organ they consider the seat or enclosure of the soul."

Sayce, in his Religion of the Ancient Egyptians, says: "Originally it was only the sun god of Upper Egypt who was represented even by the Egyptians under the form of a hawk. This was Horus, often called in later texts "Horus the elder' (Aroeris)."

This elder Horus or Aroueris, is represented by the hypotenuse of the 3-4-5 triangle, as shown in Section A. Plutarch, in Isis and Osiris, tells us, Isis and Osiris conceived the elder Horus while they were in their mother's womb." Spirit, the Father, Osiris, and Nature, the Mother, Isis, unite to produce Horus, which accounts for the Oracle's declaration that the God is "physical." For ancients did not fall into the error which has beset many who followed them. They fully understood the truth that what we call "physical" is really a self-expression of Pure Spirit.

2. Theurgist assert that He is a God, and celebrate him as both older and younger, as a circulating and eternal God, as understanding the whole number of things moving in the world, and moreover infinite through his power, and energizing a spiral force.

Theurgist assert it, please observe. They who walk in the darkness of duality cannot see the god in what they call "matter". Thus the Bhagavad-Gita says, "The deluded despise me in human form." The "circulating and eternal God" is the Eternal Pilgrim represented by the Fool in the Tarot.

3. The God of the universe, eternal, limitless, both young and old, having a spiral force.

Some versions of the Tarot represent the Fool as a youth. Others picture him as a bearded ancient.

4. For the Eternal Aeon – according to the Oracle – is the cause of never-failing life, of universal power and unsluggish energy.

Compare this with the attribution of Ruach to Aleph, the letter represented by the Fool.

5. Hence the inscrutable God is called silent by the divine ones, and is said to consent with Mind and to be known to human souls through the power of Mind alone.

6. The Chaldeans called the God Dionysus (or Bacchus) IAO in the Phoenician tongue (instead of Intelligible Light) and He is also called Sabaoth, signifying that He is above the Seven poles, that is, the Demiurgos.

7. Containing all things in the one summit of His own Hyparxis, He himself subsists wholly

beyond.

Hyparxis is a technical term of the Gnosis. By Greek Gematria it is the number 851. This reduced, is 14, and the least number is 5. 851, moreover, is 23x37, and so belongs to the great number of mystery-words which are multiplies of 37. Its meaning is existence, substance, goods, possessions. Thus Jesus' words, "All that the Father hath is mine," express the root-meaning of this Oracle.

8. Measuring and bounding all things.

This fragment brings out the idea that the Life-Power, although free in itself, works through limitation.

9. For nothing imperfect emanates from the Paternal Principle.

The commentator says, "This implies that all imperfection are derived from a succedent emanation only." We cannot admit this. From the human point-of-view, to be sure, many things are imperfect, and this relative imperfection is the consequence of limitation. But to the eye of the Creative Spirit, which sees all things in their true relations to each other, and understands that each specific phase of its self-manifestation is indispensable, necessary, inevitable stage of the creative process, everything is seen to have its rightful place in the expression of the spiral, progressive force. Nothing, therefore, being out of place, nothing can be imperfect.

10. The Father effused not Fear, but He effused Persuasion.

11. The Father hath hastily withdrawn Himself, he hath not shut up His own Fire in His intellectual power.

12. Such is the Mind which is energized before energy, while yet it had not gone forth, but abode in the Paternal Depth, and in the Adytum of God-nourished silence.

13. All things are sprung from that one Fire, for things did the Father of all things perfect, and delivered them over to the Second Mind, whom all races of men call First.

14. The Second Mind conducts the Empeyean World.

The Second Mind is what we call self-consciousness. All races of men call it first, because while many perceive the duality of self-consciousness and subconsciousness, few in these days, and fewer, when the Oracles were written, perceive the superconsciousness as the true First.

19. Natural works co-exist with the intellectual light of the Father. For it is the Soul which adorned the vast Heaven, and which adorneth it after the Father, but her dominion is established on high. (N.B. The numbering of these selections is that given in the book from which these fragments are taken.)

20. The Soul, being a brilliant Fire, by the power of the Father remaineth immortal, and is Mistress of Life, and filleth up the many recesses of the Bosom of the World.
21. The channels being intermixed, she performeth the works of incorruptible Fire.

22. For not in Matter did the Fire which is in the "Beyond" first enclose His power in acts, but in Mind. For the Framer of the Fiery World is the Mind of Mind.

23. Who first sprang from Mind, clothing the one fire with the other Fire, binding them together, so that He might mingle the fountainous craters, while preserving unsullied the brilliance of His own Fire.

24. And thence a fiery whirlwind, drawing down the brilliance of the flashing Flame, penetrating the abysses of the Universe; for thencefrom downwards, all extend their wondrous rays, (abundantly animating Light, Fire, Ether and the Universe.)

28. The Mind of the Father said that all things should be cut into Three, and immediately all things were so divided.

29. The Mind of the Father said, Into Three! governing all things by mind.

30. The Father mingled every Spirit from this Triad.

31. All things are supplied from the bosom of this Triad.

32. All things are governed and subsist in this Triad.

From 28 to 32 the Oracles speak of the Supernal Triad, figured on the Tree of Life as Kether, Chokmah and Binah.

39. The Mind of the Father whirled forth in reechoing roar, comprehending by invincible Will ideas omniform; which flying forth from that one fountain issued; for from the Father alike was the Will and the End (by which are they connected with the Father according to alternating life, through varying vehicles.) But they were divided asunder, being by Intellectual Fire distributed into other Intellectuals. For the King of all previously placed before the polymorphous World a Type, intellectual, incorruptible, the imprint of whose form is sent forth through the world, by which the universe shone forth decked with ideas all-various, of which the foundation is ONE, One and alone. From this the others rush forth distributed and separated through the various bodies of the universe, and are born in swarms through its vast abysses, ever whirling forth in illimitable radiation. They are intellectual conceptions from the Paternal Fountain partaking abundantly of the brilliance of Fire in the culmination of unresting Time. But the primary self-perfect Fountain of the Father poured forth these primogenial ideas.

40. These being many, ascend flashingly into the shining worlds, and in them are contained the Three Supernals.

41. They are the guardians of the works of the Father and of the One Mind, the Intelligible.

42. All things subsist together in the Intelligible World.

43. But all Intellect understandeth the Deity, for Intellect existeth not without the Intelligible, neither apart from Intellect doth the Intelligible exist.

44. For Intellect existeth not without the Intelligible; apart form it, it subsisteth not.

45. By Intellect He containeth the Intelligibles and introduceth the Soul into the Worlds.

46. By Intellect He containth the Intelligibles and introduceth Sense into the Worlds.

47. For this Paternal Intellect, which comprehendeth the Intelligables and adorneth things ineffable, hath sowed symbols through the World.

48. This Order is the beginning of all section.

49. The Intelligible is the principle of all section.

Oracles 48 and 49 show the Order is the Intelligible. It is the principle or beginning of "section" or division, because the idea of order necessitates a sequence or series. The Creative Thought seems to Provide the subsistent Unity into Three, and from those do proceed the Seven (according to the Gnosis and the Qabalah. Specialization, creation, section -- these are synonyms.

A consideration of this will show you, perhaps a profounder meaning in the saying, "Order is Heaven's first law."

50. The Intelligible is as food to that which understandeth.

51. The oracles concerning the Orders exhibit It as prior to the heavens, as ineffable, and they add – It hath Mystic Silence.

The "Orders" are the emanations. That which is called It is the Intelligible.

52. The oracle calls the intelligible causes Swift and asserts that, proceeding from the Father, they rush again unto Him.

Compare this with Sepher Yetzirah, 1:6:

"Ten ineffable Sephiroth (intelligible causes) appearance is like that of a flash of lightning, their goal is infinite. His word is in them when they emanate and when they return; at His bidding do they haste like a whirlwind; and before His throne do they prostrate (themselves)."

56. He gave his own whirlwinds to guard the Synoches mingling the proper force of His own strength in the Synoches.

Synoche is a Greek technical term meaning rest. It is practically equivalent with Sephira, and carries with it the idea that each of the specific self-manifestations of the Life-power is a restrain or limitation. The noun Synoche may be translated anguish, or distress, and this meaning is a clue to Jacob Boehme's use of the term "anguish," by which he designated the third property in nature.
71. Father-begotten Light, which alone hath gathered from the strength of the Father the Flower of Mind, and hath the power of understanding the Paternal Mind, and doth instil into all Fountains and Principles their power of understanding and the function of ceaseless revolution.

72. All fountains and principles whirl round and always remain in a ceaseless revolution.

This is identical with Qabalistic teaching. Kether, the Crown, is Rashith ha-Galgalim, the beginning of the whirling motion, and all the rest of the paths are manifestations of that same whirling activity. Be careful never to picture the Tree of Life to yourself as static. See each Sephirah as a whirling sphere or wheel. See each connection channel as containing a double current up toward Kether (with the exception of the Paths of Aleph and Beth, in which the current is always directed downward).

73. The principles, which have understood the intelligible works of the Father, He hath clothed in sensible words and bodies, being intermediate links existing to connect the Father with Matter, rendering apparent the images of unapparent natures, and inscribing the unapparent in the apparent frame of the world.

Note the use of the word "inscribing." The idea is the same as that which is behind Tantrik philosophy and behind the Sepher Yetzirah. It is the idea that the cosmos is, in a sense, the writing of Spirit upon the pages of the Book of Space.

78. The Father conceived ideas, and all morals bodies were animated by Him.

79. For the Father of gods and men placed the Mind (nous) in the Soul (Psyche); and placed both in the body.

80. The Paternal Mind hath sown symbols in the Soul.

All symbols know to man are reflections of these symbols which the Paternal Mind has sown in the psyche. As here used, the term Soul or psyche represents the animal sentient principle, and corresponds closely to the universal subconsciousness. It is what Eliphas Levi calls "the common and instinctive life," and of it he says:

"There are, then, in man, two lives: the individual or reasonable life, and the common or instinctive life. It is by the latter that one can live in the bodies of others, since the universal soul, of which each nervous organism has a separate consciousness, is the same for all."

This common, instinctive life, or subconsciousness, is "sown with symbols." Modern psychologist call them "complexes", or groups of ideas clustered by association around a common nucleus. Hindu psychologist call them Samskaras – impressions in the mind-stuff that produce habits.

When you make yourself familiar with a well-organized system of symbols like the Hebrew alphabet and the Tree of Life, you are in a position to make use of the psychological law that every idea has a tendency to bring to the surface of consciousness the complex with which it has affinity by association. The symbols already sown in your soul by the Cosmic Mind are, so to say, attracted by these alphabetical and numerical symbols. This is why the letter Tzaddi, the fish-hook, is the letter of meditation. When you let down the hook of a symbol into to pool of the subconsciousness, sooner or later you catch the fish. You become aware of one of the greater symbols sown in the universal soul, and through that symbol you come to understand That which cannot be expressed in human words. This is the way to the self-discovery of the Great Arcanum. And is the way to the self-discovery that the first Oracle tells us that the God is self-taught.

83. The Soul of man does in a manner clasp God to herself. Having nothing immortal she is wholly inebriated with God. For she glorieth in the harmony under which the mortal body subsisteth.

84. The more powerful Souls perceive Truth through themselves, and are of a more inventive nature. Such Souls are saved through their own strength, according to the Oracle.

MAGICAL AND PHILOSOPHICAL PRECEPTS

144. Direct not thy mind to the vast surfaces of the Earth; for the plant of truth grows not upon the ground. Nor measure the motions of the Sun, collecting rules, for he is carried by the Eternal Will of the Father, and not for your sake alone. Dismiss (from your mind) the impetuous course of the Moon, for she moveth always by the power of necessity. The progression of the stars was not generated for your sake. The wide aerial flight of birds gives no true knowledge not the dissection of the entrails of victims; they are all mere toys, the basis of mercenary fraud: flee these if you would enter the sacred paradise of piety, where Virtue, Wisdom and Equity are assembled.

Jesus summed up the gist of this Oracle in the Words, Judge not by appearances." The aim of the magician is to rise in consciousness above the sphere of necessity, above the rule of precedent, above the bondage of Karma. Omens have influence upon those who believe in them. The astrological progressions of the stars are fatal enough for one who submits to their domination. But he who has rooted his life in the center of Being behind personality can transcend what is sometimes called "the astral spirit."

145. Stoop not down unto the darkly splendid world; wherein continually lieth a faithless depth, and Hades wrapped in clouds, delighting in unintelligible images, precipitous, winding, a black ever-rolling Abyss; ever espousing a Body unluminous, formless and void.

146. Stoop not down, for a precipice lieth beneath the Earth, reached by a descending ladder which hath Seven Steps, and therein is established the throne of an evil and fatal force.

147. Stay not on the precipice with the dross of matter, for there is a place for thy Image in a realm ever splendid.

Nos. 145, 146, and 147 may be understood as referring to the dangerous psychic practices which result from a quest for power in the region of the subconsciousness. The reference to a ladder of Seven Steps in No. 146 may be compared with the Qabalistic idea that below Malkuth is the "infernal palaces" corresponding by inversion to the seven Sephiroth below the three Supernals.

148. Invoke not the visible Image of the Soul of Nature.

149. Look not upon Nature, for her name is fatal.

150. It becometh you not to behold them before your body is initiated, since by alway alluring they seduce the souls from the sacred mysteries.

151. Bring her not forth, lest in departing she retain something.

Nos. 143 to 151 indicate a subtle danger — that of investigating phenomenal relations before the mind is opened to the influx of Spirit, which alone can rightly interpret those relations.

152. Befile not the Spirit, nor deepen a superficies.

A superficies, or surface, is an appearance. To deepen a superficies is to ascribe to appearances a profundity which is not theirs, and this false judgment defiles Spirit. Never so much as in those systems of error which give power to appearances by asserting that "matter", or the sum-total of appearances, has a power which is inimical to Spirit.

155. Enlarge not thy Destiny.

A Hindu philosopher would give the same advice thus: "Do not generate unnecessary restrictive Karma."

155. Change not the barbarous names of evocation, for there are sacred names in every language which are given by God, having in the sacred rites a power ineffable.

157. Let fiery hope nourish you on the angelic plane.

158. The conception of the glowing Fire hath the first rank, for the mortal who approacheth that Fire shall have light from God; and unto the persevering mortal the Blessed Immortals are swift.

159. The gods exhort us to understand the radiating form of light.

160. It becometh you to hasten unto the Light, and to the Rays of the Father, from whom was sent unto you a soul (psyche) endued with much mind (nous).

161. Seek Paradise.

Paradise is the superconsciousness, the mystical "Garden", which is in Hebrew GN=53=ABN, the Stone of the Wise=ChMH, the Sun of the alchemists, which is in the sixth Sephira.

162. Learn the Intelligible for it subsisteth beyond the Mind.

163. There is a certain Intelligible One whom it becometh you to understand with the Flower of Mind.

Paradise is the consciousness of that Intelligible One which subsists beyond the Mind, That One Is what Herbert Spencer mistakenly calls the Unknowable. It is not to be grasped by Mind, whose highest aspect is the expression of self-consciousness in abstract mathematical ideas. It may nevertheless be known, and the knowing, or understanding, is the result of the unfoldment from the highest development of self-consciousness of something beyond Mind – the Flower of Mind. But it is to be noted that as flowers do not appear upon a plant until it has reached its perfection in stalk and branch, so the Flower of Mind does not open upon the stalk of self-consciousness until the latter has reached the limit of its development. That limit, as just indicated, is in certain forms of abstract mathematical (particularly geometrical) reasoning. This is why so much importance attaches to numbers and geometry in occult writings, including the books of the Old and New Testaments.

164. But the Paternal Mind accepteth not the aspiration of the soul until she hath passed out of her oblivious state, and pronounceth the WORD, regaining the memory of the pure paternal symbol.

Note here the importance of the Word and its pronunciation. See, too, that the enlightenment ensuing is a recollection, or "not-forgetting" (Aletheia, in Greek).

165. Unto some He gives ability to receive the Knowledge of Light; and others, even when asleep, He makes fruitful from His own strength.

The "Knowledge of Light" is a technical term of the Mysteries, Light in Greek is ΦΩΣ, by Greek Gematria the number 1500 = ΕΝΔΥΜΑ ΚΥΡΙΟΥ, Endyma Kyriou, the Robe of the Lord. The word ΕΝΔΥΜΑΤΑ, Endymata, Robes, is 601, which is the value of A plus Ω, Alpha and Omega, and also the value of ΠΕΡΙΣΤΕΡΑ, Peristera, the Dove. The Dove is the symbol of the Holy Spirit, or Ruach. The Robes, of which three are mentioned in the Pistis Sophia, are practically the same as the three veils of the Absolute (1. Ain, 2. Ain Soph, 3, Ain Soph Aur). They are robes of Lights.

The Greek word for Light, ΦΩΣ, Phos, is written with letters which are variants of the Hebrew P, O, and Sh. The Phos is the Mouth (Ph) or Utterer, the Seer (Omega, literally "Great O," or "Great Eye"), and the Devourer ("Shin", Tooth, associated with Fire.)

Note, too, that the Greek Gematria of ΦΩΣ, Phos, is related to the Hebrew Divine Name, Jah (IH), since Phos or Light is 1500, and IH=15.

Note also the last part of this Oracle, and compare with what is said of Sleep in Course A, in connection with the letter Qoph.

166. It is not proper to understand that Intelligible One with vehemence, but with the extended flame of far-reaching Mind; measuring all things except that Intelligible. But it is requisite to understand this; for if thou inclinest thy mind thou wilt understand it, not struggling; but it is becoming to bring with thee a pure and enquiring sense, to extend the void mind of thy Soul to the Intelligible, that thou mayest learn the Intelligible, because it subsisteth beyond Mind.

In some editions the word here translated "struggling is given as "earnestly," but the original Greek means "contending." The purport of the whole passage is of the same tenor as the words of the Emerald Tablet: "Separate the etherial from the gross, gently (or suavely) and with great ingenuity. It is important to keep in sight the words of the Oracle, "to extend the void mind of the Soul." This is like Lao-Tze's aphorism: "Having emptied yourself of everything, remain where you are."

167. Thou wilt not comprehend it, as when understanding some common thing.

To "comprehend" is to grasp fully. The higher understanding might be described as being comprehended, rather than as comprehension. Personal consciousness, as Paul says, is "caught up" into superconsciousness.

169. Things divine are not attainable by mortals who understand the body alone, but only by those who, stripped of their garments, arrive at the summit.

Compare this with the Qabalistic dictum, "Nulla res spiritualis deecendit sine indumento," "No spirit ever descends without a garment." Concerning this, Eliphas Levi makes the comment:

"The garments of the spirit have reference to the media through which it passes. As it is the lightness or heaviness of bodies which causes them to rise or to fall down, so the spirit clothes itself to descend and unclothes itself to go upward."

This Oracle also makes clear the distinction in consciousness between those who are on the path of return and those who are yet enmeshed in the snare of external appearances. The latter are "mortals," but the former have caught a glimpse of their immortality.

170. Having put on the completely armed vigour of resounding Light, with triple strength fortifying the soul and the mind, he must put into the mind the various symbols, and not walk dispersedly on the empyrean path, but with concentration.

Our Work aims to carry out the spirit of this Oracle. The earlier lessons have afforded you some opportunity to "sow the mind with symbols," and to learn the meaning of concentration. The symbols which are most important are those of the Hebrew alphabet. Of them it has been said, "The sacred letters are perfect hieroglyphics which express all Ideas." Eliphas Levi writes:

"Hence, by the combination of these letters, which are also numbers, are obtained combinations of ideas which are always new and always rigorously exact, like the operations of arithmetic. This is the signal wonder and the supreme power of Kabbalistic science."

172. Explore the River of the Soul, whence, or in what order you have come: so that although you have become a servant to the body, you may again rise to the Order from which you descended, joining works to sacred reason.

173. Every way unto the emancipated Soul extend the rays of Fire.

They extend even in that dimension which is held to be at right angles to our three dimensions, and it is from this Fourth Dimension that the consciousness of the practical magician works in ways which seem miracles to the uninstructed.

174. Let the immortal depth of your Soul lead you, but earnestly raise your eyes upward.

176 If thou extendeth to the fiery mind to the work of piety, thou wilt preserve the body.

178 The Oracles of the Gods declare, that through purifying ceremonies, not the Soul only but bodies themselves become worthy of receiving much assistance and health, for, say they, the mortal vestment of coarse matter will by these means be purified. And thus the gods, in an exhortatory manner, announce to the most holy of Theurgists.

179. We should flee, according to the Oracle, the multitude of men going in a herd.

One of the most important works of the practical occultist is to free himself from the dominance of the race-consciousness. This is what Jacob Boehme means by "walking in all things contrary to the world."

180. Who knoweth himself knoweth all things in himself.

181. The Oracles often give victory to our own choice, and not to the order alone of the mundane periods. As, for instance, when they say, "On beholding thyself, fear!" And again, "Believe thyself to be above the body, and thou art so." And, still further, when they assert, "That our voluntary sorrows germinate in us the growth of the particular life we lead."

185. Theurgists fall not so as to be ranked among the herd that are in subjection to Fate.

196. If thou often invokest thou shalt see all things growing dark; and then when no longer is visible unto thee the high-arched vault of heaven, when the stars have lost their light and the lamp of the moon is veiled, the earth abideth not, and around thee darts the Lightning Flame and all things appear amid thunders.

198. A similar Fire flashingly extending through the rushings of Air, or a Fire formless whence cometh the image of a Voice, or even a flashing light abounding, revolving, whirling forth, crying aloud. Also there is the vision of the fire-flashing courser of light, or also a child, borne aloft on the shoulders of the celestial steed, fiery, or clothed with gold, or naked, or shooting with the bow shafts of light; and standing on the shoulders of the horse; then if thy meditation prolongeth itself thou shalt unite all these symbols into the form of a lion.

199. When thou shalt behold that holy and formless fire shine flashingly through the depths of the universe: Hear thou the Voice of the Fire".

Fraternitas L.V.X. Occulta

--The Portal of Wisdom --

An Introduction to
The Fraternity of the Hidden Light

The Fraternitas L.V.X. Occulta (F.L.O.) is an esoteric order in the Western Mystery Tradition, tracing its lineage directly to the esteemed English tradition of the Hermetic Order of the Golden Dawn, which was founded at the turn of the twentieth century. Membership of the Golden Dawn has included notable figures such as: W. B. Yeats, George Bernard Shaw, Florence Farr, A.E. Waite, as well as many others. And, like the Golden Dawn, **F.L.O.** practices a system of spiritual disciplines best described as Hermetic Qabalah.

Hermeticism is based upon the teachings of Hermes Trismegistus, the great and legendary Egyptian Master of Masters. Hermes has been credited as being the father of Hermetic Wisdom, the founder of Astrology, and the discoverer of Alchemy.

The Qabalah is a dynamic system of Judeo–Christian theosophy, mysticism and theurgy, founded upon ancient teachings and traditions, as practiced by many traditions including the ancient Essenes whose members included John the Baptist and Jesus of Nazareth.

ESOTERICISM

Esotericism is the theory and practice of the arcane arts and sciences. Arcane by definition means "mysterious" or "secret" and these same secret arts have been practiced by the great Adepts and Masters of all ages. Furthermore, entire civilizations practiced these recondite arts, including the ancient Egyptians. In the Orient, esotericism is practiced openly as Yoga.

HISTORY

Mystery Schools, as individualized expressions of the Western Mystery Tradition, have been in existence for millennia, their origin lost in time. Tradition ascribes the founding of the first Mystery Schools to immortal beings of godlike stature, whose compassion for mankind lead them to form the Mystery Schools for the evolutionary advancement of a comparatively infant humanity.

These first Mystery Schools, having served their purpose, have long since vanished. Dying embers from their altars, how-ever, were carried to new temples and rekindled into burning flames, to be living messages to a humanity in great need. Notable among these various Schools formed through the centuries are those of Isis and Osiris, the Zoroastrian Mystery Schools, the Mysteries of Dionysus, the Mithraic Mysteries, the Eleusinian Mysteries, the Gnostics, the Essenes, the Sufis, the Knights Templar, and the Brotherhood of the Golden and Rosy Cross.

In 1888, a new and eclectic expansion of the Western Mystery Tradition for English speaking nations took form in Great Britain as the Hermetic Order of the Golden Dawn. A couple decades later an American branch was established as the Hermetic Order of the Golden Dawn in America. Reorganized under S. Liddel MacGregor Mathers, it became the Rosicrucian Order of the Alpha et Omega in America, with temples in Philadelphia, Los Angeles and San Francisco, and with its governing or mother temple in New York, the THOTH-HERMES Temple #9.

Perhaps one of the most important events for modern man in the history of the Western Mystery Tradition occurred in the 1920s when the Praemonstrator, or ruling Chief, of the Thoth-Hermes Temple, along with three other Officers, reorganized and expanded the teachings of the Alpha et Omega and formed a new Mystery School. This school operated under a new age dispensation und was a traditional order, formed to assist Piscean Age humanity into the Aquarian Age of Brotherhood and Humanitarianism

The founders of this new order have since made their own transition, but have left the vestiges of a lofty tradition intact and capable of infinite expansion by those who hold the "keys."

And now, the task has fallen to **F.L.O.**, inheritor of these "keys," to expand its tradition.

FRATERNITAS L.V.X. OCCULTA

Our name, **Fraternitas L.V.X. Occulta** (Latin for "Fraternity of the Hidden Light"), refers to that hidden light which is resident in all life, the Spirit Within.

Through application of a Qabalistic numerological system known as Gematria, "Hidden Light" equates to the phrase *"The stone which the builders rejected"*, and refers to the legend concerning the building of King Solomon's Temple, where the rejected stone became the Keystone of the Temple, the Temple of God and indwelling place of the Holy Shekinah.

Our fraternity is an order of the "Right Hand Path," and practices the Mysteries according to free will and for the purpose of uplifting all of Humanity.

STATEMENT OF PURPOSE

F.L.O. is an Aquarian Age Mystery School of the Western Mystery Tradition, organized for the following three-fold purpose:

I.   To act as a modern day repository of the Ancient Wisdom teachings of the Tarot, Qabalah, Alchemy, Astrology, and related Arcane Sciences;

II.   To train its members for unselfish service to humanity, by providing a seeding-ground for their growth and development through group and individual applications of the Wisdom teachings;

III.   To promulgate the Ancient Wisdom teachings in an effort to elevate the thought life of humanity at large, and help herald the coming of a universal brotherhood on earth.

Our Initiates advance through several grades of instruction and experience, which aid them in their quest to reach their highest potential. The common goal is illumination and the full expression of Wisdom, Love and Power. Wisdom is acquired by the experience of correct actions based upon true knowledge and insight. Love is developed through meditation, which prepares the heart for the illumination of Union with the ALL. Power is developed through the correct application of Wisdom and Love, as through Ritual. The power employed in the rituals of **F.L.O.** is the power of Love, the only true power in the Universe.

ORGANIZATION

The Fraternity of the Hidden Light does not discriminate against gender, religious or social background and status. The Order is organized into four levels. The first level is the Outer Court, which offers correspondence courses for dedicated seekers all over the world.

These courses are:

- **The Threshold Course**
- **The Path of Return**
- **Elements of Ceremonial**
- **Astrology for the Qabalist**

This preliminary level is probationary and members of the Outer Court are referred to as "Probationers". The materials they receive focus on developing a well rounded knowledge and understanding of the esoteric arts. All of the correspondence courses include theory and guided practices.

The "First" Order of **F.L.O.** is composed of the Initiates of a greater Mystery Tradition of which it is a part. The objective of the First Order is to train its members in the Lesser Mysteries and assist them to develop into balanced centers of expression for Wisdom, Love, and Power.

As Initiates progress through the curriculum and practices of the First Order they learn to develop each element of their being, resulting in balance and harmony. The goal is to be in control of ones own actions, thoughts, and emotions, and ideally, at peace with oneself, the world and all of its creatures.

The "Second" or "Inner" Order is composed of Initiates of the Greater Mysteries who not only have developed balance and harmony in themselves, but who have also received illumination. Their Higher Self is both awakened and in control of their lives. They seek to become those who truly "know" and can serve humanity.

The "Third" or "Invisible" Order is composed solely of Great Adepts and Masters throughout the ages. These great souls guide the Order, and other spiritual organizations that have similar objectives and high ideals. The Masters that guide the Fraternity of the Hidden Light serve the Will of God.

CURRICULUM

The curriculum of the **F.L.O.** is a structured, graduated system. This system utilizes the ancient grades as a means of identifying the level a student has reached for the purpose of receiving the Ancient Wisdom teachings.

The curriculum is personally guided, and consists of study, meditation, and ritual. Lessons center primarily around the Qabalah, the Tarot, Alchemy, Hermeticism, Astrology, and Esoteric Psychology. Meditation is used to bring about an in-depth understanding of the teachings and to create in the aspirant a personal communication link with the only true teacher, one's Higher Self.

Rituals are used for numerous purposes, the most frequent being initiatory, which are aimed at invoking quantum changes in consciousness. These changes lead to recognition of the inner realities behind the outward appearance of things.

An important part of our curriculum involves applications of our teachings towards healing. Through the use of Light and Sound, a harmonizing and equilibrating energy is released for all those who are in need: *be they student, friend, or foe.*

MEMBERSHIP

Membership of the outer court of the Fraternity entitles the Probationer to receive the Threshold correspondence course. This course consists of 32 Lessons of which you receive two monthly by mail. The curriculum includes the study of the Tree of Life, Tarot, Meditation, and the work of the Esoteric Orders. After completion you can continue membership and study the Path of Return, Elements of Ceremonial and Astrology for the Qabalist. The correspondence courses are different from the work of our Initiates. Only initiated members are provided with the occult knowledge of the grade work and access into a lodge.

The Fraternity of the Hidden Light is very selective in accepting members for initiation into its lodges, and seeks only those who truly desire to grow in Love and who willingly commit to serve humanity.

Before applying for Initiation into a lodge of the **FRATERNATAS L.V.X. OCCULTA,** a minimum of three months is required as a Probationer. Completion of the probationary period, however, is not an entitlement to membership. Rather, it is a condition pursuant thereto.

Members of the Outer Court who are considered for initiation will be expected to submit a proficiency examination demonstrating a basic knowledge of the esoteric science.

"At Large" membership in a working Lodge is available to sincere students who are able to travel to the nearest lodge at least twice a year. We don't perform "astral" Initiations or Attunements.

HOW TO APPLY FOR MEMBERSHIP

Apply via www.lvx.org/enroll.htm or fill in the Information on application form and mail it to:

Director of Probationers
Fraternity of the Hidden Light
P.O. Box 836432
Richardson, TX 75083-6432

Before applying, however please visit our website at www.lvx.org to learn more about the Fraternity and consider well the statements made in this brochure.

The Fraternitas L.V.X. Occulta, like all true mystery schools, never urges an aspirant to become a member. This is a step you should seriously consider without persuasion.

A well-known saying among initiates of the Western Mystery Tradition is "When the student is ready, a teacher will appear."

Are you ready?

In the meantime, may the Love and Light of the Lord of the Universe guide us all to the full realization of the Age of Brotherhood.

In L.V.X.,

The Grand Lodge

Sub Umbra Alarum Tuarum

Issued under the Authority and by Dispensation of:

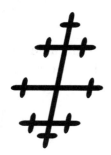

THE STEWARD
FRATERNITAS L.V.X. OCCULTA

APPLICATION FOR PROBATIONARY MEMBERSHIP

Please photocopy this page and send to address on page 180 or
apply on-line at www.lvx.org/enroll.htm

PERSONAL INFORMATION

Name: _____

Address: _____

City/State/Zip: _____

Phone Number: _____

E Mail Address: _____

Birthplace: _____

Birth date and Time: _____

Male __ Female __ Marital Status: _____

Education: _____

Occupation: _____

Interests: _____

_____

_____

If you are a member of any secret, fraternal or philosophical organizations, please give names:

_____

_____

_____

I hereby make application for probationary membership in the Fraternity of the Hidden Light. I
have enclosed my check, or money order for $15.00 to cover my first month's probationary
membership dues or $45 for a quarter year (includes receipt of our correspondence course, The
Threshold). U.S. funds please.

_____   _____

Signature   Date

CPSIA information can be obtained
at www.ICGtesting.com
Printed in the USA
LVHW012004290822
727047LV00007B/151

9 780981 897738

MW00490935

Liberated
STRING QUILTS

GWEN MARSTON

C&T PUBLISHING

© 2003, Gwen Marston, Artwork and Text

© 2003, C&T Publishing Artwork

Editor-in-Chief: Darra Williamson

Editor: Jan Grigsby

Technical Editors: Carolyn Aune, Joyce Lytle

Copyeditor/Proofreaders: Molly Greensaid, Stacy Chamness

Cover Designer: Kristen Yenche

Design Director/Book Designer: Kristen Yenche

Illustrator: Richard Sheppard

Production Assistant: Jeff Carrillo, Luke Mulks

Photography: Steven C. Tuttle, The Collection of Nancy Ray; John Boucher,
all other quilts.

Published by C&T Publishing, Inc., P.O. Box 1456, Lafayette, California, 94549

Front cover: *Amish String Quilt*

Back cover: *String Bars* and *Liberated String Basket*

All rights reserved. No part of this work covered by the copyright hereon may be
reproduced or used in any form or any means—graphic, electronic, or mechanical,
including photocopying, recording, taping, or information storage and retrieval
systems—without written permission of the publisher.

The copyrights on individual artworks are retained by the artists as noted in
Liberated String Quilts.

Attention Copy Shops: Please note the following exception—Publisher and author
give permission to photocopy pages 78, 92, and 93 for personal use only.

Attention Teachers: C&T Publishing, Inc. encourages you to use this book as a text
for teaching. Contact us at 800-284-1114 or www.ctpub.com for more information about the C&T Teachers Program.

We take great care to ensure that the information included in this book is accurate
and presented in good faith, but no warranty is provided nor results guaranteed.
Having no control over the choices of materials or procedures used, neither the
author nor C&T Publishing, Inc. shall have any liability to any person or entity
with respect to any loss or damage caused directly or indirectly by the information
contained in this book. For your convenience, we post an up-to-date listing of
corrections on our web page (www.ctpub.com). If a correction is not already
noted, please contact our customer service department at ctinfo@ctpub.com or
at P.O. Box 1456, Lafayette, California, 94549.

Trademarked (™) and Registered Trademark (®) names are used throughout this
book. Rather than use the symbols with every occurrence of a trademark and
registered trademark name, we are using the names only in the editorial fashion
and to the benefit of the owner, with no intention of infringement.

Library of Congress Cataloging-in-Publication Data

Marston, Gwen.

    Liberated string quilts / Gwen Marston.

       p. cm.

    ISBN 1-57120-207-2 (paper trade)

    1. Patchwork--Patterns. 2. Quilting—Patterns. I. Title.

    TT835.M27245 2003

    746.46'041--dc21

                                                2003002508

Printed in China

10 9 8 7 6 5 4 3 2

Dedication

This book is dedicated to my sister
Amber Joy, who, like these quilts, is
innovative, resourceful and a real scrapper.

Acknowledgements

Many thanks to Mary Ellen Dunneback,
Jan Workman, and Chris Roosien for
allowing me to show their quilts in this
book, and I thank Nancy Ray for her
generosity in sharing her spectacular
collection of antique quilts. Thanks also
to Christopher Young, whose essay added
immeasurably to the understanding of
string quilts. My additional thanks to
John Boucher of Beaver, Island Michigan,
for providing the photography of my
quilts and to Steve Tuttle of Alexandria,
Virginia, for photographing antique quilts
in the collection of Nancy Ray. I am
especially grateful to Elizabeth Bird
Noguchi who took the quilts to Steve's
studio and assisted him as he photographed
this wonderful collection. Finally, I thank
the staff at C&T Publishing for their
guidance throughout the preparation
of this book.

Table *of* Contents

INTRODUCTION

Definition 6

History of String Quilts 6

Foundation Piecing 6

String Quilts and the Great Depression 7

African-American Strings 8

Amish Strings 8

Common String Patterns 9

Liberated String Quilts: Achieving the same
look without foundation piecing 9

A Contemporary Perspective on String Quilts
by Christopher R. Young 11

CHAPTER 1—GENERAL INSTRUCTIONS

Design Principals for String Quilts 13

Fabric 13

Tools 14

Construction 14

Pressing .14

Adding Borders 15

Backing 15

Batting 15

The Summer Spread 15

Tying 15

Hand and Machine Quilting 16

Finishing a String Quilt 16

**CHAPTER 2—WORKING WITH
SHORT STRINGS**

String Quilt Set on Point 21

In the Beginning 23

Pinwheel String with String Border 25

String Bars 28

Liberated Strings and Stars 30

GALLERY 33

**CHAPTER 3—WORKING WITH
LONG STRINGS**

String Quilt with Sashing
and Corner Squares 44

Arkansas Traveler 46

String Quilt 48

Amish String Quilt 51

Bunny String Quilt with Double Sashing . .54

Mary Ellen's String with Red Center 57

Chevron String Bars 59

Slanted Bars 62

**CHAPTER 4—WORKING WITH
RECTANGLES**

Amish Rectangular String 67

Quartered String Quilt 69

CHAPTER 5—WORKING WITH WEDGES

String Tulip Block 74

Liberated Wedding Ring 76

**CHAPTER 6—WORKING WITH
TRADITIONAL BLOCKS**

Amish String Star 82

Liberated String Basket 86

Nine-Patch with String Border 89

Patterns .92

BIBLIOGRAPHY 94

INDEX .96

Introduction

LIBERATED STRING QUILTS

As a diligent collector and student of antique quilts, I've long known about string quilts; still, it wasn't until 1999 that I began to study them seriously. As my exploration continued, the powerful visual qualities of these quilts became increasingly apparent. Created without pretense, string quilts virtually personify art; I consider them the "Jackson Pollacks" of textiles, as spontaneous, vibrant, and dramatic as his paintings. Most string quilts were made by quilters with few means, unschooled in art, yet their naïve beauty can withstand the scrutiny of quilt and art critics alike. Though conceived in humble beginnings string quilts have, in my view, moved to the head of the class we now call art quilts.

Traditionally, string quilts were made from narrow pieces of fabric too small to be used for other purposes; they were stitched by women who, in many cases, had only this minimal resource to keep their families warm. They were made quickly and by necessity, sometimes crudely, sewn with available scraps. They were made without a commercial pattern, without a design wall, and well before art quilts had become a concept. Still, they take a back seat to none. Because of the way they're made, there are no duplicates; each quilt is an original work. A look at antique string quilts is a humbling experience. One after another, these pieces dazzle the eye with their unexpected brilliance.

◀ STRING QUILT, *c. 1930. Maker Unknown. Collection of Nancy Ray.*

Definition:

What one person calls a string quilt, another calls a strip quilt, and yet another calls a cotton crazy quilt. Most would agree, however, that string quilts are made with strips (strings) sewn to a foundation block, either paper or fabric, with the term "string" referring to the irregular widths of material. Some string quilts are fairly orderly, made with strings cut in similar widths. Others are made with radically different sized strings, creating a more chaotic, random effect.

History of String Quilts:

Of the many string quilts that certainly were made, few antique string quilts have survived. Made primarily for utility, most simply got worn out and used up. Those that did survive were often made in a hurry, with little attention to careful technique. Lacking in technique, they were often overlooked by quilt collectors as unworthy of serious consideration. To borrow Cuesta Benberry's words, they were "always there", but, for the most part, not taken seriously by the quilting community.

Little documentation exists on string quilts so the ability to conduct research on the subject is limited. We can talk to quilters who grew up surrounded by string quilts and who still make them. But, for the most part, we have to rely on what the quilts themselves tell us. We can date the fabrics, and we can see how they were constructed.

While not restricted to any one geographical area, string quilts are as Southern as cornbread and just as familiar to quilters from that region. As surely as country-women knew how to plant a garden in the springtime, they knew how to make this kind of quilt. String quilts were generally made by poor people living in rural areas. A major share of them came from Tennessee, Alabama, Mississippi, Kentucky, and Texas.

Foundation Piecing:

Foundation piecing begins by cutting the pattern shape from paper or fabric, called "the foundation"; this method makes it possible to construct a block from widely different sized scraps, and to control small, misshapen pieces that would otherwise be hard to use. Once sewn, any extra fabric gets trimmed away.

Foundation piecing has been used since about 1860 to make standard Log Cabin, Rail Fence and Pineapple quilts. I have several Log Cabin quilts circa 1880 that are foundation pieced on muslin, and I have two Rail Fence quilts made no later than 1910 that were constructed in the same way. While foundation pieced, these particular quilt patterns differ from string quilts in one significant way-they were made of uniformly cut pieces while string quilts were made of irregular, distinctly random pieces.

When foundations were cut from fabric, that fabric was most often recycled. I have a number of vintage quilt tops pieced on cloth foundations cut from very worn cloth. No longer of value for other purposes, the tattered cloth performed more than adequately when used as a foundation. The Rail Fence quilt, page 7, was made by sewing wool strips to clearly re-used fabric foundations.

Any and all forms of paper became foundations including newspapers, old letters, department store paper bags, grocery sacks and phone book pages. When paper was used, it was usually removed before the blocks were sewn together or quilted, but when left intact, paper foundations offer an additional advantage. If printed, paper foundations on unquilted tops can provide important historical and anecdotal information from the times and thus aid in dating a quilt. For example, the *String Star* quilt shown on page 8, was pieced on newspaper that reveals both where and when the quilt was made. It reads *"The Knoxville Journal,* Wednesday, April 17, 1957." In addition to valuable historical information, we get a picture of local events, such as this enlistment announcement:

"Hamblen Youth Enlists in Navy
Arthur Keith Knowling, son of Mr. and Mrs. Ray Jackson Knowling of Route 4, Morristown, has enlisted in the U.S. Navy. Knowling enlisted through the U.S. Navy incrutment (sic) Branch Station here in Morristown and was sworn into the Navy at Nashville on January 16, 1957."

The newspaper foundation of the star block shown on page 8 could qualify as material for a Eudora Welty short story. In this edition of the *Charlotte Observer*, under the heading "Recorder's Court," we learn that Lincoln County Recorder's Court was held Monday, January 30, 1961 and that a certain person, who shall remain unnamed, was accused of "larceny of gasoline." (The charges were dismissed when he voluntarily enlisted in the U.S. Army!) It appears that speeding was a big temptation for the residents of Charlotte, as nineteen traffic violations were also listed.

And, if you can't remember which car was voted Car of the Year in 1961, this string star foundation tells us it was Pontiac's Tempest: "Tempest is a winner. Check the facts! 110 to 155 h.p. from a gas-saving 4. Big car ride. Independent wheel suspension. 15-inch wheels at no extra cost! Priced with the compacts. See your Pontiac dealer."

String Quilts and the Great Depression:
The Great Depression brought with it an unheralded resurgence in string quilts. Hard times meant economizing. It meant using what you had around-making do, and that meant the sewing of quilts using small, odd shaped scraps. Many surviving string quilts dating from the 1930s and 1940s are sewn in the pastel cotton prints and loosely woven printed feed sacks typical of the period. Feedsack fabric, is generally loosely woven, making it hard to work with if precision piecing is the goal. Making string quilts from feed sacks, however, are a great idea as precision is much less an issue in string quilt construction.

RAIL FENCE TOP *72" x 91", c.1910. Wool. Collected in Burlington, Iowa. Collection of Gwen Marston.*

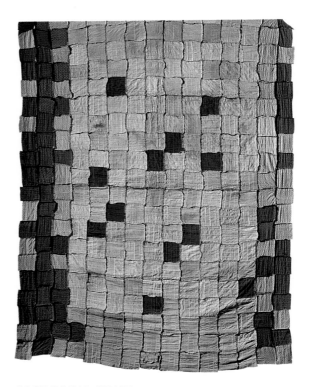

BACK OF RAIL FENCE. *Foundation patterns cut from recycled clothing.*

African-American Strings:

String quilts are well known among African-American quilters. Some sources claim they are familiar with the form because it comes directly from African textile traditions. (Vlach, John Michael. *The Afro-American Tradition in Decorative Arts,* 1978.) On a trip to West Africa, I saw weavers working on narrow looms, just as they have for centuries. They weave cloth in long narrow strips, which they stitch together to make a larger, finished textile. The long vertical strips often have horizontal designs, not unlike some string quilts.

Dr. Carolyn Mazloomi has a different view, and, as founder and coordinator of the Women of Color Quilters Network, she holds a position of authority on the subject. Reminding us that she, for example, can't remember anything about her ancient homeland, Dr. Mazloomi claims that quilting by African-Americans today "comes about from a conscious effort of studying our culture." (*A Communion of The Spirits,* p. 273.)

STRING STAR BLOCK, *front and back,* 37" wide, 1961. Charlotte, North Carolina. Collection of Gwen Marston.

While no one knows with certainty how African-Americans got the idea for making string quilts, somehow they did, and they learned the lesson very well indeed. It was a group of African-American quilters who first taught me to make a string block on foundation. In the early 1980s I attended an exhibit of African-American quilts at the Flint, Michigan Public Library. Derenda Collins and Jeffalone Rumph sat me down, handed me an eight-inch square of paper, a bundle of strings, and put me to work. In 1987 Jeffalone Rumph was responsible for organizing the Flint Afro-American Quilters Guild, which is still going strong today. Her contributions have been cited in Roland Freeman's book *A Communion of the Spirits,* and in *African-American Quiltmaking in Michigan,* edited by Marsha McDowell.

Amish Strings:

Antique Amish String quilts, made in the bold, solid, saturated colors characteristic of the sect, are nothing short of spectacular. A number of such quilts are seen in Eve Wheatcroft Granick's book *The Amish Quilt,* where they are referred to as crazy quilts, but the term "string" is justified as well. What is *crazy* and what is *string* is not clearly defined and it need not be.

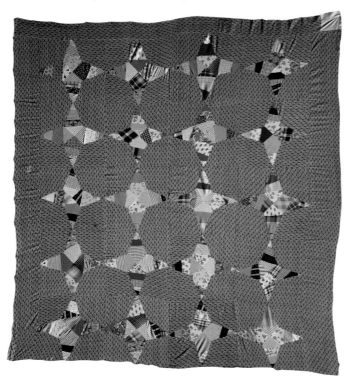

STRING STAR TOP, *80" x 86", 1957. Tennessee.* Collection of Gwen Marston.

Common String Patterns:

Perhaps the most common string quilt pattern consists of strings sewn diagonally on a square block. Nancy Ray, whose quilt collection is shown in this book, told me she spoke with one quilter who called this pattern "Road to Nowhere"; when the blocks are assembled in different ways, the results are all distinctly different. Sometimes the strings are sewn on the straight instead of on the diagonal.

Star patterns are commonly used in many variations. Other string patterns are Pieced Diamonds, Spider Web, and Snowball.

Star Variations

 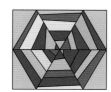

Diamond   *Spider Web*   *Snowball*

Most string quilts are block quilts, but not all. Some quilters sewed long strings together one after the other creating an entire quilt. Pat Townes made the string quilt shown here. Pat is a prolific quiltmaker. After seeing a similar string quilt she had made, I commissioned her to make one for me.

PAT'S STRING QUILT, *57" x 80", 1994. Made and hand quilted in all over fans by Pat Townes. Collection of Gwen Marston.*

Liberated String Quilts: Achieving the same look without foundation piecing

Foundation piecing was the forerunner to today's paper piecing, and like paper piecing, this technique is "slow as molasses." Over the years, I've created several alternative methods for making string quilts. All are far quicker than foundation piecing, thus "liberating" me from the tedium of that technique. Dictated in part by the patterns, I developed five different methods, all of which eliminate time-consuming foundation piecing: working with short strings, long strings, rectangles, wedges, and traditional blocks.

One of the wonderful features of string quilts is the endless diversity they offer, so any way you can think of to make the work easier or more interesting can be stirred into the mix. My methods only open the door for you to make your own discoveries. String quilts are improvisational; they are neither planned in advance nor manipulated on a design wall. Grand results come not from intellectualizing, but from letting go, letting be.

A Contemporary Perspective on String Quilts

There are many complex variables confronting us when evaluating the aesthetic merits of string quilts. Before allowing ourselves the pleasure of appreciating and understanding the intricate designs and colorist poetry of string quilts, most of us seem compelled to substantiate and justify them in terms of modern art. Several significant factors contributed to quilts moving from their domestic roles and humble beginnings as bed covers to the public walls of museum and galleries in our contemporary world.

With the ever-increasing pace of life during the twentieth century, brought about by the industrial and technological revolutions, there has been a growing view of a world moving toward self-destruction. Paralleling this escalating pace and the rise of existential anxiety came the radical breakdown of the 36,000-year-old tradition of representational picture making. It was not until the second decade of the twentieth century that the first truly abstract paintings were executed. For the first time in the history of art, pictures were not based on recognizable subjects, but on the decorative and expressive possibilities of line, color and form. While abstraction was considered revolutionary in the art world, the humble tradition of quilt making had been doing geometric, minimalist, colorfield and optical abstractions for centuries.

Another contributing factor for the current acceptance of quilts in the realm of fine arts is pop culture's assimilation of Albert Einstein's phrase "all is relative." The appropriation of this idea by the masses, disembodied from Einstein's elaborate theory, has resulted in a pervasive attitude that "anything goes." Responding to the havoc caused by new machines of destruction used in World War I and this popularized notion of relativism, Marcel Duchamp made numerous absurdist statements about aesthetics. One of his most famous and playful "ready-mades" involved a men's white-porcelain urinal, which he placed on a pedestal in a gallery and declared it a work of art. While challenging conventional standards, Duchamp's liberating example opened people's minds to new possibilities that have continued to percolate over the century. In this context another door was opened for the recognition of quilts.

In developing an abstract vocabulary, Wassily Kandinsky looked to the art of children for inspiration. He was the first of a growing number of artists who refused to be limited by the rigid academic regime. Kandinsky sought purer, soulful expressions unencumbered by art-school rhetoric and traditional chauvinisms. The dynamic asymmetry of a string quilt like Spider Web has numerous compositional similarities to Kandinsky's cosmic and celestial paintings of the mid-1920s. Both Kandinsky's paintings and this string quilt utilize unanchored, free-floating circular and biomorphic motifs that seem to mysteriously bubble up across the surface. Further, Kandinsky, who was a thoroughly trained artist, believed real expression came from an internal creative force rather than an external vision or technical skill. In this vein, Kandinsky would have tolerated, if not embraced, the obvious imperfections in the construction of some of these string quilts. This issue of technical execution is an important consideration for many contemporary quilt makers obsessed with precise technical execution to the point of denying themselves any appreciation of the inventive intricacies of design and the movingly expressive orchestration of color. When looking at the use of color in these string quilts, reflect on Kandinsky's well-known quote:

Generally speaking, color directly influences the soul. Color is the keyboard, the eyes are the hammers, and the soul is the piano with many strings. The artist is the hand that plays, touching one key or another purposely, to cause vibration in the soul. (The Effect of Color, 1911)

STRING QUILT, 81" x 82". C. 1930. Wisconsin.
Maker Unknown. Collection of Nancy Ray.

Scholarly revisionism has also aided us in developing our sensitivity to the aesthetic qualities of quilts. During the 1920s quilts gained value as folk art, but in the 1960s along with the feminist movement a significant shift occurred. Over the last four decades there has been an increasing number of articles, books and exhibitions reevaluating the merits of quilts. With this expanding interest in quilts, more people have written comparisons between traditional quilt designs and the modernist movements, such as op art, minimalism, geometric abstraction and colorfield. Since the groundbreaking exhibition Abstract Design in American Quilts in 1971, held at the prestigious Whitney Museum of American Art, the popularity of quilts has begun to soar.

Deservedly quilts have gained recognition as a valid form of artistic expression, but this appreciation is still limited to only certain types and traditions. The respected art critic Robert Hughes endorsed the progressive nature of Amish quilts in his essay for a book compiled by Julie Silber, *Amish: The Art of the Quilts* in 1990. Hughes also included an Amish quilt in his survey text, *American Visions: The Epic History of Art in America,* published in conjunction with a popular PBS series in 1997.

CRASH STRING TOP, BARS, *73" x 85", c. 1900-border possibly added later. Maker Unknown. Collection of Nancy Ray.

However, he only scratched the surface when he called Amish quilts the "first abstract art" in America and compared them to works by contemporary luminaries, such as Josef Albers, Frank Stella and Mark Rothko. While much attention has been given to the illustrious tradition of Amish quilts, little is know and even less has been written about the visually stimulating tradition of string quilts.

Among the expanding body of literature comparing quilts to modern art, I am unaware of any strong comparison with the most significant American art movement of the Twentieth century: Abstract Expressionism. The untitled quilt (no. 28) has the dynamics of totally non-objective, all-over gestural paintings made by Jackson Pollack between 1947 and 1950. Instead of the fabric being pieced together to form a distinct repeating geometric pattern common to most quilts, this example is composed of a fluid network of lines and facets of color without the normal anchoring grid. Pollack's paintings have been interpreted as a metaphor for chaos, uncertainty and existential traumas of the modern world. Along these lines, this quilt may capture the essential uncertainty and angst of a modern mother and wife, who has daily concerns about making ends meet and providing adequate care for her family in a seemingly uncaring world.

What is most remarkable about this group of string quilts is how the most basic and simple technique of sewing strips of salvaged fabric together can result in such sophisticated designs and stunning visuals. Generally, underprivileged and poorly educated women created these string quilts that rival the innovative paintings by modern artists. Without pretense and pumped up theoretical justifications, these quilts were an economic means of recycling materials to keep loved ones warm. This selection of quilts provides a rare opportunity to expand our understanding of another facet of quilt making and to view yet another group in terms of modernist achievements.

Christopher R. Young
Adjunct Lecturer
Art Department
University of Michigan-Flint

▲ STRING QUILT, *58" x 71½", c. 1910. Tied, with feather stitching.*

Maker Unknown. Collection of Nancy Ray.

It's safe to say that, in the past, the general instructions for making a string quilt went something like this: "Just make it. Figure it out for yourself. After all, how hard can it be?" I'm tempted to leave it at that. Still, if you've never made a string quilt, certain questions are bound to arise. What follows are general guidelines, giving you license to experiment with fabric, construction, and design as you see fit. There are no hard and fast rules to follow, no prescribed technique to confine you. Looking at the antique string quilts, I would guess they were made by resourceful and inventive problem-solvers, working without benefit of written instructions. It's a good idea to remember this as you make your first string quilt; just do what makes sense to you.

Design Principals for String Quilts

Rather than planning the quilt in advance, string quilts have traditionally been designed as they were being made. Instead of pre-cutting all the strings, cut some and begin to sew them together. Once the work is in progress you can better tell what other fabrics you need to stir into the mix. You might decide you need to add a bright color to spice things up, or you need more variation in the width of the strings. It's like making chili; you start with the major ingredients, and once it's cooking you can taste it and tell what needs to be added to make it utterly delicious.

Work intuitively. Don't overintellectualize. The antique string quilts shown in this book were not the result of laborious study and meticulous stitching, in the same way as abstract painters were not struggling to stay inside the lines. String quilts have always been made by sewing strings together randomly, and that very randomness is an essential artistic characteristic of string quilts. The thing about random is that you can't plan it.

STRING WITH RED CENTER, 37½" x 50½", C. 1940.
Flint Michigan. Maker unknown. Collection of Gwen Marston.

Fabric

Taking a cue from antique string quilts, which were made of every conceivable fabric, I suggest that you follow suit. As with the technique, no rules apply to fabric selection for string quilts. While my preference is for 100% cotton fabrics, wools, silks, and vintage feed sacks pose no problems when used, and actually add to the random design appeal of the quilt. In my collection I even have a string quilt that could have been made from 1955 prom dresses-taffetas, laces and tulle!

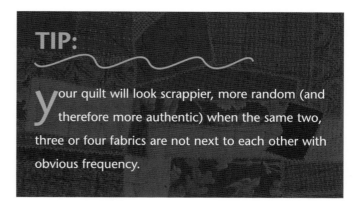

TIP:

Your quilt will look scrappier, more random (and therefore more authentic) when the same two, three or four fabrics are not next to each other with obvious frequency.

Tools

The tools I recommend for string quilting are a rotary cutter, quilter's rulers and a cutting mat.

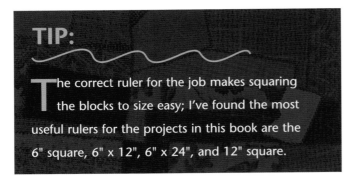

TIP:

The correct ruler for the job makes squaring the blocks to size easy; I've found the most useful rulers for the projects in this book are the 6" square, 6" x 12", 6" x 24", and 12" square.

Beyond these recommendations, I suggest you just use the quilting and sewing tools that are most comfortable for you—nothing fancy is required. Even a very modest sewing machine will suffice. All my quilts are pieced on an old, but very reliable, straight stitch sewing machine.

Construction

Although I've allowed a standard ¼" seam in my projects, precise seam allowances are not critical. Unlike traditional blocks, string blocks are all squared to size once finished and pressed, taking care of any irregularities in size and shape.

I used chain piecing to make all the quilts for this book, sewing one unit after another continuously, saving both time and thread.

Piece the blocks, press well and square blocks to same size.

Pressing

Every block or unit should be pressed before it is joined to another block or unit.

String pieced blocks often have bias edges and many seams. Therefore, it's important to press and handle blocks carefully to avoid stretching them out of square.

Pressing blocks correctly is key for the blocks to lie flat and join together with ease. The goal is to press the block so all the strings lay flat without pleats or folds, in a manner that won't stretch the blocks out of square. Here's the system that works best for me:

- Mist the blocks with a light spray or steam iron.
- Press on wrong side first with a firm but gentle touch.
- Turn block right side up and press again.

I don't fight the seam allowances; I let them turn either way. With string piecing there is no right or wrong way the seams should turn. The important thing is to make sure each seam goes in one direction only and doesn't change its mind half way along.

Adding Borders

The most accurate way to measure for borders is to measure through the center of your quilt. Add the long sides of your quilt first. Pin both ends and then the midpoint of the border. Place additional pins about every 2" between the first pins. Careful measuring and pinning make sure your borders lie flat and won't waffle. It is worth taking the extra time and care to make sure you get the borders sewn on right the first time.

Backing

The backing should be about 1½" to 2" larger than the quilt top all the way around. In other words, cut the backing about 4" longer and wider than the top. If you need to piece the back to make it wide enough, remember there are no rules for how the backing should be pieced. Quilters have traditionally chosen the most practical, most obvious way to piece their backings.

Batting

I prefer to use 100% cotton batting because I like the flat look of antique quilts, and I like natural fibers. Others prefer polyester because of the loft, and because it is easier to needle and doesn't require as close quilting as cotton.

My method for cutting the batting is to lay it over the stretched backing, smooth it out and trim off the extra. This method requires no measuring.

The Summer Spread

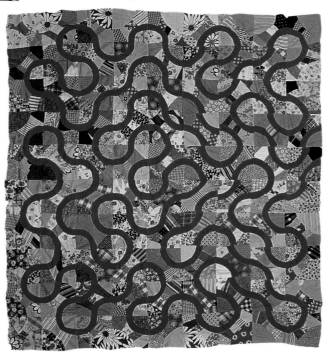

STRING TOP, *73" x 81½", c. 1950. Oklahoma. Maker Unknown. Collection of Nancy Ray.*

The summer spread is a traditional bed covering for warm summer nights, and what a great idea it is—no batting and little or no quilting. It's also a good way to get a quilt finished.

I have several antique summer spreads in my collection; some have backs and some don't. A backing is preferable because the seams are protected and won't fray. I either minimally machine quilt, or tie, summer spreads. The edges can be finished by bringing backing around to the top, (or the top around to the back) folding under the raw edges and machine stitching it in place.

Tying

Remember the saying "it's not a quilt unless it's quilted?" I believed it myself until I realized how many wonderful string quilts were tied, and how much fun the ties could be; they add texture and color. They seem playful, even entertaining. Antique string quilts that were tied looked good then and they look good now.

Out of necessity, quilts were tied with every conceivable type of thread. Some that were commonly used are cotton embroidery floss, pearl cotton, crochet thread, tatting thread, and wool yarn (both light and heavy weight). Wool has a distinctive quality that once washed, the fibers lock together keeping the ties tied. Silk also has a distinctive quality that makes it unsuitable for tying—it doesn't stay tied.

My favorite way to tie a quilt is using six strands of cotton embroidery floss to create a square knot. Sometimes I use a single color that compliments the quilt, and other times I combine colors. Ties can be cut short or left long and can be spaced close together or far apart.

Hand and Machine Quilting

COMPOSITION STRING, 42" x 49", C. 2000.
Made and handquilted by Gwen Marston.

When hand-quilted, string quilts were done in a very simple pattern. Fan quilting, (another Southern tradition) with its graceful concentric arches, was a favorite choice of pattern for heavily pieced string quilts. Its simplicity made it a comfortable companion to the patterns of string quilts.

I used outline quilting on some of my string quilts, quilting ¼" away from the seam line to avoid the extra layers of fabric. For borders I chose common designs such as cables and continuous feathers. In general, I kept the quilting simple and informal.

A few of my quilts are machine quilted. Once again, simple, straight-line quilting is appropriate. My thread preference is cotton in a color that blends well with the colors in the quilt.

Finishing a String Quilt

My string quilt projects recommend one of three methods to finish the quilt: the back to front finish, the pillowslip method and adding a separate binding.

The Back to Front Finish:

STRING QUILT, 65½" x 82", C. 1930. Lookout Mountain, Tennessee.
Maker Unknown. Collection of Nancy Ray.

In times past, bringing the back around to the front was a popular way to finish the edges. The backing was brought around to the top side, the raw edge folded under and either hand stitched or top stitched in place.

This method made sense because it saved fabric using what was already there instead of cutting a separate binding. While not common today, this method seems especially appropriate for string quilts as it echoes the sensibilities of antique quilts made for utility.

The trick to a neat finished edge is in following these steps with care. Don't rush. Take your time and trim the batting and backing accurately.

- Using scissors, carefully trim away the batting to the edge of the quilt top.

- Using a quilter's ruler and rotary cutter, trim the backing to ¾" beyond the edge of the quilt top all the way around.

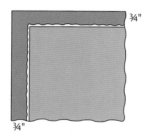

- Fold the backing around to the top so the raw edge of the backing comes to the raw edge of the quilt top. Fold the edge over again making a finished edge. Pin thoroughly, about every 2½".

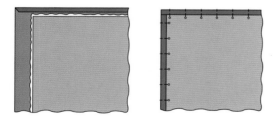

- Using matching thread, sew the edge down by hand or machine.

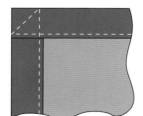

The Pillowslip Method:

STRING TOP, *59" x 72½". C. 1930. Missouri. Maker Unknown. Collection of Nancy Ray.*

1. Cut the backing larger than the top, adding 2" all the way around.

2. Press both top and backing *thoroughly*.

3. Lay the backing on a hard surface and position the top on the back, *right sides together*.

4. Smooth it out, smooth it out, and smooth it out again.

5. With fine silk pins, pin every 2½" all the way around the edges.

6. Beginning and ending with a backstitch, machine stitch ¼" from the edges all around the quilt, leaving a large enough opening so the quilt can be turned right side out.

7. Trim the corners. Turn the quilt right side out. Press thoroughly.

8. Hand stitch the opening closed with a slipstitch or the stitch of your choice.

9. Stabilize the summer spread with either minimal hand or machine quilting, or by tying it.

Binding:

You can use a separate binding, either single or double-fold.

The vast majority of nineteenth century quilts had a single-fold binding cut on the straight of the goods. That is my preference too. A single-fold binding is easy to handle and it gives a fine line to the edge of the quilt. While popular today, the double-fold binding looks too bulky for my taste.

- Rotary cut 1¼" strips and join them together on the diagonal. A diagonal cut will help the finished seam lie flat.

- Lay the binding along the edge of the quilt right sides together.

- Miter the corners. Sew to exactly ¼" from the edge of the quilt. Backstitch, lift the presser foot and pull the quilt away from the sewing machine. Fold the binding up and away from the quilt at a 45° angle.

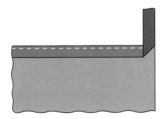

- Fold the binding down and carefully place the needle ¼" in from both sides of the corner. Line up the binding with the outer edge of the quilt and continue stitching.

start ¼" in from edge

- To join the two ends of the binding, stop sewing about 5" away from your stitches. Remove the quilt from the sewing machine.

  Lay both ends along the edge of the quilt, overlapping each other. Draw a pencil line at a 45° angle along the edge of the binding laying on the top. Add ½" beyond the drawn line and cut off extra binding.

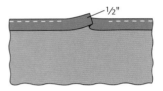
½"

- Join the ends with a ½" seam and finger press the seam open.

  Finish stitching the binding. Press the seam open.

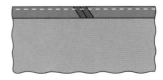

- Bring the binding to the backside, fold the raw edge under and stitch the binding in place.

Chapter 2

STRING QUILT, 65½" x 75½", c. 1930.
Maker Unknown. Collection of Nancy Ray.

SHORT STRINGS

The primary characteristic of the traditional string quilt is randomness. The short string method of construction insures the most random, original, and traditional results. It uses totally miscellaneous fabrics cut into short, irregular-width strips, then sewn together intuitively. The six projects that follow use short strings cut in lengths from 5" to 14".

Sew the short strips into fabric. Trim to size.

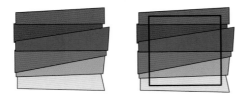

Cut some of the strings on an angle.
Sew angled pieces to individual strings. Press and trim even.

Variation:

Here are some possible variations when working with short strings.

You can sew small lengths together to make longer lengths and then sew the strips into fabric. Trim to size.

Piece the leftover parts together
to make some of the strings.

Re-cut some of the strings on an angle. To make sure the angle will fit the next piece to be added, lay the two together, *right sides up* and cut an angle. Flip one piece over and the two strings will line up perfectly.

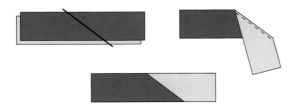

STRING QUILT, *Nine-patch variation,*
57½" x 75", c. 1940. Mississippi. Made by Mrs. Johnson.
Collection of Nancy Ray.

STRING QUILT, *71" x 77½",*
c. 1910. Pennsylvania. Maker Unknown.
Collection of Nancy Ray.

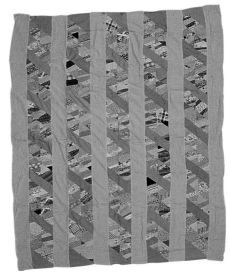

STRING TOP, *strippy set, 66"x 80",*
c.1930. Kentucky. Maker Unknown.
Collection of Nancy Ray.

made each of these blocks oversize and squared them to 7" once they were pieced and pressed. The string blocks are then set on point into Square-in-a-Square blocks. I framed half of the string blocks with white triangles and the other half with yellow triangles. When the blocks are sewn together, the triangles create the appearance of alternating pieced blocks.

String Quilt
Set *on* Point

47" x 60⅝" (20 blocks—6½" finished), 1999.
Made and hand quilted by Gwen Marston.

FABRIC REQUIREMENTS:

Yardage based on 42"-wide fabric

Assorted Fabrics for Strings:
Approximately 2½ yards (total)

White Triangles: ⅔ yard

Yellow Triangles: ⅔ yard

Yellow Border: 1½ yards

Pink Border: ¼ yard

Binding (optional): ½ yard

Backing: 3 yards

Batting: 51" x 65"

CUTTING INSTRUCTIONS:

String Blocks
Start by cutting 50-60 strings (1"-2½" wide x approximately 8½" long)–you will need 130-145 total

White Triangles
20 squares (5½"), then cut diagonally into 40 half-square triangles

Yellow Triangles
20 squares (5½"), then cut diagonally into 40 half-square triangles

Yellow Border—*cut crosswise*
5 strips (5½" wide), then cut 2 strips in half to measure 5½" x 21"

2 strips (7¾" wide)

Pink Border—*cut crosswise*
2 strips (2¾" wide)

MAKING THE BLOCKS:

1. Chain piece strings into pairs, and then join them into fours. Add additional strips until the blocks are at least 7" square. Make 20 blocks.

2. Press and trim the blocks to 7" square.

Trim each block to 7" square.

ASSEMBLING THE QUILT:

1. Sew 2 yellow triangles to opposite sides of a string block and press. Then sew 2 additional yellow triangles to the remaining sides of the block and press. Make 10 Square-in-a-Square blocks. Repeat with the white triangles to make the other 10 blocks.

Make 10.   *Make 10.*

2. Arrange 5 rows of 4 blocks each, alternating the white and yellow blocks. Sew the blocks into rows and press. Sew the rows together and press.

NOTE: Notice that the direction of the strings varies in the quilt. Some strings angle to the right and others to the left. While you could organize them all in one direction, or alternate them systematically, the unorganized system adds to the scrappy, random look.

4. See Adding Borders page 15. Sew three 5½"-wide yellow border strips to two 5½"-wide half strips end to end to make pieced strips for the side borders. Measure the length of the quilt top and cut 2 side borders this measurement.

5. Measure the width of the quilt top and cut a 5½"-wide yellow border strip to this measurement. Sew to the top of the quilt. Press.

6. Sew the 7¾"-wide yellow border strips and the pink border strips together end to end to make a yellow bottom border strip and a pink border strip. Measure the width of the quilt top and cut a yellow and a pink bottom border to this measurement. Sew the pink and yellow borders together, then sew to the top of the quilt. Press.

FINISHING THE QUILT:

See page 16 for finishing options.

Assembly Diagram.

This quilt was fun to make-inspired by the many messages printed on fabric selvages, I decided to incorporate them into a quilt of their own. Titled *In the Beginning,* the selvage used in the first block, it's an interesting and amusing quilt, with messages that include "essentials," "my heart," "romancing the sea," "100% cotton," and "crafted with pride in the U.S.A." My favorite reads, "SILK, INC 100% COTTON."

In the *Beginning*

33½" x 39" (20 blocks—5½" finished), 1999.
Made and machine quilted by Gwen Marston.

We have been taught to cut the selvage off because it is known to shrink. This was definitely an issue in the past when fabrics themselves shrunk, in which case selvages had a tendency to pull up or pucker slightly. So, why am I using selvages in my quilts? I use it because I want to use the words on the selvages and because shrinkage isn't a big issue when using today's fabrics in these informal scrappy quilts. I've been using the words on the selvage in my quilts for years now and I haven't had any problem with it.

The border complements the unique quality of the quilt. Used on many antique quilts, I call it an "interrupted border." I like the way it looks and I use it often.

FABRIC REQUIREMENTS:

Yardage based on 42"-wide fabric

Assorted Fabrics for Strings:
Approximately 1½ yards (total)

Red Border: ⅓ yard

Blue Border: ⅝ yard

Binding (optional): ⅜ yard

Backing: 1⅓ yards

Batting (optional): 38" x 44"

CUTTING INSTRUCTIONS:

String Blocks

Start by cutting 50–60 strings (1"–2" wide x approximately 7" long). You will need 130–145 total.

Red Border—*cut crosswise*

4 strips (2" wide)

Blue Border—*cut crosswise*

4 strips (4½" wide)

TIP:

When sewing a selvage to a raw edge, place the very edge of the selvage just outside the stitching line, leaving the normal ¼" seam allowance on the fabric piece with the raw edge. By doing this, you will show as much of the selvage as possible and will still have an adequate seam allowance on the raw edge of the other fabric piece.

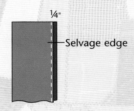

¼"

—Selvage edge

Sew a ¼" seam but catch only the very edge of the selvage.

MAKING THE BLOCKS:

1. Chain piece strings into pairs, then join them into fours. Add additional strips until the blocks are at least 6" square. Make 20 blocks.

2. Press and trim the blocks to 6" square.

6" square

ASSEMBLING THE QUILT:

1. Arrange 5 rows of 4 blocks each, alternating the direction of the strips. Sew the blocks into rows and press.

2. Sew the rows together and press.

3. See Adding Borders, page 15. Cut 2 red border strips and 2 blue border strips to this measurement. Sew the red borders and the blue borders together in pairs. Sew to the sides of the quilt. Press.

4. Measure the width of the quilt top. Cut 2 red border strips and 2 blue border strips to this measurement. Sew the red borders and the blue borders together in pairs. Sew to the top and bottom of the quilt. Press.

Assembly Diagram

FINISHING THE QUILT:

See page 16 for finishing options.

Pinwheel String
With String Border

NOTE: If you want the pinwheels to show up more clearly than they do in my quilt, make your new fabric from 19" strings, placing the colors you want to show most prominently at the top and bottom. Cut the new fabric into squares and cut the squares diagonally. If you choose to put the same colors at the top and bottom of your new fabric, both blocks will have prominent pinwheels that are the same color. If you use different colors, each block will have a different color pinwheel.

28½" x 35" (12 blocks—5" finished), 1999.
Made and machine quilted by Gwen Marston,

FABRIC REQUIREMENTS:

Yardage based on 42"-wide fabric

Assorted Fabrics for Block and Border Strings:
   Approximately 2 yards (total)

Cream Print Sashing and Border:
   ½ yard

Rust Sashing Corner Squares:
   ⅛ yard

Purple Border Corner Squares:
   ⅛ yard

Binding (optional): ⅜ yard

Backing: 1¼ yards

Batting: 33" x 40"

CUTTING INSTRUCTIONS:

String Blocks and String Border
   Start with 35-40 strings (1"-1½" wide x approximately 15" or 19" long). You will need 70-80 total.

Cream Sashing
   3 strips (2" wide), then cut into 17 pieces (5½" long)

Cream Inner Border—
cut crosswise
   3 strips (2" wide), then cut one strip in half to measure 2" x 21"

Rust Sashing Corner Squares
   6 squares (2")

Purple Inner Corner Squares
   4 squares (2")

Purple Outer Corner Squares
   4 squares (4")

MAKING THE BLOCKS:

1. Sew the strings together to make a new fabric piece that measures 4½" x 15". Make 8 pieces of new fabric. (You will be able to make 1½ blocks from each new fabric piece.)

NOTE: For blocks with prominent pinwheels (see Note, page 25), make 6 new fabric pieces that measure 4½" x 19". You will be able to cut 8 triangles to make 2 blocks from each fabric piece.

2. Press and cut each fabric piece into 4½" squares. Cut the squares diagonally, all in the *same direction* to make 6 triangles from each fabric piece, 48 total.

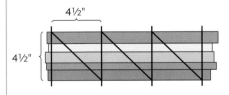

2. Arrange the triangles into Pinwheel blocks, then sew together two pairs of triangles. Sew the pairs together. Press the blocks carefully since the edges are on the bias. Trim the blocks to 5½" square. Make 12 Pinwheel blocks.

Make 12.

MAKING THE STRING BORDER:

1. Stitch together 2 to 5 strings, off-setting each by about ½". Press and cut on an angle into 4" units.

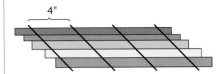

2. Sew the angled string sets together to make two new pieces of fabric that measure at least 4" x 32" and two new pieces of fabric that measure at least 4" x 28". Press carefully. The ends of these pieces will be squared off before being sewn to the quilt.

NOTE: The strings making up the border of the *Pinwheel* quilt are at differing angles; to achieve this effect, cut the next strip of new fabric into 4" units, but change the angle of the cut.

TIP:

Two units cut at different angles cannot be sewn together. To make them fit, lay them on top of each other *right sides up* and re-cut an angle. This method works anytime you have to join two different angles.

Place the two pieces on top of each other,

Sew the pieces together, right sides together,

Press.

ASSEMBLING THE QUILT:

1. Sew sashing and corner squares to 11 string blocks as shown. One block has no sashing added. Press.

Make 3   *Make 2*

Make 6

2. Arrange 4 rows of 3 blocks each. Sew the blocks into rows. Press.

3. Sew the rows together and press.

4. See Adding Borders, page 15. Measure the width and length of the quilt top. Cut 2 side cream borders and 2 top and bottom cream borders to these measurements. Sew the side borders to the sides of the quilt. Press.

5. Sew an inner corner square to each end of the top and bottom borders. Press and sew to the top and bottom of the quilt. Press.

6. Measure the width and length of the quilt top. Cut 2 side string borders and 2 top and bottom string borders to these measurements. Sew the side string borders to the sides of the quilt. Press.

7. Sew an outer corner block to each end of the top and bottom borders. Press and sew to the top and bottom of the quilt. Press.

FINISHING THE QUILT:

See page 16 for finishing options. On this quilt I machine quilted in the ditch with white thread, quilting on both edges of the sashing and along the edges of the borders, and I used the Back to Front method.

Assembly Diagram

I made this quilt from 50 different leftover strips of fabric of various lengths, between 1" and 3" wide. I wanted a sense of spontaneity and surprise in this particular quilt, and I got it by simply sewing strings together randomly. Random design cannot be planned, nor can the surprising results of random arrangements be anticipated.

String Bars

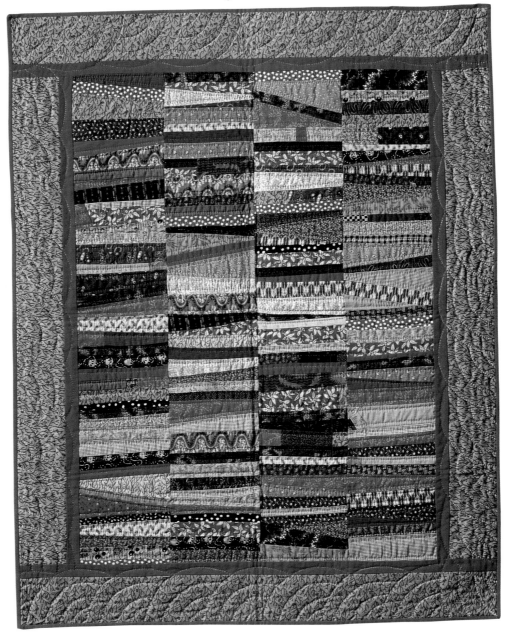

32" x 46½", 1999.
Made and hand quilted by Gwen Marston.

FABRIC REQUIREMENTS:

Yardage based on 42"-wide fabric

Assorted Fabrics for Strings:
Approximately 2 yards (total)

Red Border: ¼ yard

Gold Border: ⅝ yard

Binding (optional): ½ yard

Backing: 1½ yards

Batting: 36" x 51"

CUTTING INSTRUCTIONS:

String Bars

Start with 60–70 strings 160–170 strings (1"–3" wide x approximately 7" long). You will need 160–170 total.

Red Border—*cut crosswise*

4 strips (1½" wide)

Gold Border—*cut crosswise*

4 strips (4¼" wide)

MAKING THE STRING BARS:

1. Chain piece the strings first into pairs and then into fours and so on. Add additional strings with little concern about organizing their order until each bar is at least 37" long. Make 4 bars.

2. Press and trim the bars to 6" x 37".

TIP:

With so many seams these long bars are not unlike an accordion. They can easily stretch out of shape resulting in a quilt that doesn't lie flat. To maintain control, follow these steps.

Press carefully and thoroughly.

Lay two bars together with the right sides together. Pin both ends and the middle, and then fill in with pins about 2" or 2½" apart.

Be careful not to stretch the bars as you sew.

ASSEMBLING THE QUILT:

1. Sew the bars together and press.

2. See Adding Borders, page 15. Measure the length of the quilt top. Cut 2 red and 2 gold border strips to this measurement. Sew the red and gold borders together in pairs, then sew to the sides of the quilt. Press.

3. Measure the width of the quilt top. Cut 2 red and 2 gold border strips to this measurement. Sew the red and gold borders together in pairs, then sew to the top and bottom of the quilt. Press.

FINISHING THE QUILT:

See page 16 for finishing options.

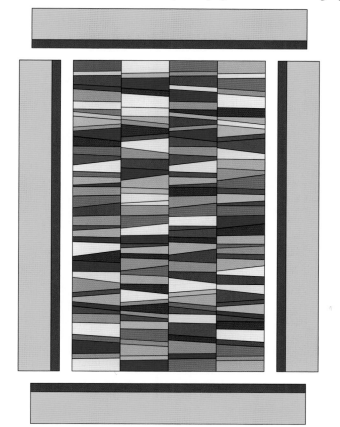

Assembly Diagram

S tring blocks alternate with traditional blocks within the same quilt. This particular quilt demonstrates how compatible and complementary the two styles can be. The stars are easy and fun to make using my liberated process.

Liberated
Strings and Stars

36½" x 42½" (20 blocks–6" finished), 1999.
Made and machine quilted by Gwen Marston.

FABRIC REQUIREMENTS:

Yardage based on 42"-wide fabric.

Assorted Fabrics for Strings and Stars:

Approximately 1¾ yards (total)

Green Border: ½ yard

Cream Border: ⅝ yard

Border Corner Squares: ¼ yard

Backing: 1½ yards

Binding (optional): ⅓ yard

Batting: 41" x 47"

CUTTING INSTRUCTIONS:

String Blocks

Start with 20-25 strings (1"-2½" wide x 7" long). You will need 40-50 total.

Star Centers and Backgrounds

108 squares (2½")

Star Points

48 squares (3"), then cut each square diagonally to make 96 half-square triangles

NOTE: You will need 1 center square, 8 side background squares, and 8 star points for each block. You may choose to make each block from two or three fabrics, or for a more random look, interchange the centers, backgrounds, and points among the blocks.

Green Border—*cut crosswise*

4 strips (3" wide)

Cream Border—*cut crosswise*

4 strips (4" wide)

Border Corner Squares

4 squares (6½")

MAKING THE BLOCKS:

1. To make the star points for each block, sew a triangle to the corner of 4 squares.

Sew 4 for each block, 48 total.

NOTE: You can make the star points vary by changing the placement of the triangle.

Adjust the angle of the triangle as you wish.

2. Press. Turn the square over and trim the triangle even with the edge of the square.

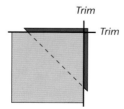

Trim
Trim

3. Trim background square seam allowance to ¼". (If you don't trim away the extra fabric, the layers of fabric at all seam junctions will be double and the block is less likely to lie flat).

Trim the background seam allowance to ¼".

4. Repeat Steps 1-3 to add a second star point to each of the background squares.

Sew 4 of each block, 48 total.

5. Sew 4 star point units, a center square and 4 background squares together into rows. Press and then sew the rows together to make each finished star block. Press. Make 12 Star blocks.

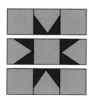

Make 12.

6. To make the string blocks, chain piece strings together randomly, as for the quilts shown in *String Quilt Set on Point,* page 21 and *In the Beginning,* page 23 to make pieces approximately 7" square.

7. Press and trim to 6½" square.

ASSEMBLING THE QUILT:

1. Arrange 5 rows of 4 blocks each, randomly mixing the string and star blocks. Sew the blocks into rows and press.

2. Sew the rows together and press.

3. See Adding Borders, page 15. Measure the length and the width of the quilt top. Cut 2 green and 2 cream side borders, and cut 2 green and 2 cream top and bottom borders to these measurements.

4. Sew side borders together into pairs. Sew to the sides of the quilt. Press.

5. Sew top and bottom borders together into pairs. Sew the border corners to the ends of each border pair. Sew to the top and bottom of the quilt. Press.

FINISHING THE QUILT:

See page 16 for finishing options.

Assembly Diagram

STRING TOP,
69" x 71", c.1920. East Tennessee.
Maker Unknown. Collection of Nancy Ray.

STRING QUILT,
64" x 79½", c. 1920. Virginia.
Maker Unknown. Collection of Nancy Ray.

STRING TOP,
73" x 89", c. 1930.
Maker Unknown. Collection of Nancy Ray.

CRAZY STRING QUILT, BARS,
62" x 81½", c. 1920. Midwest.
Maker Unknown. Collection of Nancy Ray.

STRING QUILT, STRIPPY SET,
62" x 77½", c. 1920. Southwestern Virginia. Maker
Unknown. Collection of Nancy Ray.

STRING QUILT,
65" x 81½", c. 1959. Wisconsin.
Maker Unknown. Collection of Nancy Ray.

STRING QUILT, ALTERNATING PIECED STARS
AND STRING BLOCKS,
70½" x 81", c. 1970. Kentucky.
Maker Unknown. Collection of Nancy Ray.

STRING QUILT, SAMPLER,
75" x 85", c. 1920. Virginia.
Maker Unknown. Collection of Nancy Ray.

STRING QUILT,
71" x 84", c. 1900.
Maker Unknown. Collection of Nancy Ray.

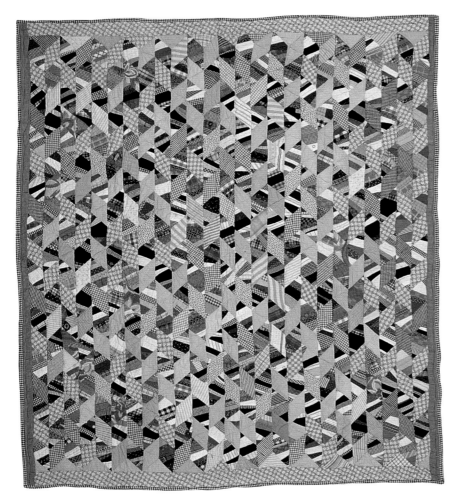

STRING QUILT,
70" x 80", c. 1920.
Maker Unknown. Collection of Nancy Ray.

STRING QUILT,
70" x 78", c. 1930. Tennessee.
Maker Unknown. Collection of Nancy Ray.

STRING QUILT, SAMPLER,
62" x 75", c. 1950. Cookeville, Tennessee.
Maker Unknown. Collection of Nancy Ray.

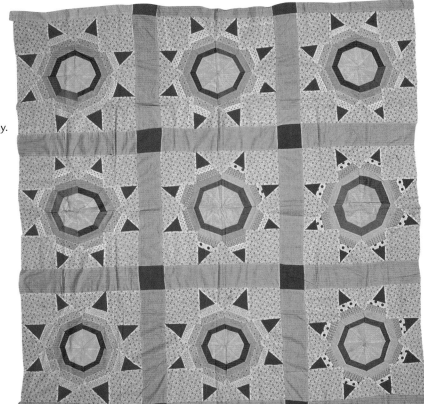

STRING STAR TOP,
77" x 80", c. 1910. East Tennessee.
Maker Unknown. Collection of Nancy Ray.

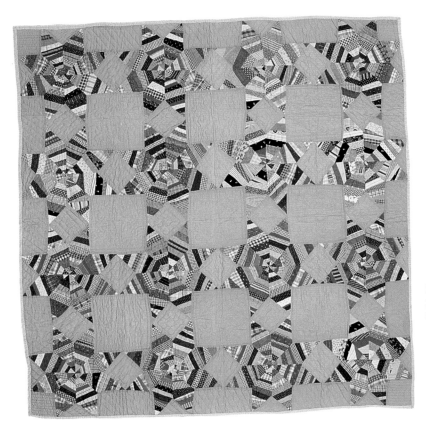

STRING STAR QUILT,
75" x 79", c. 1920.
Maker Unknown. Collection of Nancy Ray.

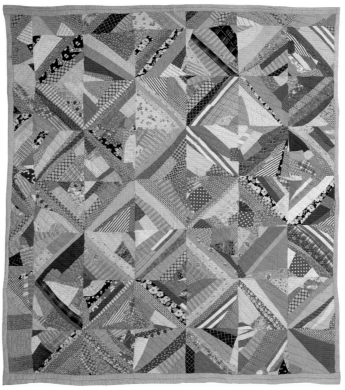

STRING QUILT,
68" x 80", c. 1930.
Maker Unknown. Collection of Nancy Ray.

STRING TOP, STRIPPY SET,
63" x 90½", c. 1940.
Maker Unknown. Collection of Nancy Ray.

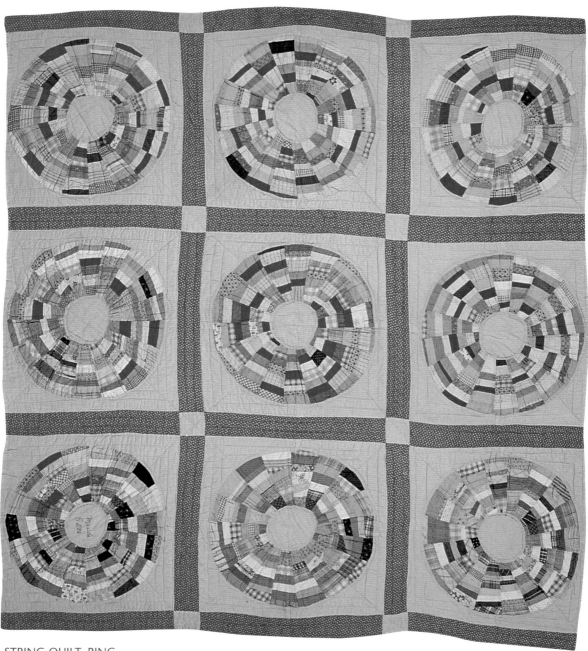

STRING QUILT, RING,
71½" x 80", c. 1930. Eastern Kansas, close to the Oklahoma
and Missouri borders. Maker Unknown. Collection of Nancy Ray.

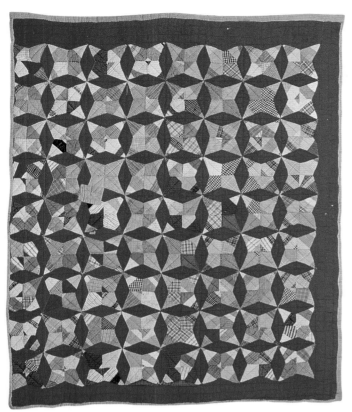

STRING QUILT, ROCKY ROAD TO KANSAS,
59½" x 74", c. 1930. Tennessee.
Maker Unknown. Collection of Nancy Ray.

STRING QUILT,
65½" x 79", c. 1920. Indiana.
Maker Unknown. Collection of Nancy Ray.

WORKING WITH LONG STRINGS

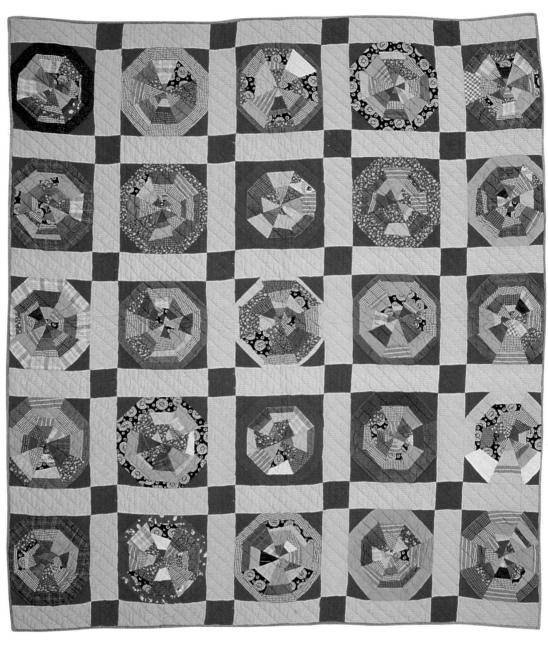

Chapter 3

▲ STRING QUILT, *72½" x 85", c. 1950. West Tennessee.*

Maker Unknown. Collection of Nancy Ray.

enerally speaking, quilters today are no longer limited to the tiniest of fabric scraps. We can afford to work from larger leftovers or to purchase yardage for specific projects. This being the case, I developed the long string method, which uses strips ranging from 22" to 45" to create a "new" piece of fabric. It's a faster method, yet still offers the "scrappiness" that distinguishes string quilts.

Sew the long strings into fabric.

You can also use short strings to make a long string, and insert these pieced strings randomly as you piece the new fabric. Intermittently, I joined the short pieces at an angle for additional effect, as well.

Sew short strings together to make a long string.

STRING DIAMOND TOP, *78" x 82½", c.1920.*
Maker Unknown. Collection of Nancy Ray.

STRING TOP, *78" x 76",c. 1930. Midwest.*
Maker Unknown. Collection of Nancy Ray.

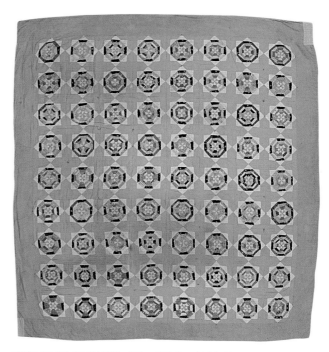

STRING STAR QUILT, *72" x 79½", c.1900. Upper East Tennessee.*
Maker Unknown. Collection of Nancy Ray.

This is a very easy quilt to make, a fact that in no way diminishes its effectiveness. The design principle of "less is more" has survived for good reason, and it applies to quiltmaking as well as other media. This quilt was made with reproduction fabrics from the 1930s, using the left-over pieces to create the sashing corner squares. Most blocks are set horizontally. Setting some blocks vertically give the quilt additional energy and interest.

String Quilt
with Sashing and Corner Squares

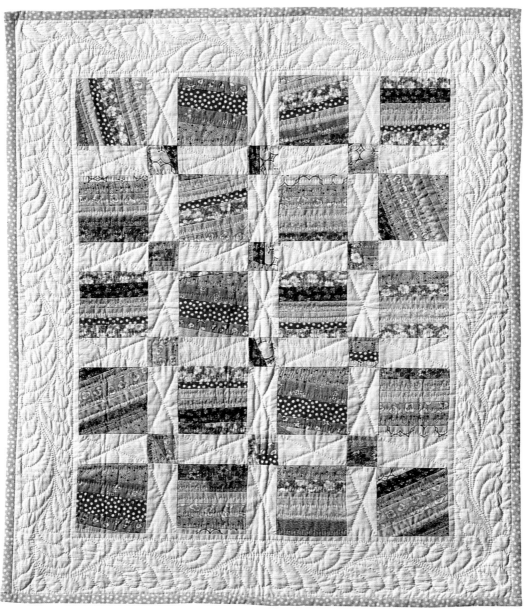

33½" x 40" (20 blocks–4½" finished), 1999.
Made and hand quilted by Gwen Marston.

FABRIC REQUIREMENTS:

Yardage based on 42"-wide fabric

Assorted Fabrics for Strings:
Approximately 1½ yards (total)

White Sashing and Border: 1 yard

Backing: 1⅓ yards

Binding (optional): ½ yard

Batting: 38" x 44"

CUTTING INSTRUCTIONS:

String Blocks
20-25 strings 1 (1"-2" wide x 42" long)

White Sashing
4 strips (2½" wide), then cut the strips into 31 sashing pieces (2½" x 5")

White Border—*cut crosswise*
4 strips (5" wide)

MAKING THE BLOCKS:

1. Make new fabric by sewing the 42" strings together until you have a piece that measures approximately 6" wide. You will need to make 3-4 new fabric pieces.

NOTE: To increase the scrappy look, cut some of the 42" strings into two 21" lengths, then sew together 2 different 21" long strings into pairs and use them as a single string.

2. Press and cut the new fabric into 5" segments. Square up to make 20-5" blocks.

TIP:

To create blocks with slanted strings, make the new fabric approximately 7½" wide (if you offset the ends of the strings about ½", you will conserve fabric). Again, cut 5" blocks, but this time at slight angles.

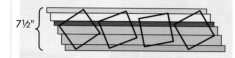

3. Cut 12 sashing corners, 2½" square, in the same manner, either straight or on an angle, from the remaining new string fabric.

ASSEMBLING THE QUILT:

1. Sew sashing and corner squares to the string blocks as shown. One block has no sashing added. Press.

Make 4.   *Make 3.*   *Make 12.*

2. Arrange 5 rows of 4 blocks each. Sew the blocks into rows. Press.

3. Sew rows together and press.

4. See Added Borders, page 15. Measure the length of the quilt top. Cut 2 side borders to this measurement, and sew to the sides of the quilt. Press.

5. Measure the width of the quilt top. Cut 2 borders to this measurement and sew to the top and bottom. Press.

FINISHING THE QUILT:

See page 16 for finishing options. I finished this quilt with a ¾"-wide binding cut on the straight grain, an idea I borrowed from old Amish quilts. It gives the quilt a nice strong finished edge.

NOTE: For a ¾"-wide single binding, trim batting and backing ½" larger than the quilt top all around and cut the binding strips 2¾" wide.

Assembly Diagram

This quilt was made from strips left by students in a class I taught in Little Rock, Arkansas in 1999. I wouldn't ordinarily have chosen all the fabrics in this quilt, but it demonstrates an important design truism. Individual fabric matters less when there are so many of them.

Arkansas Traveler

36¾" x 41⅞" (42 blocks–5⅛" finished), 1999.
Made and machine quilted and tied by Gwen Marston.

FABRIC REQUIREMENTS:

Yardage based on 42"-wide fabric

Assorted Fabrics for Strings:
Approximately 1⅝ yards (total)

Assorted Light Fabrics:
1¼ yards (total)

Lavender Print Corner Squares:
Scraps

Yellow Print Border: ½ yard

Binding (optional): ½ yard

Backing: 1⅓ yards

Batting (optional): 41" x 46"

Green and Lavender perle cotton

CUTTING INSTRUCTIONS:

String Blocks
20 strings (1½" wide x 42" long)

Light Fabrics
42 squares (4½"), then cut diagonally to make 84 half-square triangles (two per block).

Lavender Print Corner Squares
2 squares (3¼")

Yellow Print Border
4 strips (3¼" wide)

NOTE: If your light fabrics are not striped, you may choose to avoid having bias on all the edges of the block by cutting 21 squares (6⅜") then cutting each square twice diagonally into quarters to make 84 quarter-square triangles.

MAKING THE BLOCKS:

1. Sew 4 strips together randomly by grabbing two strips, without looking, and sewing them together, then sew two of these units together into a set of 4 to make new fabric. You will need to make 5 pieces of new fabric.

2. Press the new fabric and measure the width. Four 1½" strips sewn together should measure 4½". Cut the new fabric into 42 segments (4½" square).

3. Cut the resulting squares on the diagonal, *all in the same direction,* as shown.

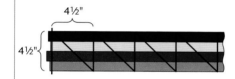

4. Sew 2 light triangles to 2 string triangles to make a block. Make 42 blocks. Press.

NOTE: Handle these blocks very carefully when pressing and sewing them together because they have bias outside edges.

ASSEMBLING THE QUILT:

1. Arrange 7 rows of 6 blocks each, turning alternate blocks a quarter turn. Sew the blocks into rows and press.

2. Sew the rows together and press.

3. See Adding Borders, page 15. Measure the width of the quilt top. Cut 1 border to this measurement and set aside for the bottom border. Press.

4. Measure the length of the quilt top. Cut 2 borders to this measurement. Sew to the sides of the quilt. Press.

5. Measure the width of the quilt top. Cut 1 border to this measurement and sew to the top of the quilt. Press.

6. Sew the corner squares to the ends of the bottom border, and sew to the bottom of the quilt. Press.

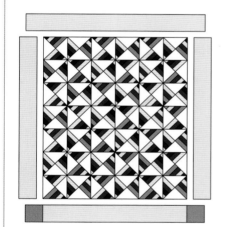

Assembly Diagram

FINISHING THE QUILT:

See page 16 for finishing options.

I machine quilted in the ditch around the inside of the border and tied the corners and center of every block with either lavender or green perle cotton.

ade with 1930s reproduction prints, this quilt uses units cut at different angles, a technique that increases the abstract nature of the piece.

String Quilt

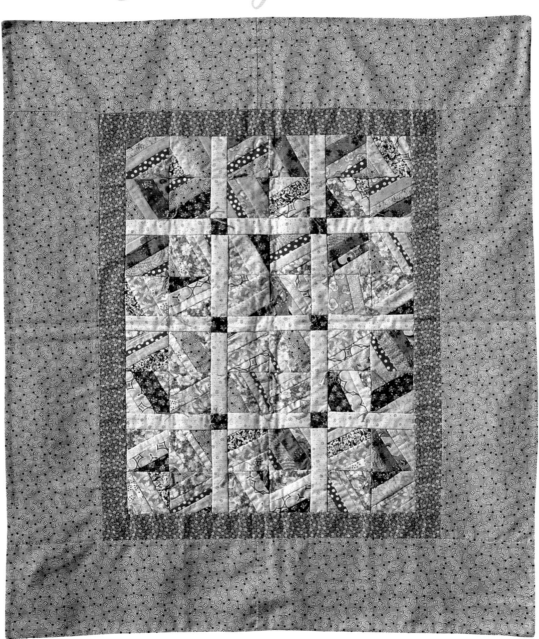

31½" x 37½" (12 blocks–5" finished), 1999.
Made and machine quilted and tied by Gwen Marston.

FABRIC REQUIREMENTS:

Yardage based on 42"-wide fabric

Assorted Fabrics for Strings:
Approximately 1⅜ yards (total)

Cream Print Sashing: ¼ yard

Purple Sashing Corner Squares:
scraps

Turquoise Border: ⅓ yard

Rose Border: ⅞ yard

Binding (optional): ⅓ yard

Backing: 1¼ yards

Batting (optional): 36" x 42"

Pink Embroidery Floss

CUTTING INSTRUCTIONS:

String Blocks

12-20 strings (1"-2" wide x 42" long), then cut the strings in half so they all measure approximately 21" long.

Cream Print Sashing

3 strips (1½" wide), then cut the strips into 17 sashing pieces (1½" x 5½").

Purple Sashing Corner Squares

6 squares (1½")

Turquoise Border—*cut crosswise*

4 strips (2" wide)

Rose Border—*cut crosswise*

4 strips (6" wide)

MAKING THE BLOCKS:

1. Sew the strings together, off-setting them about ½" to 1" to make a new piece of fabric measuring approximately 21" x 24". Make 2 pieces of new fabric using this method.

2. Once the new fabric is sewn and pressed, cut 3"-wide strips at *approximately* a 60° angle. Cut the strips from the second piece of new fabric at a slightly different angle.

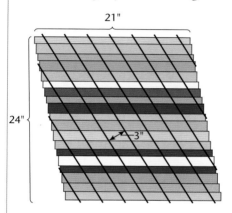

NOTE: Since all sides of the blocks are on the bias, they tend to stretch, so cut and press them carefully. *Make the blocks fit the sashing by pinning carefully and easing, if necessary.*

3. Cut each of the 3"-wide strips into 3" squares, 48 total.

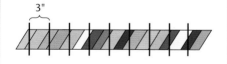

4. Sew 4 squares together to make a block. Make 12 blocks total. Press.

Make 12.

ASSEMBLING THE QUILT:

1. Sew sashing and corner squares to the blocks as shown. One block has no sashing added. Press.

Make 3.   *Make 2.*   *Make 6.*

2. Arrange 4 rows of 3 blocks each. Sew the blocks into rows and press.

3. Sew the rows together and press.

4. See Adding Borders, page 15. Measure the length of the quilt top. Cut 2 turquoise borders to this measurement and sew to the sides of the quilt. Press.

5. Measure the width of the quilt top. Cut 2 turquoise borders to this measurement and sew to the top and bottom of the quilt. Press.

6. Add the rose borders in the same manner.

FINISHING THE QUILT:

NOTE: I made this into a summer spread without batting and used the pillow slip method to finish the edges before quilting and tying.

See page 16 for finishing options.

I machine quilted in the ditch on both edges of the inner border with pink cotton thread that hid in the seams. The blocks are tied with pink embroidery floss.

String Doll Quilt, summer spread,

15½" x 17", 1999. Made and machine quilted by Gwen Marston.

This quilt was made from leftover units and scraps from the String Quilt, page 48. Small, but full of energy, it demonstrates that even the "scraps of scraps" can be used to make an interesting project. Use your imagination and skills to re-cut, stitch and add borders to some of the leftovers from your string quilts.

I simply machine quilted in white thread around each block and both edges of the inner border, then completed it with zigzag quilting line on the border. I finished the edges with the Back to Front method, page 16.

Made in the style of early Midwest Amish quilts, even the quilting and wide borders comply with Amish sensibilities. This quilt was made using the same basic method as the String Quilt shown on page 48, but in this instance, the blocks are set with scrap sashing, which is another way to increase the informality of the quilt.

Amish String Quilt

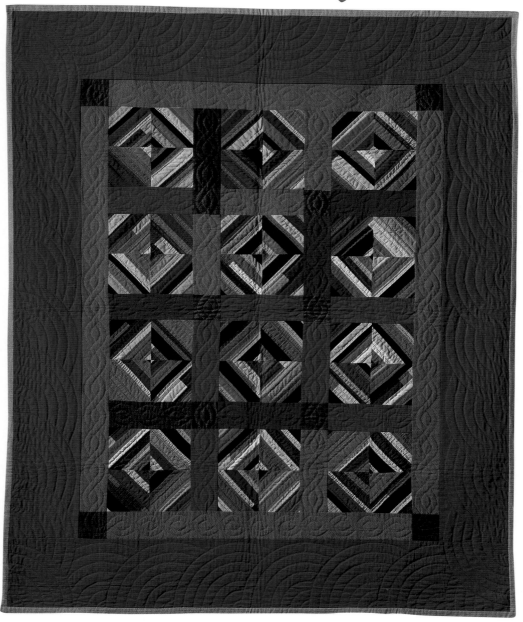

54½" x 66½" (12 blocks–9" finished), 1999. Made and hand quilted by Gwen Marston.

FABRIC REQUIREMENTS:

Yardage based on 42"-wide fabric

Assorted Fabrics for Strings:
Approximately 1½ yards (total)

Assorted Fabrics for Sashing:
Approximately ⅝ yard (total)

Olive Green for Sashing Corner squares and Border Corner Squares:
⅛ yard

Red Border: ⅝ yard

Blue Border: 1⅝ yards

Binding (optional): ⅝ yard

Backing: 3½ yards

Batting: 59" x 71"

CUTTING INSTRUCTIONS:

String Blocks

12-20 strings (1"-2½" wide x 42" long), then cut the strings in half so they all measure approximately 21" long.

NOTE: Use the short strings to make a long string, and insert these pieced strings randomly as you piece the new fabric. Intermittently, I joined the short pieces at an angle for additional effect. See page 20 for more information.

Sashing

5 strips (3½" wide), then cut the strips into 17 sashing pieces (3½" x 9½").

Olive Green Sashing Corner Squares and Border Corner Squares

One strip (3½" wide), then cut the strip into 10 squares (3½")

Red Border—*cut crosswise*
5 strips (3½" wide), then cut 1 strip in half to measure 3½" x 21"

Blue Border—*cut crosswise*
6 strips (8" wide), then cut 2 strips in half to measure 8" x 21"

MAKING THE BLOCKS:

1. Chain piece the strings together, off-setting each string about 1", until the new fabric piece measures 21" x 24". Make 2 new fabric pieces.

2. Once the new fabric is sewn and pressed, cut 5"-wide strips at *approximately* a 45° angle.

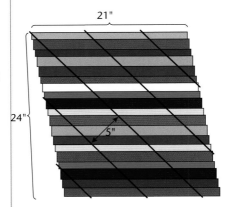

NOTE: Since all sides of the blocks are on the bias, they tend to stretch, so cut and press them carefully. Make the blocks fit the sashing by pinning carefully and easing, if necessary.

3. Cut each of the 5"-wide strips into 5" squares, 48 total.

4. Sew together 4 squares to make a block. Make 12 blocks total. Press.

Make 12.

ASSEMBLING THE QUILT:

1. Sew sashing and corner squares to the blocks as shown. One block has no sashing added. Press.

Make 3.   *Make 2.*   *Make 6.*

2. Arrange 4 rows of 3 blocks each. Sew the blocks into rows. Press.

3. Sew the rows together and press.

4. See Adding Borders, page 15. Sew 2 red border strips to 2 half strips end to end to make pieced strips for red borders. Measure the width and length of the quilt top. Cut 2 side red borders and 2 top and bottom red borders to these measurements.

5. Sew the side red borders to the sides of the quilt. Press.

6. Sew the border corners to the ends of each top and bottom red border. Sew to the top and bottom of the quilt. Press.

7. Sew 4 blue border strips to 4 half strips end to end to make pieced strips for the outer borders. Measure the length of the quilt top. Cut 2 side blue borders to this measurement. Sew to the sides of the quilt. Press.

8. Measure the width of the quilt top. Cut top and bottom blue borders to this measurement. Sew to the top and bottom of the quilt. Press.

FINISHING THE QUILT:

See page 16 for finishing options.

I hand-quilted ¼" along the seam of each string, then quilted a single cable on the sashing and inner borders and, finally, I quilted fans around the outer blue border.

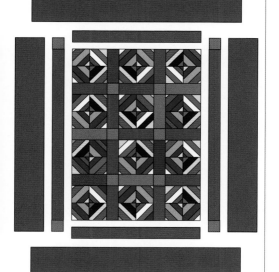

Assembly Diagram

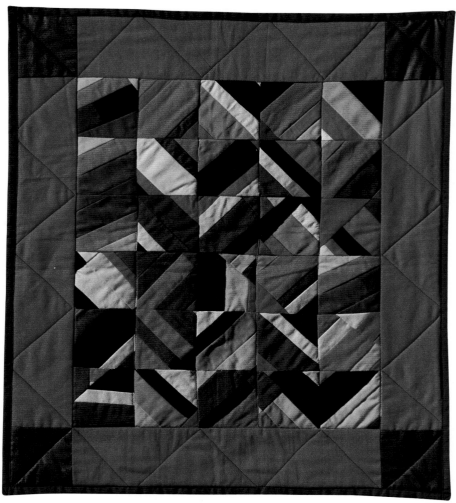

AMISH DOLL QUILT,

18" x 20". Made and machine quilted by Gwen Marston.

This quilt is made from scraps left over from the *Amish String Quilt,* page 51. Simply take all the leavings, sew them together the best you can, do some simple quilting, add a border, and that's it—you have a true string scrap quilt.

This quilt, a favorite of mine, is the sweetest one I ever made. I cut the fabric in fairly wide strips to keep the images intact because I wanted to showcase these appealing 1930-style bunny and dog prints. This quilt is a reminder that quilts made with wide strings are just as successful as those using narrow strings.

Bunny String Quilt
with Double Sashing

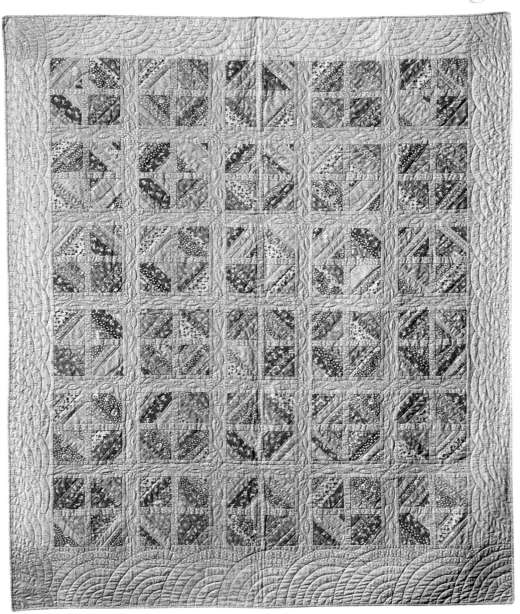

49¼" x 60" (30 blocks–7¾" finished), 1999.
Made and hand quilted by Gwen Marston.

Fabric Requirements:

Yardage based on 42"-wide fabric

Assorted Fabrics for Strings:
 Approximately 2½ yards (total)

Pink Wide Sashing, Narrow Sashing Corner Squares, and Border Corner Squares:
 1⅛ yards

Dark Yellow Narrow Sashing and Border:
 ⅞ yard

Light Yellow Border:
 1⅛ yards

Binding (optional): ½ yard

Backing: 3⅔ yards

Batting: 62" x 74"

NOTE: When using a predominantly pastel palette, include a little bit of zip with a touch of dark fabric, as quilters often did in the 1930s. Notice the red in this pink and yellow quilt.

Cutting Instructions:

String Blocks
 Start with 15–20 strings (1¼"–2½" wide x 42" long). You will need 35–40 total.

Pink Center Squares and Corner Squares
 1 strip (1¼" wide), then cut into 30 squares (1¼")

 10 strips (2½" wide), then cut into 49 sashing pieces (2½" x 8¼")

 4 squares (5½")

Dark Yellow Sashing and Border—*cut crosswise*
 12 strips (1¼" wide), then cut into 120 sashing pieces (1¼" x 4")

 2 strips (2½" wide), then cut into 20 squares (2½")

 2 strips (3" wide)

Light Yellow Border—*cut crosswise*
 6 strips (5½" wide), then cut 2 strips in half to measure 5½" x 21"

Making the Blocks:

1. Chain piece the strings together, off-setting each string about 1", until the new fabric piece measures approximately 23" x 42". Make 3 new fabric pieces.

2. Once the new fabric is sewn and pressed, cut 4" strips at *approximately* a 45° angle with a quilter's ruler and rotary cutter. If you cut the angles by eye at "about" 45°, they will be slightly off, adding to the scrappy look of the quilt.

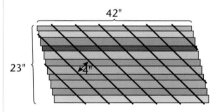

3. Cut each of the 4"-wide strips into 4" squares, 120 units total.

NOTE: Since all sides of the blocks are on the bias, they tend to stretch, so cut and press them carefully. Make the blocks fit the sashing by pinning carefully and easing, if necessary.

4. Join 4 units with 4 narrow sashing pieces and 1 narrow sashing corner to make the complete block. Make 30 blocks total.

Make 30.

TIP:

When adding the narrow sashing to the blocks, make sure all four parts are placed in the correct position. It's easy to get one turned the wrong way. I lay the whole block out on my sewing table to make sure each part is turned the right way.

Assembling the Quilt:

1. Sew sashing and corner squares to the string blocks as shown. One block has no sashing added. Press.

Make 5.   *Make 4.*

Make 20.

2. Arrange 6 rows of 5 blocks each. Sew the blocks into rows and press.

3. Sew the rows together. Press.

4. See Adding Borders, page 15. Sew 4 light yellow border strips to 4 half strips and the 2 dark yellow border strips end to end to make pieced strips for the borders.

5. Measure the length of the quilt top and cut 2 side borders to this measurement. Measure the width of the quilt top and cut top and bottom borders to this measurement and set aside.

6. Sew the side borders to the sides of the quilt. Press.

7. Measure the width of the quilt top and cut the dark yellow border to this measurement. Sew the dark yellow border to the bottom of the quilt. Press.

8. Sew the border squares to the ends of each top and bottom outer border. Sew to the top and bottom of the quilt. Press.

FINISHING THE QUILT:

See page 16 for finishing options.

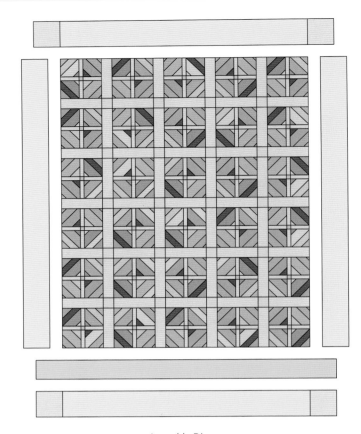

Assembly Diagram

Mary Ellen Dunneback, a student at my string quilt retreat 0n Beaver Island quilt in 1999, liked the old quilt top on page 13. She succeeded in capturing the essence of the old piece in her own wonderful version.

Mary Ellen's
String *with* Red Center

53½" x 74½" (54 blocks–7" finished), 1999.
Made by Mary Ellen Dunneback, machine quilted by Tammy Finkler.

Here's what Mary Ellen says about her quilt: "When trying to come up with an idea for Gwen's 'String Quilt Retreat' in 1999, I wanted to create a block that, when set side by side, would create a completely differently look. After seeing Gwen's antique quilt, I knew the idea would work. Because of the theme for the retreat, I chose 1930s reproduction fabrics thinking they would be fitting for that year's theme. It was fun sewing the strips, cutting the blocks and setting them as I watched the design come alive."

FABRIC REQUIREMENTS:
Based on 42"-wide fabric

Assorted Fabrics for Strings:
   Approximately 4 yards (total)

Red Strings and Border: ¾ yard

Yellow Border: 1¼ yards

Backing: 3½ yards

Binding (optional): ½ yard

Batting: 58" x 79"

Template plastic (optional)

CUTTING INSTRUCTIONS:
String Blocks
   Start with 25-30 (1¼"-2½" wide x 42" long). You will need 55-65 total

Red strings and Border—
cut crosswise
   25 strips (1" wide), then cut into 54 strips (12½" long). Use the remaining strips for the red border. Cut 1 of the remaining strips in half to measure 1" x 21".

Yellow border—*cut crosswise*
   7 strips (5½" wide), then cut one strip in half to measure 5½" x 21"

MAKING THE BLOCKS:
Cut a 7⅞" square of paper or template plastic, then cut in half diagonally to use as a template.

1. Chain piece the strings together, off-setting each string about 1", until the new fabric piece measures approximately 6" x 42". Make approximately 18 new fabric pieces.

NOTE: Since all sides of the blocks are on the bias, they tend to stretch, so cut and press them carefully.

2. Press the new fabric. Lay the template along its length and cut out string pieced triangles. Cut 108 triangles total.

6"

Cut 108 triangles.

3. Sew a 1" red strip to the long side of one triangle. You will have approximately a 1" overhang at each end. Press and sew the second triangle to the other side of the red strip.

Press.

4. Press and trim the blocks to 7½" square. Make 54 blocks.

Make 54.

ASSEMBLING THE QUILT:
1. Referring to the diagram and the quilt photo, arrange the blocks. Sew the blocks together into 9 rows of 6 blocks each. Press.

Mary Ellen chose to miter the corners of the borders. The directions below are for borders with straight corners.

2. See Adding Borders, page 15. Sew 2 red border strips to 2 half strips end to end and sew 4 red border strips end to end in pairs to make pieced strips for the inner borders.

3. Measure the length of the quilt top. Cut side red borders to this measurement. Sew to the sides of the quilt. Press.

4. Measure the width of the quilt top and cut top and bottom red borders to this measurement. Sew to the top and bottom of the quilt. Press.

5. Piece and add the yellow borders in the same manner.

FINISHING THE QUILT:
See page 16 for finishing options.

Assembly Diagram

For this quilt, I used what I call my "surprise" method, which I devised to guarantee absolute randomness. I put strings into a bag, draw them out without looking, and sew them together. Using a variety of colors and size of strings, this random piecing method guarantees the look of early string quilts, and it reinforces one of my string quilt beliefs: you don't have to struggle to make a nice-looking quilt.

Chevron String Bars

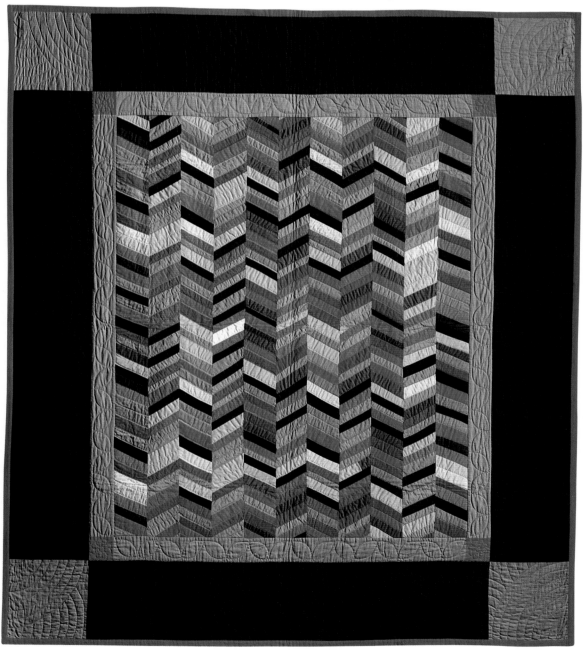

70½" x 77½", 1989.
Made and hand quilted by Gwen Marston.

The instructions may seem a little loose, and they are. The way this quilt works is that you get started, make a bunch of units, start joining them into rows, and if you need more—just make more. It's simple and fun.

FABRIC REQUIREMENTS:

Yardage based on 42"-wide fabric

Assorted Fabrics for Strings:
3½ yards (total)

Turquoise Borders:
¾ yard

Red Border Corner Squares:
⅛ yard

Black Borders: 2⅛ yards

Taupe Border Corner Blocks:
⅓ yard

Binding (optional): ⅔ yard

Backing: 4⅝ yards

Batting: 75" x 82"

CUTTING INSTRUCTIONS:

String Bars

Start with 25-30 strings (1¼"-2" wide x 42" long). You will need 60-65 total.

Turquoise Border—*cut crosswise*

6 strips (3½" wide), then cut 2 strips in half to measure 3½" x 21"

Red Corner Squares

4 squares (3½")

Black Border—*cut crosswise*

6 strips (10½" wide), then cut 2 strips in half to measure 10½" x 21"

Taupe Corner Squares

4 squares (10½")

MAKING THE PIECED BARS:

1. Place the strings into a paper bag, and mix together.

2. Pull 2 strings out without looking. Offset the strings about 1" and sew them right sides together.

3. Repeat until all strings are sewn into pairs. You will need to make approximately 30 string sets. Press.

4. To create the chevron effect, you need both a right and a left unit. With a quilter's ruler, cut a 60° angle at one end of a string set. Move the ruler along at 4½" increments and cut units. Repeat at the reverse angle on a second string set. Continue until you have the number of units needed.

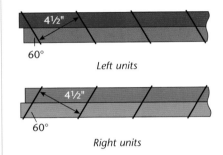

Left units

Right units

5. Put all the left units in one paper bag and the right units in another. From the bag of lefts, pull out 2 units and sew them together. Continue chain piecing the units: first into pairs, then joining into fours and so on until you have a bar approximately 54" long. Repeat with the right bars. Make a total of 11 bars, 5 going right and 6 going left. Press the bars very carefully to prevent stretching.

See Tip on page 29 for hints on pressing. Square up the ends of the bars to 51½" long.

Sew pairs of units together.

Make 5.

Make 6.

ASSEMBLING THE QUILT:

1. Carefully pin and sew the bars together, alternating the right and left bars. Do not try to line up the unit seams. Press.

NOTE: With so many seams, the bars are stretchy. It's a good idea to pin carefully before sewing the bars together. Pin both ends and the middle and then add subsequent pins every 3" or so.

2. See Adding Borders, page 15. Sew 4 turquoise border strips to 4 half strips end to end to make pieced strips for borders. Measure the width and length of the quilt top. Cut 2 side turquoise borders and top and bottom inner borders to these measurements.

3. Sew the side borders to the sides of the quilt. Press.

4. Sew the red border corner squares to the ends of each top and bottom border. Press. Sew to the top and bottom of the quilt. Press.

5. Add the black borders in the same manner.

FINISHING THE QUILT:

See page 16 for finishing options. I hand quilted around all the blocks and inside border and added a separate binding—finished 1" wide (cut 2½").

Assembly Diagram

made this quilt from left over strips from a number of classes I taught. No one wanted them so I hauled them home. The idea for this quilt came from classes in which I was teaching quilters how to make the *Chevron* quilt (see page 59). On several occasions, quilters forgot to cut both the right and left unit and ended up cutting them all the same direction. The original plan had to be abandoned and a new one formed. In light of the fact that the units were all cut going in one direction, the obvious solution was to sew them together that way. For me, this was another opportunity to create a new design from an existing "mistake".

Slanted Bars

59½" x 62½", 1997.
Made and hand quilted by Gwen Marston.

FABRIC REQUIREMENTS:

Yardage based on 42"-wide fabric

Assorted Fabrics for Strings:
1⅞ yards (total)

Rose Border: ½ yard

Purple Border: ¾ yard

Gold Border: 1⅞ yards

Binding (optional): ⅝ yard

Backing: 3⅞ yards

Batting: 64" x 67"

CUTTING INSTRUCTIONS

String Bars

Start with 20-25 strings (1½" wide x 42" long). You will need 40-45 total.

Red Border—*cut crosswise*
5 strips (3" wide)

Purple Border—*cut crosswise*
5 strips (4" wide), then cut one strip in half to measure 4" x 21"

Gold Border—*cut crosswise*
7 strips (8" wide), then cut one strip in half to measure 8" x 21"

MAKING THE STRING BARS:

NOTE: The string bars for this quilt are made the same as the Chevron quilt except for two things: the strings are all cut the same size and the units are all cut in the same direction.

Cutting the strings varying widths as I did for the *Chevron* quilt will also work and would result in an even more random appearance.

1. To sew the string sets follow Steps 1 and 2 on page 60. You will need approximately 20 string sets.

2. To cut the bar units, see Step 4 on page 60. Cut all units the same direction.

3. Put all the units in a paper bag. Pull out 2 units and sew them together. Continue chain piecing the units: first into pairs, then joining into fours and so on until you have a bar approximately 39" long. Make 8 bars.

4. Press the bars very carefully to prevent stretching. See Tip on page 29 for hints on pressing. Square up the ends of the bars to 35½" long.

ASSEMBLING THE QUILT:

NOTE: With so many seams, the bars are stretchy. It's a good idea to pin carefully before sewing the bars together. Pin both ends and the middle and then add subsequent pins every 3" or so.

1. Pin carefully and sew the bars together. Do not try to line up the unit seams; leaving them a bit offset is one of the interesting features of this quilt.

2. See Adding Borders, page 15. Sew 2 red border strips to 2 half border strips end to end, and sew 2 purple border strips to 2 half border strips end to end to make pieced strips for the inner borders.

3. Measure the length of the quilt top. Cut 2 red borders and 2 purple borders to this measurement. Sew a rose border to a purple border. Sew the paired borders to the sides of the quilt. Press.

4. Measure the width of the quilt top. Cut 2 red borders and 2 purple borders to this measurement. Sew a red border to a purple border, then sew the paired borders to the top and bottom of the quilt. Press.

5. Sew 4 gold border strips together into pairs end to end to make 2 outer border strips. Sew 2 additional gold border strips to 2 half strips end to end to make 2 pieced strips for the outer border.

6. Measure the length of the quilt top and cut 2 gold borders to this measurement. Sew to the sides of the quilt. Press.

7. Measure the width of the quilt top and cut 2 gold borders to this measurement. Sew to the top and bottom of the quilt. Press.

FINISHING THE QUILT:

See page 16 for finishing options. I hand quilted around all the blocks and inside border, and used a separate binding—finished 1" wide (cut 2½" wide).

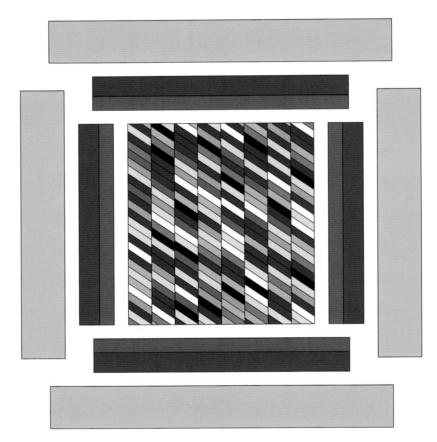

Assembly Diagram

Chapter 4

▲ STRING QUILT, *35" x 35", 1999.*

Made and hand quilted by Gwen Marston.

When working with rectangles, I essentially reverse the process of the traditional string quilt. Rather than begin with the smallest of scraps, I start with good-sized rectangular shapes, cut them into smaller pieces, mix up the shapes, rearrange them like puzzle pieces, and re-sew into new blocks.

An easy way to make triangular units is to cut rectangles of different fabrics and layer them one upon the other right sides up.

Make some blocks with 2 cuts resulting in 3 sections: Use a quilter's ruler as a straight edge and cut 2 angles. Rearrange the cut parts and sew them together to make 2 reconstructed rectangles.

Make some blocks with 3 cuts, resulting in 4 sections: Stack rectangles, then position your ruler on the stacked rectangles and make 3 angled cuts into 4 parts.

The resulting parts of each rectangle are interchangeable with the same parts of the other rectangles. Rearrange the cut parts. Sew them together to make 4 reconstructed blocks. The newly created blocks will be wider than they are long because you have lost seam allowances (½" for each seam) in the length only.

Make some blocks with 4 cuts, resulting in 5 sections.

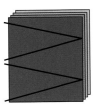

To make the variation on page 65, cut some narrow strips, about 1" wide, and insert them here and there. Mixing in just a few prints also adds interest.

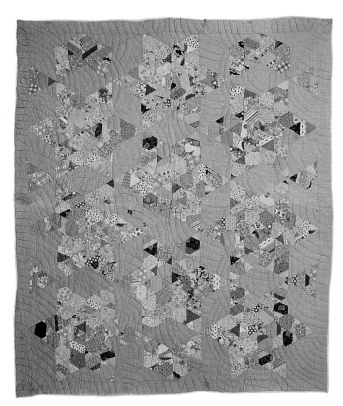

STRING QUILT, SIX-POINTED STAR,
67" x 82", c. 1930. Texas.
Maker Unknown. Collection of Nancy Ray.

T his quilt was easy to make. It is a bit more systematically constructed than the usual string quilt. I layered fabric, cut it into sections, and reorganized the resulting corresponding shapes back into new units. Make the units larger than you need so they're easier to square up and, more importantly, give you leeway to cut the finished blocks at different angles for a random look.

Amish Rectangular String

51" x 66" (48 blocks–6½" finished), 1999.
Made and hand quilted by Gwen Marston.

FABRIC REQUIREMENTS:

Yardage based on 42"-wide fabric

Assorted Fabrics:
  Approximately 2½ yards (total)

Yellow Border: ¼ yard

Red Border: 1¼ yards

Binding (optional): ½ yard

Backing: 3⅓ yards

Batting: 55" x 70"

CUTTING INSTRUCTIONS

String Blocks

48 rectangles (approximately 8" x 9") (If you choose to make more than 3 angled cuts, see page 66 to determine approximately rectangle sizes.)

Yellow Border—*cut crosswise*
2 strips (2½" wide)

Red Border—*cut crosswise*
6 strips (6¼" wide), then cut 2 strips in half to measure 6¼" x 21"

MAKING THE BLOCKS:

NOTE: To create the really random look of this quilt, make 3 or 4 angled cuts in the rectangles. See page 66 for information on cutting and sewing the rectangles. To add more variation, cut some narrow strips, about 1" wide, and stick them in here and there. The instructions below are for 3 angled cuts.

1. Stack the rectangles and make 3 angled cuts into 4 parts.

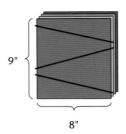

2. Rearrange the rectangle parts and sew them together to form new blocks. Make 48 blocks.

3. Press the new blocks and trim to 7" square.

TIP:

Accuracy in cutting and sewing the seam allowance isn't important for these blocks. Once sewn and pressed, they will be squared to make them equal in size. The easiest way to cut big rectangles and to square finished blocks to size is to use a 12" square quilter's ruler.

ASSEMBLING THE QUILT:

1. Sew the blocks together into 8 rows of 6 blocks each, alternating the direction of the blocks. Press.

2. Sew the rows together. Press.

3. See Adding Borders, page 15. Sew 4 red border strips to 4 half strips end to end and sew 2 yellow borders end to end to make pieced strips for the borders.

4. Measure the length of the quilt top and cut 2 red side borders this measurement. Sew to the sides of the quilt. Press.

5. Measure the width of the quilt top. Cut 1 yellow border and 2 red borders to this measurement. Sew the yellow border and a red border together, sew to the bottom of the quilt. Pin and sew a red border to the top of the quilt. Press.

FINISHING THE QUILT:

See page 16 for finishing options.

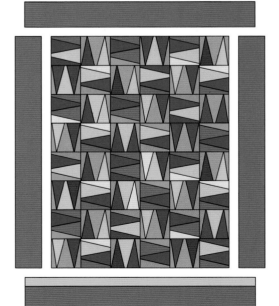

Assembly Diagram

This block began as a rectangle and ended as a quartered string block with an inserted sashing forming an "X". This method created a quilt with unique shapes and all the variation one could hope for. It began exactly as the Amish Rectangular String.

Quartered String Quilt

33½" x 39" (30 blocks–5½" finished), 1999.
Made and machine quilted by Gwen Marston.

To guarantee variation within each block, I made many triangles and stirred them well before constructing the block. I added interest to this predominantly brown quilt by inserting accent colors occasionally, or I mixed up the prints and colors used in the sashing and corners.

FABRIC REQUIREMENTS:

Yardage based on 42"-wide fabric

Assorted Fabrics for String Blocks: Approximately 1½ yards (total)

Assorted Fabrics for Sashing and Corner Squares: ¾ yard (total)

Border: ½ yard

Border Corner Squares: ⅛ yard

Binding (optional): ⅓ yard

Backing: 1¼ yards

Batting: 38" x 43"

CUTTING INSTRUCTIONS

String Blocks

30 rectangles (7" x 9")—If you choose to make more than 3 angled cuts, see page 66 for determining approximate rectangle sizes.

Sashing

Cut 15 strips (1¼" wide), then cut into 120 pieces (1¼" x 5" long)

Sashing Corner Squares

30 squares (1¼")

Border—*cut crosswise*

4 strips (3¼" wide)

Border Corner Squares

4 squares (3¼")

MAKING THE BLOCKS:

1. Stack the rectangles and make 3 angled cuts into 4 parts.

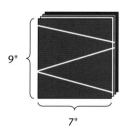

2. Rearrange the rectangle parts and sew them together to form new blocks. Make 30 blocks.

3. Press the blocks and trim to 6" square.

4. Cut the 6" squares twice diagonally to create 4 triangles.

5. Mix up the triangles and sew the sashing between 2 pairs of triangles. Press seams towards the sashing. The sashing length is slightly longer than needed, and will be trimmed after the block is assembled.

6. Sew a sashing corner square between two sashing strips. Press.

7. Sew the sashing/corner square unit between two halves of the block. Make 30 blocks.

TIP:

To insure accuracy, line up the sashing seams with the center square and pin.

8. Press the blocks and trim to 6" square.

NOTE: If you want the center square to be *exactly* in the center, use a 6" wide quilter's ruler to square up the blocks. Line up the 3" line with the center of the square and trim the block to size.

Make 30.

ASSEMBLING THE QUILT:

1. Arrange 6 rows of 5 blocks each. Sew the blocks into rows and press.

2. Sew the rows together and press.

3. See Adding Borders, page 15. Measure the length and the width of the quilt top. Cut 2 side borders and top and bottom borders to these measurements. Sew the side borders to the sides of the quilt. Press.

4. Sew the border squares to the ends of each top and bottom border. Press. Sew to the top and bottom of the quilt. Press.

FINISHING THE QUILT:

See page 16 for finishing options.

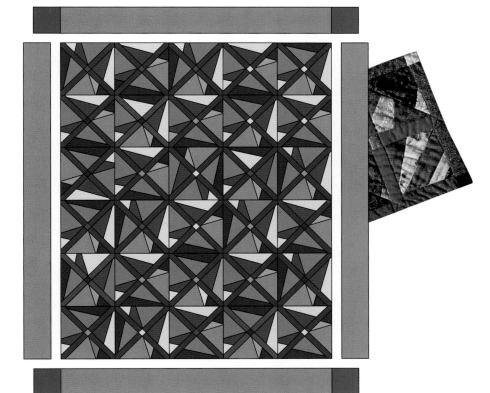

Assembly Diagram

Chapter 5

▲ STRING TOP, *69½" x 80", c. 1940. Oklahoma.*
Maker Unknown. Collection of Nancy Ray.

More than with other string methods, the wedge method is very much dictated by the design of the quilt; i.e., the shape of the block pre-determines the size of the wedges and how they are sewn together. Both the String Tulip block and the *Liberated Wedding Ring* quilt call for the wedge; it's the most appropriate shape for creating the shape of the tulip and the modified shapes used in this Wedding Ring. In addition to being appropriate to the shape, wedges are easy and efficient to cut.

The wedges will fit together almost any way you choose. Unlike the rectangle strings in Chapter 4, all the parts (not just the corresponding parts) are interchangeable.

Layer the rectangles and make angled cuts.

Reorganize the wedges in a pleasing order.

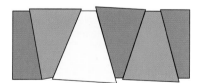

Sew the wedges together. Note that the edges of the newly pieced fabric will not be perfectly straight.

Place the template on top of the newly pieced fabric and cut.

When cutting rectangles for making wedges, determine the width and length of the template for the block you are making. Cut the rectangles you will use for the wedges at least that wide. Sew the wedges together into lengths long enough to accommodate the template.

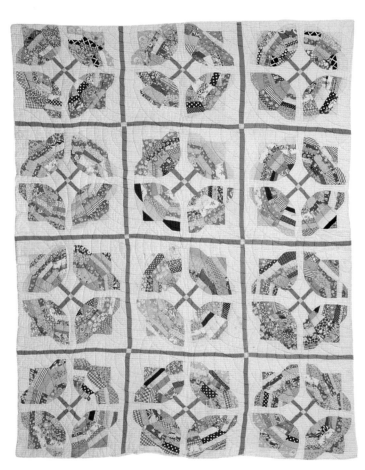

STRING TULIP QUILT, *60½" x 81½", c. 1940.*

Maker Unknown. Collection of Nancy Ray.

I came across this design when I spotted a pile of string tulip blocks on a
visit to Missouri; I thought it was a very clever variation on string quilting.
Since then, I've seen several more string pieced tulips.

String Tulip Block

65" x 75", c. 1900. Dallas Texas.
Maker Unknown. Collection of Nancy Ray.

String Tulip, pieced by Gwen Marston.

NOTE: This is my variation of the Antique block.

FABRIC REQUIREMENTS:

Yardage based on 42"-wide fabric

The yardage below will make 4 Tulip blocks.

Assorted Fabrics for String Tulip Blocks: Approximately ¾ yard (total)

Background: ½ yard

Template plastic (optional)

CUTTING INSTRUCTIONS FOR FOUR STRING TULIP BLOCKS

String Tulip Petals

8–12 rectangles (4" x approximately 10½")

NOTE: You may choose to use more rectangles for an even scrappier look. The leftover wedges can be used to make other Tulip blocks, or they can be saved for other string quilts.

Center Section of the String Tulip

4 scraps (at least 4" x 8")

Background

4 squares (10")

MAKING THE BLOCK:

Trace and cut out templates using the String Tulip patterns A/Ar and B on page 93.

1. Layer 4 to 6 rectangles at a time and cut at various angles to make random wedge shapes.

2. Rearrange the wedges, organizing the colors in a way that looks good to you. Chain piece the wedges together, into new pieces of fabric at least 8½" long. Press.

3. Lay template A on the newly pieced fabric and cut a left petal for each tulip. Turn the template over and cut a right petal for each tulip.

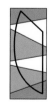 

4. Lay template B on a 4" x 8" piece and cut one center section for each tulip.

5. Sew the 2 side petal pieces to the center section to complete the tulip. Press.

6. Use your favorite method to appliqué the tulip to the background block. Press and trim the background to 9" square.

VARIATION

You may choose to change the size of the background fabric and add appliquéd stems and leaves to the tulip. Make as many block as you like and arrange as you wish.

The basic unit of this block is fairly narrow, so wedge shapes help to achieve variation within each block. As with most string quilts, variety of fabrics is a key element; every pieced section of this quilt is different. I chose brown as the predominant color, but randomly added accent pieces in red, pink, blue and yellow. The background is made from a variety of shirting fabrics.

Liberated Wedding Ring

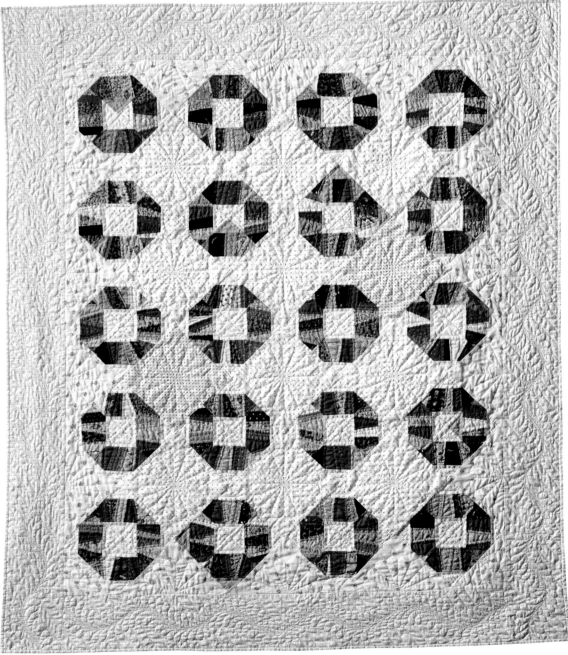

61" x 72¾" (20 blocks–8½" finished), 1999.
Made and hand quilted by Gwen Marston.

FABRIC REQUIREMENTS:

Yardage based on 42"-wide fabric

Assorted Fabrics for Strings:
2¼ yards (total)

Assorted Fabrics for Block Background: ⅞ yard

Alternate Blocks: 1⅓ yard

Setting Triangles: 1 yard

Border: 1¾ yards

Binding (optional): ½ yard

Backing: 3⅞ yards

Batting: 65" x 77"

CUTTING INSTRUCTIONS

String Blocks

18–20 strings (at least 4" wide x 22" long)

Block Background Triangles

7 strips (3½") Cut into 80 squares (3½"), then cut diagonally into 160 half-square triangles

Alternate Blocks

3 strips (8¾"), then cut into 12 squares (8¾")

Side Setting Triangles

4 squares (13"), then cut twice diagonally into 16 quarter-square triangles (You will not use 2 triangles.)

Corner Setting Triangles

2 squares (6¾"), then cut diagonally into 4 triangles

Border—*cut crosswise*

7 strips (7½" wide), then cut one strip in half to measure 7½" x 21"

MAKING THE BLOCKS:

Trace and cut out a template using the Wedding Ring pattern on page 78.

1. Layer 4 to 6 strings and cut wedge shapes at various angles and sizes.

2. Rearrange the wedges so they look pleasing. Sew them together into lengths large enough to accommodate the Wedding Ring template (approximately 6½"–6¾"). Press. Make 80 lengths.

3. Lay the template on the newly pieced fabric and cut a string unit. Cut 80.

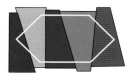

TIP:

You may choose to cut the template from muslin; the natural friction of fabric on fabric holds it in place nicely. Credit for this great idea goes to Nancy Ray, whose quilt collection is featured throughout the book.

4. Sew the block background triangles to the 2 sides of each pieced unit. The triangles will be a bit oversize. Press.

5. Trim the units to 4⅝" square.

6. Sew 4 units together to make the block. Press.

ASSEMBLING THE QUILT:

1. Arrange corner setting triangles, side setting triangles, and Wedding Ring blocks into diagonal rows. Sew the rows and press.

2. Sew the diagonal rows together. Press.

3. See Adding Borders. page 15. Sew 2 border strips to 2 half strips end to end to make 2 pieced strips for the top and bottom borders. Measure the width of the quilt top and cut 2 borders that length. Sew to the sides of the quilt.

4. Sew 2 pairs of border strips end to end to make 2 pieced strips for the top and bottom borders. Measure the width of the quilt top and cut 2 borders to that length. Sew to the top and bottom of the quilt.

FINISHING THE QUILT:

See page 16 for finishing options. This quilt is hand quilted with pin-wheels in the alternate blocks, and a continuous feather on the border. The wedges in the pieced blocks are outline quilted.

Assembly Diagram

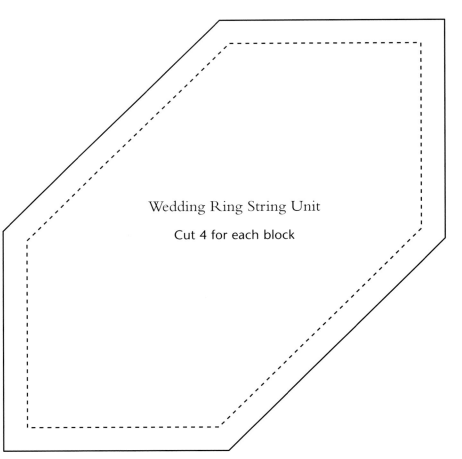

Wedding Ring String Unit

Cut 4 for each block

Chapter 6

WORKING
WITH

TRADITIONAL BLOCKS

▲ **STRING QUILT, FOUR-PATCH WITH STRING BLOCKS,** *67½" x 76", c.1920. Kentucky.*
Maker Unknown. Collection of Nancy Ray.

Working with Traditional Blocks

String quilts are indeed liberating. They are endlessly versatile, and seldom restrict our sense of imagination and spirit of invention. Even when making a traditional, structured quilt, tucking in a little string piecing is sure to enliven it. And don't be afraid to add a "new" twist to a "conventional" quilt by string piecing a simple, traditional quilt pattern. I hope the following blocks and quilts will inspire you to take the string quilt lessons of this book and combine them with more structured quilt techniques.

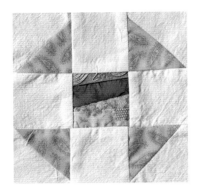

Shoo Fly

This Shoo Fly block has a string pieced center square. It is made of little leftover scraps, sewn together, pressed and squared to size. Again, you have the option of string piecing all or some of the parts that make up this block.

Variable Star

The center square as well as several points in this Variable Star are string pieced. Feel free to string piece all of the parts or some of the parts of this pattern.

STRING PINWHEEL TOP,
71½" x 80", c. 1950. South Georgia.
Maker Unknown. Collection of Nancy Ray.

Four-Patch

This Four-Patch is made with two string pieced squares and two plain squares.

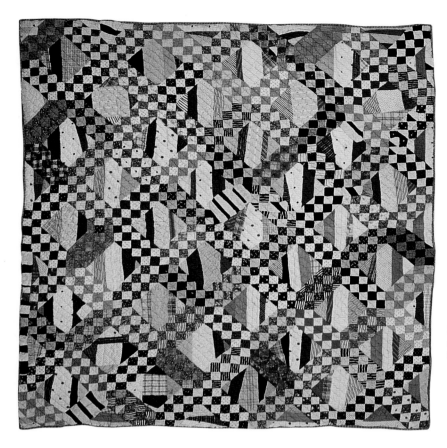

STRING QUILT,
69" x 76½", c.1920. Kentucky.
Maker Unknown. Collection of Nancy Ray.

STRING QUILT, TRIANGLES,
63" x 79", c. 1900, Maker Unknown.
Collection of Nancy Ray.

tars have long been a popular string quilt pattern. The distinguishing feature of this particular quilt is the placement of the black string at the midpoint of each star, an idea picked up from a 1890 Indiana Amish quilt shown in the 1991 *Quilt Engagement Calendar*, plate 21, published by Dutton, 1991. While this placement slightly complicates the construction process, it's well worth the effort.

Amish String Star

NOTE: String stars made without a consistent center string, are easier when made with long strings. See Long Strings, Chapter 3, page 43.

55" x 71" (4 blocks–19" finished), 1999.
Made by Gwen Marston, machine quilted by Sue Nickels.

FABRIC REQUIREMENTS:

Yardage based on 42"-wide fabric

Assorted Fabrics for String Block:
Approximately 2¾ yards (total)

Black Background, Border, and Binding: 3¼ yards

Red Sashing and Corner Squares: ⅓ yard

Rust Sashing Corner Square: scrap

Fuchsia Border: ½ yard

Blue Border: ⅝ yard

Binding (optional): ½ yard

Backing: 3½ yards

Batting: 59" x 75"'

Template Plastic (optional)

CUTTING INSTRUCTIONS:

String Blocks

Start with 50-60 strings (1"–4" wide x 6" long). You will need 200–220 total

Black Strings

Cut 6 strips (1½" wide), then cut into 32 strings (1½" wide x 6" long)

Black Background

Cut 3 strips (6¾" wide) then cut into 16 squares (6¾")

4 squares (10"), then cut twice diagonally for 16 quarter-square triangles

Black Borders—*cut crosswise*

4 strips (4¼" wide)

4 strips (7¾" wide)

Red Sashing and Corner Squares

2 strips (3½" wide), then cut into 4 pieces (3½" x 19½")

4 squares (3½")

Rust Sashing Corner Square

1 square (3½")

Fuchsia Border—*cut crosswise*

4 strips (3½" wide)

Blue Border—*cut crosswise*

3 strips (5" wide), then cut 1 strip in half to measure 5" x 21"

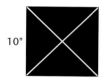

10"

Cut 10" background squares twice diagonally.

MAKING THE DIAMONDS:

Trace the pattern on page 92 and cut a template. Mark the position of the black string.

1. Sew enough short strings on either side of a 1½" wide black string to make a fabric piece large enough for the diamond template, approximately 7" x 12½". Press

2. Place the template on the fabric piece, with the black string in position, and cut. Make 8 diamonds for each block, 32 total.

MAKING THE BLOCKS:

1. Sew 2 sets of 4 diamonds together, and then join to form the star. Press.

2. Mark a dot ¼" from the point of each background square and triangle, and ¼" from the edge at each star seam.

Mark dots at each corner.
Sew in the direction of the arrows.

3. To set in a background triangle, sew one edge of the triangle to the star edge starting at the dot, backstitching, and then sewing to the outer edge. Note that the triangles are cut oversize so the edges will go beyond the star points.

4. Repeat Step 3 to set in the other side of the triangle. Be sure to line up the dots of the star and the triangle exactly. Press the seams toward the triangle. Repeat for all the background triangles.

Set in the background squares in the same manner. The squares are also cut oversize.

5. Trim the blocks to 19½" square.

ASSEMBLING THE QUILT:

1. Sew the blocks and red sashing together to make 2 rows of 2 blocks each. Press.

2. Sew red sashing on either side of a corner post. Press.

3. Sew the rows together. Press.

4. See Adding Borders, on page 15. Measure the length and width of the quilt top. Cut 2 fuchsia side borders and fuchsia top and bottom borders to these measurements.

5. Pin thoroughly and sew the side inner borders to the sides of the quilt. Press.

6. Sew a red corner square to the ends of each top and bottom fuchsia border. Sew to the top and bottom of the quilt. Press.

7. Sew 2 blue border strips to 2 half strips end to end to make the pieced strips for the blue border. Measure the width of the quilt top and cut 2 borders to this measurement. Sew to the top and bottom of the quilt. Press.

8. Sew 2 black 4¼"-wide side border strips end to end in pairs to make the pieced border strips needed for the side borders. Measure the length of the quilt top and cut 2 borders to this measurement. Sew to the sides of the quilt. Press.

9. Sew 2 black 7¾" border strips end to end in pairs to make the pieced border strips needed for the top and bottom borders. Measure the width of the quilt top and cut 2 borders to this measurement. Sew to the top and bottom of the quilt. Press.

FINISHING THE QUILT:

See page 16 for finishing options.

Assembly Diagram

String Star Quilts by Students

Jan Workman and Chris Roosien, who attended the Beaver Island Quilt Retreat in 1999, made wonderful String Star quilts. Both women used nineteenth century reproduction fabrics, and sewed 45" long strings of varying widths together to make their new fabric as described for the other projects in this book. They then cut diamonds for the stars, and pieced some strings for added variation.

Jan and Chris both like to make bed size quilts and both are marvelous hand quilters. These two quilts are certain to be enjoyed and treasured for years to come by the Workman and Roosien families.

Jan Workman's quilt consists of twelve 20" blocks on a red background with a blue print sashing and red corner squares.

Chris made a classic Four-Block quilt by piecing four 32" blocks and setting them on a cheddar background joined by pieced sashing with Nine-Patches at the junctions. Her pieced borders are a nice finish.

JAN WORKMAN'S STRING STARS,
70" x 90", 2002.
Made and hand quilted by Jan Workman.

CHRIS ROOSIEN'S STRING STARS,
80" x 87", 2000.
Made and hand quilted by Chris Roosien.

Liberated String Basket

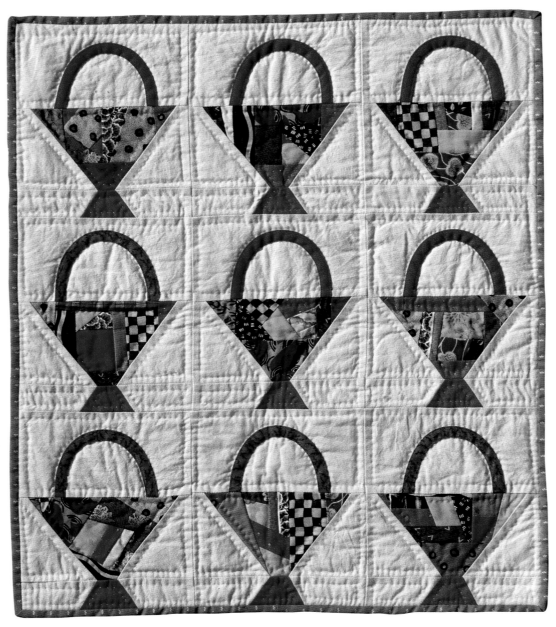

18½" x 21½" (9 blocks–6" x 7" finished), 1997.
Made and hand quilted by Gwen Marston.

FABRIC REQUIREMENTS:

Yardage based on 42"-wide fabric

Assorted Fabrics for Strings:
Approximately 1¼ yards (total)

Light Background: ⅝ yard

Assorted Reds for Basket Bases and Handles: ⅜ yard (total)

Binding (optional): ¼ yard

Backing: ¾ yard

Batting: 23" x 26"

CUTTING INSTRUCTIONS:

Trace and cut templates using patterns A, B, C, and D on page 93.

String Baskets

Start with 25–30 randomly shaped pieces (approximately 2"–3" x 3"–4"). You will need 65–70 total

Background

9 rectangles (3" x 6½")

9 Basket Side B and 9 Basket Side B reversed

9 Basket Base Side D and 9 Basket Base Side D reversed

Red Basket Bases and Handles

9 Basket Base C

9 bias strips (approximately 1¼" wide x 8" long)

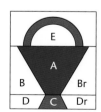

Basket block

MAKING THE BLOCKS:

1. Using your favorite method make ⅜"-wide bias. Use your favorite method to appliqué them to the 3" x 6½" basket handle backgrounds to complete Section 1. Use pattern E on page 93 as a guide for placing the handle.

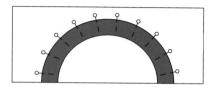

Section 1

TIP:

Here is a quick and easy way to make the bias stems on the sewing machine. Set the machine to the longest stitch. Machine-baste the edges under, turning both raw edges in, overlapping them slightly. You can do this as you sew. You don't need to press them, and you don't need any special equipment. Turn the edges under about 3" at a time, stitch, then stop and prepare the next 3". Press the finished appliqué strips. Appliqué the stems in place and remove the basting stitches.

I machine appliquéd the basket handles using an old method common on many nineteenth century quilts. I pinned the handles in place, set the machine for a short straight stitch (about 15 stitches per inch). I top stitched the handles with matching thread, sewing right along the *very* edge of the appliqué. If you stay right on the edge, your work will look neat.

2. Sew together a number of randomly shaped scraps any way you can until you make a fabric piece large enough to accommodate Basket template A, approximately 4½" x 6½".

3. Press the fabric, lay the template on top, and then cut out the basket shape.

4. Sew the Basket Sides B and Br to each side of the Basket to complete Section 2. Press.

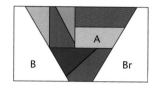

Section 2

5. Sew the Basket Base Sides D and Dr to each side of the Basket Base C to complete Section 3. Press.

Section 3

6. Sew together Sections 1, 2, and 3 to complete the Basket block. Press. Make 9 Baskets.

Make 9.

ASSEMBLING THE QUILT:

1. Arrange 3 rows of 3 blocks each. Sew the blocks into rows and press.

2. Sew the rows together and press.

FINISHING THE QUILT:

See page 16 for finishing options.

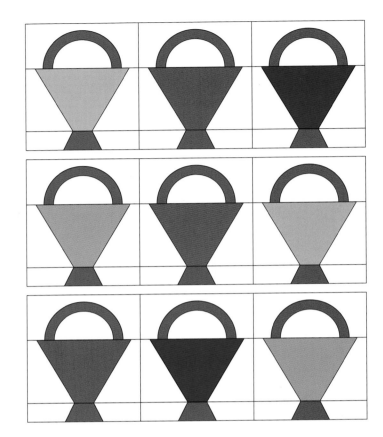

Assembly Diagram

A string pieced border can enliven a conventional pieced quilt. Here's one used in combination with Nine-Patch blocks set with sashing and corner squares.

Nine-Patch
with String Border

31½" x 35½" (20 blocks–3" finished), 1999.
Made and hand quilted by Gwen Marston.

FABRIC REQUIREMENTS:

Yardage based on 42"-wide fabric

White for Nine-Patches, Sashing and Border: ¾ yard

Assorted Pinks for Nine-Patches and Sashing Corner Squares: ⅜ yard (total)

Assorted fabrics for String Border: 1¾ yards (total)

Backing: 1¼ yards

Binding (optional): ⅓ yard

Batting: 36" x 40"

CUTTING INSTRUCTIONS:

White Nine-Patch Strips, Sashing, and Border

7 strips (1½" wide), then cut 31 sashing pieces (1½" x 3½"). The remainder of the strips will be sewn into strip sets for the Nine-Patch blocks.

4 strips (2½" wide)

Assorted Pink Nine-Patch Strips and Sashing Corner Squares

6 strips (1½" wide), then cut 12 squares for the sashing corner squares. The remainder of the strips will be sewn into strip sets for the Nine-Patch blocks.

NOTE: For a more random look reverse the positions of the pink and white squares in some of the Nine-Patch blocks. If you choose to do this, you will need more white strips and fewer pink strips.

String Border

Start with 35-40 strings (1"–3" wide x 4"–9" long). You will need 100-120 total

MAKING THE NINE-PATCH BLOCKS:

Sew the 1½" white strips to assorted 1½" pink strips into strips sets and cut into 1½" segments. Sew the segments together. Press. Make 20 Nine-Patch blocks.

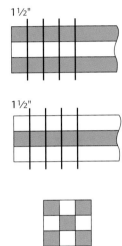

MAKING THE STRING BORDER

NOTE: I used the short string, long string, and rectangle string techniques to create the pieces in this border.

1. Sew the short strings end to end into long pieced strings about 45" in length (piecing the strings creates variation and randomness). For the basic unit, sew 5 or 6 pieced strings together to make a 6½" wide piece of new fabric. Press and cut into 6½" sections.

2. To create an even more random look, cut sewn strings into smaller sections and then resew them together with strings running both horizontally and vertically. Just be sure that your resulting border section is at least 6½" wide.

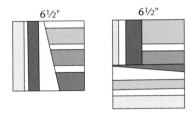

3. To make the triangular units, cut one white and one pink rectangle, 5" x 6½".

4. Lay the 2 rectangles on top of each other, right sides up. Cut a triangle shape. Interchange the pieces as you do for rectangle strings. See page 66. Sew the triangles together to make two triangular units with reversed colors. Press.

NOTE: For different sized triangular units, make the rectangle narrower or wider. Because the finished unit needs to fit into the 6"-wide border, the vertical dimension needs to be 6½". If it is shorter, you can add strips to the top to make the segment 6½" high.

5. Join the various units together randomly to form 2 border strips at least 26" long and 2 border strips at least 34" long. Press and, if needed, trim each strip to 6½" wide.

ASSEMBLING THE QUILT:

1. Sew sashing and corner squares to the blocks as shown. One block will not have sashing. Press.

Make 4.   *Make 3.*

Make 12.

2. Arrange 5 rows of 4 blocks each. Sew the blocks into rows and press.

3. Sew the rows together. Press.

4. See Adding Borders, page 15. Measure the length of the quilt top. Cut 2 white borders to this measurement. Sew to the sides of the quilt. Press.

5. Measure the width of the quilt top. Cut 2 white borders to this measurement. Sew to the top and bottom of the quilt. Press.

6. Measure the length of the quilt top. Cut 2 string borders to this measurement. Sew to the sides of the quilt. Press.

7. Measure the width of the quilt top. Cut 2 string borders to this measurement. Sew to the top and bottom of the quilt. Press.

FINISHING THE QUILT:

See page 16 for finishing options. This quilt is hand quilted. The blocks are criss-crossed and the shapes making up the string borders are outline quilted.

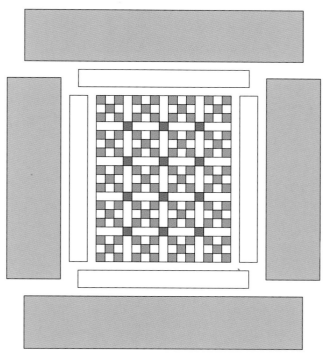

Assembly Diagram

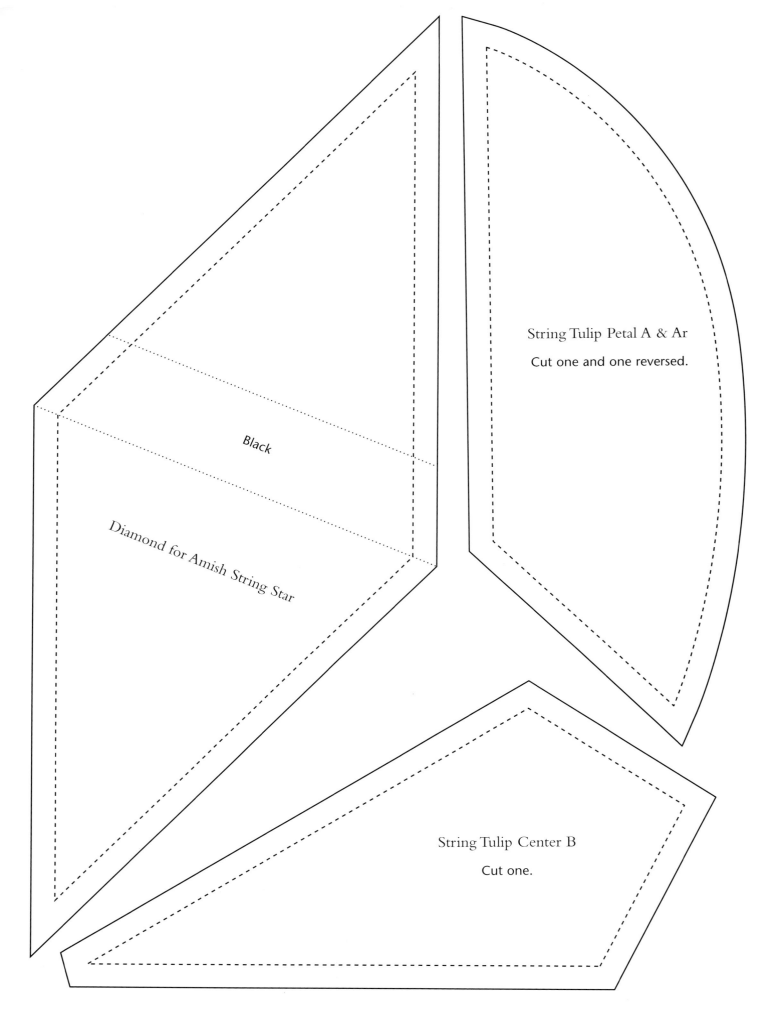

String Tulip Petal A & Ar

Cut one and one reversed.

Black

Diamond for Amish String Star

String Tulip Center B

Cut one.

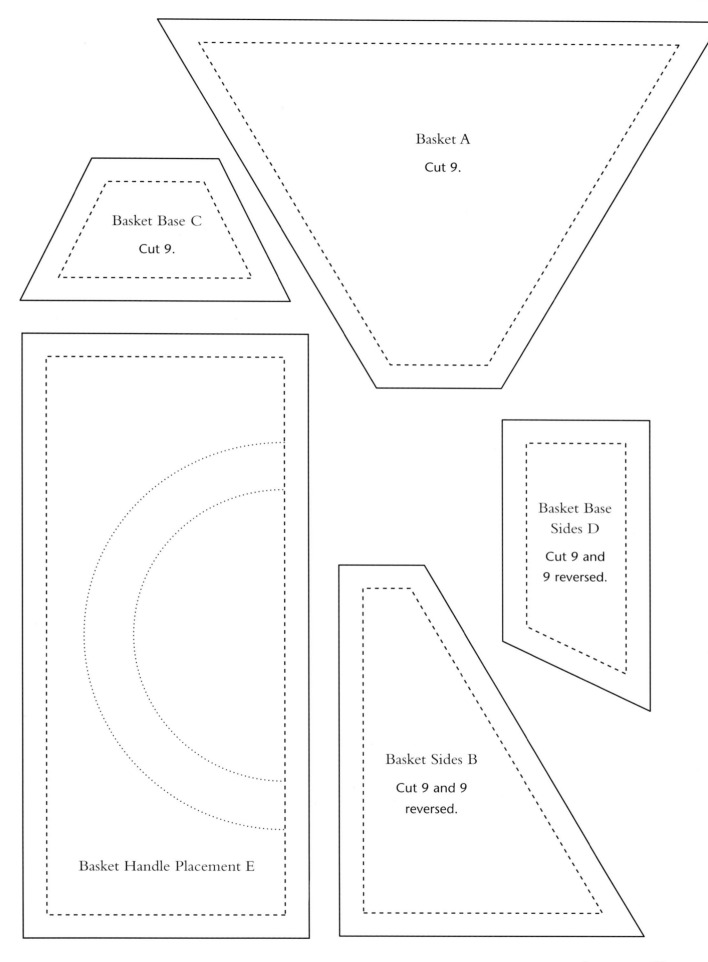

Basket A

Cut 9.

Basket Base C

Cut 9.

Basket Base
Sides D

Cut 9 and
9 reversed.

Basket Sides B

Cut 9 and 9
reversed.

Basket Handle Placement E

Bibliography

Vlach, John Michael. *The Afro-American Tradition in Decorative Arts,* Cleveland, Ohio: The Cleveland Museum of Art, 1978.

Freeman, Roland L. *A Communion of the Spirits,* Nashville, Tennessee: Rutledge Hill Press, 1996.

Granick, Eve Wheatcroft. *The Amish Quilt,* Intercourse, Pennsylvania: Good Books, 1989.

Leon, Eli. *Who'd A Thought It: Improvisation in African-American Quiltmaking,* San Francisco, California: Published in conjunction with the exhibition on view at the San Francisco Craft & Folk Art Museum from December 31, 1987 to February 28, 1988.

MacDowell, Marsha L., editor. *African American Quiltmaking in Michigan,.* East Lansing, Michigan: Michigan State University Press, 1997.

Nickols, Pat. *Uncoverings,* 1982. Mill Valley, California: American Quilt Study Group. 1983.

Ramsey, Bets and Merikay Waldvogel. *The Quilts of Tennessee,.* Nashville, Tennessee: Rutledge Hill Press, 1986.

Wahlman, Maude Southwell. *Signs and Symbols: African Images in African-American Quilts,* New York: Studio Books in Association with The Museum of American Folk Art, 1993.

Waldvogel, Merikay. *Soft Covers For Hard Times: Quiltmaking & The Great Depression,* Nashville, Tennessee: Ruthledge Hill Press, 1990.

Watts, Katherine with Elizabeth Walker. *Anna Williams: Her Quilts & Their Influences,* Paducah, Kentucky: American Quilter's Society, 1995.

For more information, write for a free catalog:
C&T Publishing, Inc.
P.O. Box 1456
Lafayette, CA 94549
(800) 284-1114
Email: ctinfo@ctpub.com
Website: www.ctpub.com

For quilting supplies:
Cotton Patch Mail Order
3405 Hall Lane, Dept.CTB
Lafayette, CA 94549
(800) 835-4418
(925) 283-7883
Email:quiltusa@yahoo.com
Website: www.quiltusa.com

Note: Fabrics used in the quilts shown may not be currently available since fabric manufacturers keep most fabrics in print for only a short time.

Other Fine Books From C&T Publishing

24 Quilted Gems: Sparkling Traditional & Original Projects, Gai Perry

All About Quilting from A to Z, From the Editors and Contributors of Quilter's Newsletter Magazine and Quiltmaker Magazine

An Amish Adventure, 2nd Edition: A Workbook for Color in Quilts, Roberta Horton

Art of Classic Quiltmaking, The, Harriet Hargrave & Sharyn Craig

Art of Machine Piecing, The: How to Achieve Quality Workmanship Through a Colorful Journey, Sally Collins

Block Magic: Over 50 Fun & Easy Blocks from Squares and Rectangles, Nancy Johnson-Srebro

Block Magic, Too!: Over 50 NEW Blocks from Squares and Rectangles, Nancy Johnson-Srebro

Celebrate the Tradition with C&T Publishing: Over 70 Fabulous New Blocks, Tips & Stories from Quilting's Best, C&T Staff

Civil War Women: Their Quilts, Their Roles & Activities for Re-Enactors, Barbara Brackman

Contemporary Classics in Plaids & Stripes: 9 Projects from Piece 'O Cake Designs, Linda Jenkins & Becky Goldsmith

Cozy Cabin Quilts from Thimbleberries: 20 Projects for Any Home, Lynette Jensen

Crazy Quilt Handbook, The: Revised, 2nd Edition, Judith Baker Montano

Easy Pieces: Creative Color Play with Two Simple Quilt Blocks, Margaret Miller

Elm Creek Quilts: Quilt Projects Inspired by the Elm Creek Quilts Novels, Jennifer Chiaverini & Nancy Odom

Free Stuff for Quilters on the Internet, 3rd Edition, Judy Heim & Gloria Hansen

Free Stuff for Sewing Fanatics on the Internet, Judy Heim & Gloria Hansen

Great Lakes, Great Quilts: 12 Projects Celebrating Quilting Traditions, Marsha MacDowell

Heirloom Machine Quilting, Third Edition: Comprehensive Guide to Hand-Quilting Effects Using Your Sewing Machine, Harriet Hargrave

Hidden Block Quilts: • Discover New Blocks Inside Traditional Favorites • 13 Quilt Settings Instructions for 76 Blocks, Lerlene Nevaril

Lone Star Quilts and Beyond: Step-by-Step Projects and Inspiration, Jan Krentz

Magical Four-Patch and Nine-Patch Quilts, Yvonne Porcella

Make Any Block Any Size: Easy Drawing Method, Unlimited Pattern Possibilities, Sensational Quilt Designs, Joen Wolfrom

Mariner's Compass Quilts: New Directions, Judy Mathieson

New England Quilt Museum Quilts, The: Featuring the Story of the Mill Girls, with Instructions for 5 Heirloom Quilts, Jennifer Gilbert

Patchwork Persuasion: Fascinating Quilts from Traditional Designs, Joen Wolfrom

Q is for Quilt, Diana McClun & Laura Nownes

Quilting Back to Front: Fun & Easy No-Mark Techniques, Larraine Scouler

Quilting with Carol Armstrong: •30 Quilting Patterns•Appliqué Designs•16 Projects, Carol Armstrong

Quilts from the Civil War: Nine Projects, Historic Notes, Diary Entries, Barbara Brackman

Quilts, Quilts, and More Quilts!, Diana McClun & Laura Nownes

Ultimate Guide to Longarm Quilting, The: •How to Use Any Longarm Machine •Techniques, Patterns & Pantographs •Starting a Business •Hiring a Longarm Machine Quilter, Linda Taylor

Scrap Quilts: The Art of Making Do, Roberta Horton

Thimbleberries Housewarming, A: 22 Projects for Quilters, Lynette Jensen

Tradition with a Twist: Variations on Your Favorite Quilts, Blanche Young & Dalene Young-Stone

About the Author

Gwen Marston is a professional quilt-maker, teacher and author. Since 1981 she has had nineteen solo exhibits and participated in many group shows. She maintains a busy teaching and lecture schedule across the United States and has twice taught in Japan. For the past twenty years she has conducted quilt retreats on Beaver Island, Michigan, her year-round home. She was a regular columnist for Ladies Circle Patchwork Quilts for twelve consecutive years. This is her sixteenth book.

Index

Abstract Expressionism, 11

African-American string quilts, 8

Afro-American Quiltmaking in Michigan, 8

American Visions: The Epic History of Art in America, 11

Amish Quilt, The, 8

Amish: The Art of the Quilts, 11

Amish string quilts, 8

Antique string quilts, 5

Backing, 15

Back to front finish, 16

Basket patterns, 93

Basket quilt, 86

Batting, 15

Benberry, Cuesta, 6

Bias stems, by machine, 87

Binding, 18

Block quilts, 9

Borders:

    adding, 15

    string pieced, 89

    Chris Roosien's String Stars, 85

    Collins, Derenda, 8

        Communion of the Spirits, A, 8

    Construction, 14

    Contemporary perspective, 10

Crazy vs. string quilts, 6, 8

Definition of string quilts, 6

Design principles, 13

Diamond pattern, 92

Duchamp, Marcel, 10

Dunneback, Mary Ellen, 57

Fabric tips, 13

Feed sacks, used as fabric, 7

Flint Afro-American Quilters Guild, 8

Foundation piecing, 6, 9

Four-Patch block, 80

Freeman, Roland, 8

Granick, Eve Wheatcroft, 8

Great Depression, 7

Hand quilting, 16

History of string quilts, 6

Hughes, Robert, 11

Jan Workman's String Stars, 85

Kandinsky, Wassily, 10

Long bars, tips for sewing together, 29

Long string method, 43

McDowell, Marsha, 8

Machine quilting, 16

Mazloomi, Dr. Carolyn, 8

Muslin, using for templates, 77

Narrow sashing, adding, 55

Newspaper, as foundation, 6

Nine-Patch blocks, 89

Pat's String Quilt (Pat Townes), 9

Patterns, common, 9

Pieced Diamonds, 9

Pillowslip method of finishing, 17

Pollack, Jackson, 11

Pressing, 14

PROJECT QUILTS:

    Amish Rectangular String, 67

    Amish String Quilt, 51

    Amish String Star, 82

    Arkansas Traveler, 46

    Bunny String Quilt with Double Sashing, 54

    Chevron String Bars, 59

    In the Beginning, 23

    Liberated String Basket, 86

    Liberated Strings and Stars, 30

    Liberated Wedding Ring, 76

    Mary Ellen's String with Red Center, 57

Nine-Patch with String Border, 89

Pinwheel String with String Border, 25

Quartered String Quilt, 69

Slanted Bars, 62

String Bars, 28

String Quilt, 48

String Quilt with Sashing and Corner Squares, 44

String Quilt Set on Point, 21

String Tulip, 74

Ray, Nancy, 9, 77

Rectangles, 66

Reproduction prints, 48, 54

Road to Nowhere, 9

Rumph, Jeffalone, 8

Sashing seams, lining up, 70

Selvages, using in quilts, 24

Shoo Fly block, 80

Short string construction, 20

Silber, Julie, 11

Snowball, 9

Spider Web, 9, 10

Star block, 82

Summer spread, 15

Tools, 14

Traditional blocks, 80

Triangular units, 66

Tulip patterns, 92

Tying, 15–16

Variable Star block, 80

Wedding Ring block, 73, 77

Wedge method, 73

Whitney Museum of American Art, 11

Young, Christopher R., 11